OUR ELEVEN CHIEF JUSTICES

OUR ELEVEN
CHIEF JUSTICES

———

A History of the Supreme Court
in Terms of Their Personalities

———

BY

Kenneth Bernard Umbreit

ILLUSTRATED

VOLUME I

KENNIKAT PRESS/PORT WASHINGTON, N. Y.

To the Memory of My Mother

MARY AMANDA BAUERNFEIND UMBREIT

OUR ELEVEN CHIEF JUSTICES

Copyright 1938 by Kenneth B. Umbreit
Reissued in 1969 by Kennikat Press by arrangement with
Harper and Row, Publishers
Library of Congress Catalog Card No: 75-86069
SBN 3046-0593-9

Manufactured by Taylor Publishing Company   Dallas, Texas

ESSAY AND GENERAL LITERATURE INDEX REPRINT SERIES

CONTENTS

ILLUSTRATIONS

PROLOGUE

"Lawyers," it is said, "are divided into two classes—those who know the law and those who know the judge." The division is not so clearly marked. To know the law it is also necessary to know the judge.

The most abstract of the exact sciences, astronomy, first discovered the need for the use of a personal equation in checking the results of observation. The very exactness of that science called attention to the failure of all men to observe the movements of the stars in precisely the same way. The traditional machinery of the law long tended to conceal a similar situation. That the line of precedent does grow was an observed phenomenon; that individual judges frequently followed precedents with which they expressed their personal dissatisfaction was likewise an observed phenomenon. In time, a school of thought arose which directed its attention only to the first of these phenomena. "Tell me," it said, "what the judge had for breakfast and I will tell you what his decision will be." Marshall's decisions are airily dismissed, by the followers of this hypothesis, as the machinations of a land speculator. Taney is regarded as simply an anti-Marshall, elevated to the Chief Justiceship by the public disgust at the property consciousness of the Virginian. Ignorance was the answer of this school of thought to Marshall's action in trying to bring about the confirmation of Taney's appointment as an Associate Justice; to the loud disappointment expressed by some of Marshall's old opponents over Taney's failure to write the doctrines of state sovereignty into the law, and to the ease with which the doctrines contained in the opinions of the two judges may be reconciled. Nor, so far as I know, has any member of this school ever offered an explanation of how Waite, after his career as a railroad and utilities lawyer, established his judicial reputation by upholding the first governmental attempts at rate regulation.

The failure of the breakfast theory of jurisprudence to explain anything was due in part to the use of an impossible psychology; in part to a failure to realize that the legal tradition is not merely a rationalization but has a real vitality of its own—that there really is a common law even if it is not as precedent bound as Lord Coke thought—but above all to the failure of its hypothesis to fit the facts. This last, on elementary principles of scientific thought, should dispose of any hypothesis and the continued belief by any number of intelligent people, including thousands of lawyers, that the course of American constitutional law, in particular, can be interpreted in terms of the group prejudices and interests of the judges of the Supreme Court, can be explained only in the light of the almost total absence of facts by which any such hypothesis could be tested. Curiously enough, while there is a widespread belief that constitutional decisions can be interpreted in terms of judicial biography, there is almost no such thing as judicial biography. While the Chief Justices have been more written about than the Associates, an examination of the bibliography printed at the end of this volume will indicate the paucity of material even in regard to them. What there is, is for the most part to be found only in obscure periodicals and out-of-print books. This volume is an attempt to bring that material together, to analyze and sift it, and to reduce it to usable form. It is written, for example, in the belief that many who will never take the trouble to find and read the only full-length, and now out-of-print, life of Ellsworth will be interested in a short sketch of the author of the Judiciary Act.

I have not attempted to explain the judicial decisions of my subjects in terms of their psyches. My purpose has been to write biography, not the history of constitutional law. Cases, when referred to at all, have been treated as themselves factors in the illumination of character rather than as the facts to be explained by the knowledge derived from the study of character. Yet the consecutive biographies of all the Chief Justices necessarily include an outline history, even if sketchy and imperfect, of American constitutional law.

This factor of temporal continuity was important in my choice of subject. Yet the Chief Justices, with the exception of Fuller, were not merely the Court's presiding officers but, in their individual right, among its strong members. Even if this were not so, the powers which go with the Chief Justiceship give the holder of that office a more than ordinary influence on the decisions of the Court. He is the presiding officer both in the court room and in the conference room. As such, he has considerable control both over the course of the argument before the judges and over the course of the discussion among the judges. He can direct attention to a point or away from it more easily than any of his colleagues. He it is who assigns the writing of opinions except when he himself is in the minority. This last power gives him in a sense a form of patronage but it also gives him a tremendous influence over the development of the law. Two members of the Court may agree as to the disposal of a particular case but they may differ widely in their approach to the problem. The Chief Justice, knowing the mental processes of his brethren intimately, may assign the writing of the opinion to the judge whose approach he prefers. It is true that the other judge may write a separate opinion if he chooses, setting forth his personal views, but the writing of separate opinions, like the writing of dissents, is in the nature of extra work; they do not carry the same weight as majority opinions, and when a man must work as one of a group of nine he cannot always be complaining about his colleagues.

The consecutive portrayal of the eleven men who on the whole have been most influential in the development of one of the three coordinate branches of our government has other advantages. It is a cross-section of American history cut at a new angle. That sameness which is so apparent in similar accounts of English judges and chancellors is lacking. Our Chief Justices have come from backgrounds whose diversity reflects the growth of the nation. Jay and Rutledge were by birth colonial aristocrats; Ellsworth a Yankee farmer; Marshall a frontiersman; Chase, Waite and Fuller, New Englanders who went west to seek their fortunes; and Mr. Hughes' metropolitan background seems fitting for an age in which America is no longer dominantly agricultural. This diversity of background is important in the growth of the law, which is neither a science nor a theology but, like grammar, the orderly expression of a living and growing social tradition. But the Chief Justices have not been mere symbols. They have reached the Court from different parts of the country and by routes that have varied widely. They have been alike in their integrity and in their devotion to the public good, and their comparative historical anonymity may be ascribed to that similarity. The similarity extends no further. A study of other aspects of their character, of their views on public questions and of their careers before their appointments shows each of them to have been a vital and remarkable man. The cross-section which is revealed by cutting American history at the point at which I have attempted to cut it, is a rich one.

New York, N. Y.

September, 1938

K. B. U.

Chapter I.

JOHN JAY

Born, New York City, December 12, 1745.

Graduated, King's College, New York City, 1764.

Admitted to New York bar, 1768.

Married Sarah Livingston, 1774.

Delegate to First Continental Congress, 1774.

Delegate to Second Continental Congress, 1775.

Delegate to New York Provincial Congress (subsequently called the Convention), 1776-1777.

Chief Justice of Supreme Court of New York, 1777-1779.

Elected President of the Continental Congress, December 10, 1778.

Elected minister to Spain, September 27, 1779.

Arrived at Cadiz, Spain, January 22, 1780.

Elected one of the commissioners to negotiate peace with Great Britain, June, 1781.

Arrived at Paris, France, June 23, 1782.

Returned to New York City, July 24, 1784.

Secretary for Foreign Affairs and Secretary of State *ad interim*, 1784-1790.

Chief Justice of the United States, 1789-1795.

Special Envoy to Great Britain, 1794-1795.

Governor of New York, 1795-1801.

Appointed Chief Justice of the United States, 1800 but declined appointment.

Died at Bedford, N. Y., May 17, 1829.

JOHN JAY

From a portrait by Gilbert Stuart

When George Washington took the oath of office as President at the corner of Broad and Wall Streets in New York in the spring of 1789, the federal government had neither judges nor courts. The constitution under which that government was then going into operation merely stated that there was to be a Supreme Court and a Chief Justice. The number of associate justices and the power to establish inferior courts were left in the discretion of that Congress which was now meeting in its first session. That discretion was speedily exercised and Senate Bill No. 1, which later became the Judiciary Act of 1789, remains the basis of our judicial system.

But Washington did not defer his thinking about judicial appointments until after the passage of that act. He himself had not contributed deeply to the theory of the Revolution or to the thought which had gone into the formation of the new government in the endeavor to avoid the defects which that theory had uncovered in the empire from which the Americans had broken away. It was his function to put thought into action. While he had not contributed to the development of the theory of the Revolution he thoroughly understood that theory. An essential part of the American position had been that the powers of government are limited and that those powers, in the case of the old British Empire, were not all vested in one place. Certain powers appertained to the Crown and others to Parliament. That much had been settled by the expulsion of the Stuarts.

The theory of the American Revolution went a step further. The Americans claimed that not only the powers of the Crown but also those of Parliament were limited. At the beginning of the trouble the Americans had agreed that broad questions of imperial policy were properly within the jurisdiction of the government in London but that Parlia-

3

ment had no authority in matters which the Americans
considered to be essentially local. The dispute had followed
the same course as the previous ones between King and
Parliament. Like the Roundheads of the seventeenth century the Americans appealed to precedent, to Magna Charta
and to common law. They got their arguments out of Locke
and they magnified an obscure dictum of Lord Coke, to the
effect that a court could in certain cases disregard an Act
of Parliament, into a fundamental principle of the British
constitution. The American Revolution was not the precursor of the French Revolution. It was the third act of
the drama in which the Great Rebellion and the Glorious
Revolution were the first and second acts.

In each of those acts the question of constitutional interpretation had been settled on the battlefield. So when the
Americans set about the organization of a central government to exercise those powers which they were willing to
concede had formerly been properly exercised in London
they endeavored to provide a less bloody method of determining the limitations on power. There can be no doubt
that the judiciary was set apart as one of the three independent and coordinate branches of the government with
this end in view. It was to be, as Washington phrased it,
"the keystone of our political fabric."[1]

This conception of the functions of the new Court determined Washington's choice of the man to head it. He did
not, it is true, visualize the precise method in which events
proved that the judiciary was going to perform its functions any more than he visualized party government. But
his conception of those functions has proved sound. The
judiciary was to draw the limitations on power between
the Congress and the President, between the national government and the states, and between all forms of government and individuals. The new Supreme Court would be

---

[1] Letter from Washington to Jay, Oct. 5, 1789. JOHNSTON, III
at 378.

different from any court that had heretofore existed. A lifetime spent at the bar or on the bench was not necessarily the best preparation for its judges. Deep learning in the precedents could not be demanded for there were no precedents for this kind of a court. It had to make its own law by the application of that technique which had resulted in the common law. It demanded a statesman with a knowledge of that technique but above all with an unimpeachable character. The Court had no physical power at its command. Whether it succeeded in performing its functions in the new system of government depended entirely on the moral power it succeeded in building up for itself.

The man was at hand to answer these specifications. John Jay had practiced law altogether about six years and had been Chief Justice of his state for a brief period when so much of the state had been in the possession of the enemy that the courts had scarcely functioned. But there was not an American, except possibly Washington himself, whose reputation for integrity was higher. Jay had filled a long succession of important civil offices to the general satisfaction. He had first gained a national reputation, while still in his twenties, by the ability he showed, as a member of the first Continental Congress, in the drafting of state papers. He had been a member of the next Continental Congress, the virtual draftsman of the New York State constitution, the first Chief Justice of that state, President of the Continental Congress, minister to Spain, the most influential member of the American delegation which negotiated peace with Great Britain and, from the peace until the adoption of the Constitution, the most important official of the government of the Confederation. In all these positions he had evidenced that strong sense of responsibility which is the foundation of great statesmanship. It was the combination of that sense with indubitable practical abilities which determined the President's choice. Washington appointed three of the Chief Justices and in every instance he applied the same general conception. It is the conception which has been most usually followed by succeeding Presidents.

Jay had become a revolutionary leader almost by accident. By all the rules of birth and upbringing he should have been among those who regretted the actions of the home government but who could not bring themselves to rebel. The Tories were probably stronger in New York than in any other colony and their strength there was made up of the very segment of the population to which Jay belonged. The politics of that province were dominated by ecclesiastical divisions and family feuds. The first of these arose out of the efforts of the imperial government to establish the Church of England in the colony. The Dutch had their own church, which was tolerated as a long established evil, and the British who immigrated into the colony perversely insisted on being Presbyterians. The latter church was given no legal status and was even denied the right to own land. This mild persecution did not seem to help the Church of England whose membership remained largely limited to the officials sent out from London. It would probably have remained so limited indefinitely had not the fairly numerous Huguenot churches in and about New York City been induced, despite their theological affinity to the Dutch Reformed and Presbyterian churches, to become parishes of the Church of England. The Anglicans thus made were the special favorites of the royal governors and they returned the favor by staunchly supporting the prerogative. During the Revolution they were almost to a man Tories.

Jay was the most conspicuous exception. His ancestors had been prosperous merchants in La Rochelle when the revocation of the Edict of Nantes forced them to flee from France. His grandfather, Augustus, had, after various wanderings, settled in New York. Here he set up as a merchant and prospered to such an extent that, to quote his grandson, his daughters married into "the most respectable families of the province." Augustus' only son, Peter, did likewise and married a Van Cortland, through whom the Jays became related to the De Lanceys, the recognized leaders of the Anglicans. Peter followed his father's occupation for a time but when he was about forty he retired to a country estate at Rye in Westchester County. John, the eighth of his ten children, was born in 1745, just before the family left the city.

As soon as John was old enough his mother began his schooling by teaching him "the rudiments of English and the Latin grammar" with such success that, by the time he was seven, his father wrote to an elder son, James, who was then studying medicine in Scotland, that "Johnny is of a very grave disposition and takes to learning exceedingly well, he will be soon fit to go to grammar school." The grammar school to which he was sent was kept by the minister of the Anglican Huguenot church in nearby New Rochelle. The minister and his wife were of such an eccentric disposition that after a few years John's family took him home. But the experience was invaluable to him in his later years as a diplomat for during the time he spent in New Rochelle, which was then practically a French village, he acquired a knowledge of that language which he never lost. A few years more were spent with a private tutor and then, at fourteen, he was considered ready for King's College.

The founding of that institution, which had occurred a few years previously, had been the subject of a bitter political fight. The opposition to the establishment of the college was led by Jay's future father-in-law, William Livingston, between whose family and the De Lanceys, who like the Jays were of Huguenot extraction, there was a feud of long standing. The Livingstons were Whigs and Presbyterians, words which at one time were synonymous. Jay always remained a devout member of the Church of England but it was the intimate association which he later had with

William Livingston which made him break politically with
the group to which he naturally belonged. Although Whigs,
the Livingstons were by no means democrats. The family
had been founded by the son of a Scotch Presbyterian
minister who had been forced to leave his manse and flee to
the Netherlands by the Stuart efforts to impose episcopacy
on the northern kingdom. This son, Robert Livingston the
elder, the first lord of the manor of Livingston, arrived in
New York about the time it became an English colony. His
equal familiarity with the Dutch and English languages put
him in an extremely favorable position which, aided by his
native shrewdness, enabled him to die possessed of a landed
estate which stretched from the Hudson River to the Massachusetts boundary. The manor was even entitled to a seat
in the Assembly and William Livingston, like a true aristocrat, sat in the legislature as the member for the family
estate. Livingston had a ready pen and both in and out of
the Assembly he opposed the extension of the Church of
England. The charter of the proposed college was designed
to keep it always under the control of that church. This
Livingston readily saw and rallied the opposition with the
watchword "non-sectarian education." The newspaper he
founded to further his cause was suppressed; the printers
were so terrified that he could get no one to print his pamphlets; and an Anglican clergyman named him from the pulpit
as Gog and Magog. The Presbyterian clergy replied to
these ecclesiastical thunders with the old charge that the
Church of England was a rag of the whore of Babylon.
The upshot of the matter was that half the funds which had
been raised for the proposed college by means of a public
lottery were used instead to build a new pesthouse. The
Presbyterian view was that the lottery funds had been used
to build two pesthouses.[2]

Jay was only a boy during the struggle over the founding of the college but his family was so little in sympathy

[2] *Levermore.*

with Livingston that John's elder brother, James, now went to England to solicit funds for the new college. He did this so much to the satisfaction of the royal government that the King personally knighted him.

It was in this hotbed of Toryism, King's College, which proudly boasted that it was "copied in the most material parts from Queen's College, Oxford"[3] that Jay received his early education. He was a good student and justified his father's boast that he was "a youth remarkably sedate and well disposed." Only one circumstance distinguished his college career and that is that in his last year he was suspended.

Their Toryism did not prevent the students of the college from holding the immemorial undergraduate opinion of the college commons. One day they expressed their feelings by breaking the dining tables. This led, according to the traditional custom of schools, to an investigation by the faculty in the course of which President Myles Cooper lined up the students and asked them, one by one, to name the culprits. One by one they denied all knowledge of the affair until John Jay's turn came. It is unlikely that he had had anything to do with the committing of the offense but he had an ample share of that argumentative legalism which was such a prominent characteristic of many of those who led the American Revolution. Perhaps in the present instance it was helped by the fact that he had already decided to enter the law and was at the time engaged in the study of Grotius with that end in view. In any event he now flatly refused to answer on the ground that, under the statutes of the college, neither the president nor any of the other members of the faculty had a right to call on the students to testify against each other. It was the type of argument which Jay was later to apply to King and Parliament but if the spark of rebellion in his character had not later been fanned by William Livingston it would probably have been

[3] PINE.

stifled by Jay's Tory environment. Jay speedily learned the consequences of rebellion, however legalistic, for he was promptly rusticated.

The rustication was only a suspension and not an expulsion, so after a short time the culprit was allowed to return and to take his degree with his class. The question of presidential jurisdiction was never ruled on any further but John kept a copy of the college statutes and long after he had retired from the Chief Justiceship he was still willing to prove that President Cooper had exceeded his authority in asking the obnoxious question.

His reading of Grotius had not been Jay's only private study while in college. The gravity which his father had noted in the child had now resulted in a shyness which Jay felt to be an acute handicap. To overcome this he took private lessons in elocution. These were so far successful that, although he never acquired a reputation as a great orator, he seems early to have learned to speak in public with ease and distinctness. But his shyness was not overcome. As a young man he felt ill at ease in the social gatherings of the gay little provincial capital. When he first started to practice law he constantly envied the social graces of his partner, Robert R. Livingston, later chancellor of the state. By the time of Jay's marriage, which occurred in his twenty-ninth year, his constant attendance at the functions of New York society had in appearance destroyed his shyness. The trait had been sublimated, not eradicated. It remained a part of his character but in a disguised form and is the unquestionable explanation of the disinclination for elective office and of the dignified reserve which characterized him in his maturity. His enemies attributed both these traits to pride.

His reserved nature may also have had something to do with his choice of an occupation. Their alliance with the Van Cortlands had not caused the Jays to look down on their ancestral occupation as merchants and at least one of

John's brothers followed it. But in those days of a limited
bar and sharp class distinctions the law probably allowed
one to preserve his dignity more easily than did trade. It is
probable, too, that Jay's choice of an occupation was moti-
vated by the hope of becoming a judge, again a method of
shielding himself from the scramble of the market place.
He had hardly begun practice when he made some efforts
to obtain a minor judicial appointment and in later life,
whenever he had a choice of positions, he always indicated
a decided preference for a judgeship.

His early legal ambitions were modest and reflected the
mercantile origin of the family. The only method of studying law in the colony was by clerking in a lawyer's office.
But Manhattan was apparently as overrun with lawyers then
as now and a few years before Jay's graduation from college
the lawyers decided to keep down the number of members of
their profession by entering into an agreement not to take
any clerks who hoped to become members of the bar. Jay
therefore made preparations to go to England. It is note-
worthy, however, that he seems never even to have contem-
plated entering the inns of court which was the only way
one could become a barrister. His ambitions were more
modest. What he intended to do was to study in a solicitor's
office in Bristol. The barristers were the only ones considered learned in the law and the only class eligible to
appear in the superior courts or to become judges. The
solicitors performed minor legal functions and many of the
semi-legal functions which are now undertaken by certified
public accountants and trust companies. It was the branch
of the legal profession which a member of a mercantile
family such as the Jays would most naturally enter.

Just as Jay was about to depart for Bristol the New York
lawyers changed their attitude so far as to agree to take
law students "under such restrictions as will greatly impede
the lower class of the people from creeping in."[4] Under

[4] PELLEW, at 14-15.

this arrangement, Jay, who certainly did not belong to the prohibited class, started to clerk in the office of Benjamin Kissam, an eminent lawyer of the town. By the articles of his clerkship Jay was required to pay two hundred pounds down and anything which required the payment of a thousand dollars must have been sufficiently exclusive to keep "the lower class of the people from creeping in." The fact that he was of the upper class and that he was paying for the privilege of clerking did not relieve Jay from any drudgery. Despite the lack of typewriters and stenographers even the argument of points of law before the supreme court of the province was conducted to a great extent in writing and Jay and his fellow clerk, Lindley Murray, afterwards famous as a grammarian, had to do all this writing by hand. After doing this for four years Jay was admitted to the bar in 1768.

It is doubtful whether this training made Jay a very profound lawyer. His successor in the Chief Justiceship, Rutledge, once pretty plainly expressed his opinion that his own training in the inns of court gave him a much better claim to "law knowledge" than did Jay's and he was unquestionably right. Law as practiced in colonial New York was not a very complicated science. Equity was almost non-existent, being administered, if at all, by the governors who were much more likely to be retired army officers or broken-down politicians than lawyers. The few available records of the colonial courts, as well as the correspondence between Jay and Kissam, show that the law as it passed through their office was confined almost entirely to the standard common law actions such as trover, debt, assault, trespass *quare clausum fregit* and ejectment. The latter two much more commonly turned on questions of surveying than on subtle questions of feudal land law. Nor was it easy for Jay, who was always of a studious disposition, to make up for the deficiencies of Kissam's practice through the use of books for, while Lord Holt had started the practice of writing truly critical opinions, their number was still few and there were as yet no critical legal texts.

Neither Jay's few reported decisions nor his numerous letters and other writings indicate any special knowledge of, or interest in, the common law. At two periods of his life he spent considerable time in England and on one of these visits he was actually holding the office of Chief Justice of the United States but on neither occasion did he show any interest in the judicial system of that country. Nor was this because he was so engrossed with his other duties for he devoted a good deal of attention to the Royal Agricultural Society and to other activities.

While the conclusion is irresistible that Jay was never a profound common law lawyer, he received no bad training for the work he was actually called upon to do. Kissam's office taught him the technique of the common law and his extensive reading in political science taught him the principles on which the future constitutional law was to be based. There was no place where he could learn how to fuse the two, for that had not yet been done. He himself was to begin the task. In both the judicial offices which he held, that of Chief Justice of New York and that of Chief Justice of the United States, his work was to breathe life into a new government rather than to decide whether A or B was entitled to grow corn on a particular plot of ground. He might have been qualified to be a great Chief Justice of the King's Bench and still have failed lamentably in both these positions. For what he had to do Grotius, Locke, Vattel, Pufendorf and Montesquieu, whom he read, were better than a critical treatise on the law of contracts. In America in the latter part of the eighteenth century questions of the nature of law and of the bases of authority were not material for doctoral theses but the warp and woof of politics.

Jay had not yet broken with his Anglican friends and the furor over the Stamp Act did not disturb him. Although

the Congress of the colonies was held in his own small town
he paid little attention to its doings. Indeed, his only interest
in the whole proceeding seems to have been with reference
to its effect on his own legal business. But his Tory background was gradually losing its grip on him. The first
public sign of this was when, shortly after his admission to
the bar, he went into partnership with Robert R. Livingston,
another young lawyer of about the same age. Law partner-
ships were not very common in those days and this one
seems to have been based on the belief that since neither
of them, alone, was likely to have sufficient business to keep
him busy the wisest thing to do was to join forces and both
work on every case that came in. Both of them were, however, able and well-connected and it was not long before
they had sufficient practice so that they deemed it wise to
separate. Their friendship continued for many years, however, and was only the beginning of Jay's connection with
the family.

William Livingston, in addition to being the leading
Whig in the colony, had a ready pen and was generally regarded as the town's chief literateur. It was Jay's
love of books which first brought him into intimate contact
with the older man. But Jay did not leave his family connections in a hurry. They were still so close that he proposed in succession to two girls of the De Lancey family.
He was refused by both, perhaps because of his lack of
social grace, and, in after years, the Tory pamphleteers
blamed his Whiggism on these two refusals. They were
partly right. Jay was incapable of the mean spirit of
revenge which they imputed to him but his subsequent
political course was undoubtedly influenced by these refusals for he next proposed to, and was accepted by,
Livingston's daughter Sarah. The marriage, which occurred
in 1774, brought Jay into intimate family contact with the
most outspoken Whig in the Middle Atlantic colonies, for
such his father-in-law unquestionably was. When the parting of the ways came John Jay did not, like John Dickin-

son, have his wife at his elbow exclaiming, "Johnny, you will be hanged; your estate will be forfeited and confiscated; you will leave your excellent wife a widow, and your charming children orphans, beggars and infamous."[5]

Livingston, who was not the eldest son and therefore had not inherited the family manor, had, shortly before the marriage, retired from New York politics and settled near Elizabeth, New Jersey. He named the mansion which he built here Liberty Hall and speedily became a power in New Jersey for he had retired from New York politics, not from politics in general. The difficulty he found with New York politics was that the Dutch and German population, for the royal government had aided in the establishment of a considerable number of German Lutherans in the colony, too often allowed their antipathy to Yankees, and such most of the Presbyterians were, to overcome their antipathy to Tories.

During the next twenty years Liberty Hall was a second home to Jay. His wife, to whom he remained devotedly attached, made frequent visits there and his own character and that of his father-in-law were so similar as to draw them ever closer together. Both were distinguished primarily by an inflexible honesty; an honesty which led Livingston to be described as the "Don Quixote of the Jerseys" and which led Jay later to attempt to administer the governorship of New York with the same high-minded disregard for party interests that Washington showed in his administration of the presidency. Livingston would certainly have applauded the manner in which, after his death, his son-in-law turned down a plea from Hamilton that he use his power as governor to reduce, in a strictly legal manner, Jefferson's electoral votes from New York. The Jeffersonians had for years advocated the election of presidential electors in districts directly by popular vote. The Federalists, so long as they had control of the legisla-

---

[5] Diary of John Adams. ADAMS, II at 408.

ture, opposed this but when it became apparent that they were about to lose this control, Hamilton wrote Jay an urgent letter suggesting that the latter convene a special session of the lame-duck legislature to change the method of electing presidential electors. The latter simply indorsed on this letter, "Proposing a measure for party purposes which I think it would not become me to adopt."

His marriage was Jay's break with his past. Many others of the Anglican party in New York objected to the tax on tea and the Boston Port Bill; many of them even sat on the early revolutionary committees but in the end they nearly all remained loyal to the Crown. Even his brother, Sir James, after sitting in the first state senate, deserted to the British, an action whose only apparent effect on Jay was to call forth the statement that "I shall endeavor to forget that my father has such a son."

The first Continental Congress met within a year of Jay's marriage. The election of delegates from New York took place in an atmosphere of intense political bickering which was increased by the fact that the whole proceeding was extra-legal. It may have been due to his rapidly increasing professional reputation that Jay, who was not yet thirty, was one of the conservative nominees, but it was certainly due to his father-in-law that his election was not opposed by the radicals. Their action was wise. Jay traveled to Philadelphia by way of Liberty Hall and made the rest of the journey in the company of his father-in-law who was a delegate from New Jersey. It was due to the influence of the latter that, by the time they arrived, Jay was irretrievably committed, with all the strength of his deep sense of responsibility, to opposition to the measures of the imperial government.

The Congress to which Jay and his father-in-law were delegates was more in the nature of a convention of an embryo political party than anything else. The delegates from the few colonies, such as Connecticut, which were practically self-governing could claim in a real sense that they represented the people whom they claimed to represent. At the other extreme were the delegates from New York and South Carolina, who really represented nothing but a more or less substantial group among the citizens of their leading cities. The Congress was not a governmental body. Even its right to speak for the people of British America was open to question. But just because of its irregularity it had attracted an extraordinarily high quality of membership. Many responsible men had sought membership simply because the situation was so grave that it could not be left to political hacks. As there was no certainty that the members of the Congress would reap either glory or money but, instead, at least a remote possibility of hanging, the usual type of office-seeker was not much in evidence.

Constituted as it was, the Congress faced three important tasks. It had to justify its claim that it spoke for the people of America; it had to articulate their desires, and it had to devise means for compelling the Crown to respect those desires. The first two naturally merged into one. If the platform adopted by the Congress appealed to the people the Congress claimed to represent, those people would acknowledge that the Congress represented them. And whatever platform the Congress adopted would be likely to be accepted by a substantial proportion of the population partly because, however unrepresentative the Congress might be, it was still the most representative body available and partly because of the weight which the names of many of its delegates carried in their respective home communities. None of the subsequent congresses was so strong in this last respect as the first. "Jay," said Gouverneur Morris some thirty years later when they were reminiscing over their churchwardens, "what a set of damned scoundrels we had in that second Congress." "Yes," said Jay, "that we had."

As in the case of a convention of an embryo political party, the first work before the Congress was to formulate a platform; a statement of what it wanted and why. The opportunity was made for Jay. He apparently had some literary ambition for there is evidence that in his college days he had devoted some effort to the acquisition of an English style. His wide reading in the classics had helped him in this and his careful study of the political philosophers had furnished him with an armory of arguments. There were few men in the Congress better prepared than he was to set forth the American position on paper. That position was not enunciated in any one document but in a series of declarations, petitions and memorials. Jay, along with his father-in-law and very probably through the latter's influence, was placed on the committee to prepare an Address to the People of Great Britain, certainly one of the most important of these documents. The first draft was prepared by a more mature and better known member of the committee, Richard Henry Lee. It was reported but was not well received by the Congress. Jay, young and unknown, had been anxiously looking for an opportunity to show his skill; so anxiously that he had secretly prepared a draft himself. He did not dare to rise among such a gathering of distinguished men to present it. Instead, he gave it to Livingston, who now rose and read it to the Congress without saying anything about its author. The old and distinguished Whig was listened to with attention, for everyone took the draft to be the product of his pen. The draft he had read pleased the Congress and was approved and ordered to be printed and distributed. Jefferson wrote that it was "a production certainly of the finest pen in America."[6] But Livingston was too honest a man to attempt to steal his son-in-law's glory. He let everyone know who the real author was. Jay became a national figure almost overnight. No longer would the Congressmen dismiss the young New York delegate with his long, lean figure, slight stoop, prominent nose, black eyes and high forehead,

[6] Quoted in PELLEW, at 40.

from which the hair was already receding, simply as Livingston's son-in-law. Jay was now of importance in his own right. He always had a rather self-satisfied opinion of his own abilities, although the trait was not yet so marked as it was later to become, and the regard in which he was held by the revolutionary leaders, when compared with his comparative insignificance among his Tory friends, was probably a factor in his increasing Whiggism.

Jay sometimes struck the more radical members of the Congress as overly conservative but it was the conservatism of a naturally cautious man with a strong sense of responsibility, not the conservatism of a man who is horrified by change simply because it is change. Throughout the growth of the revolutionary movement he never hesitated, although there were many among the radicals who went back to their allegiance when they decided that the possibilities of hanging were getting too serious. While Jay did not falter, his conscience demanded that no opportunity for a peaceful settlement of the difficulty should be overlooked and his naturally legalistic temperament demanded that the American position be buttressed on good logic. After he had thoroughly satisfied himself of the morality and legality of their cause he took a very practical attitude as to the means.

In his zeal to make his interpretation of the imperial constitution effective, Jay's rather argumentative legalism disappeared from sight for the next two years. On his return from the first Congress he struck many of his intimate friends as a changed man, particularly that numerous group among them who were gradually becoming more and more Toryish and some of whom were later arrested by Jay's personal order.

The constitution of the old empire, with its lack of a tribunal to interpret it, was singularly like the international law of today, so much so that the Congress had adopted a very modern means of enforcing its interpretation of that constitution. The American interpretation was to be made effective through economic sanctions, specifically the non-importation of British goods. This was the only possible means except war although the American experience, like subsequent experience, showed that in practice economic sanctions and war were likely to prove to be much the same. Probably because he realized that war was the only alternative, Jay entered wholeheartedly into the non-importation plan. His doing so can only be explained by the earnestness with which he had entered into the American cause. Due to the control of the official colonial government by the Tories non-importation could be enforced only by means which in practice smacked of Judge Lynch. With his gravity and his refined looks Jay must have seemed a queer ally to the mob of "Liberty Boys" who did the rough and tumble work. The incongruity was very real. Both Jay's life prior to this period and his life subsequent to it were distinguished by an extreme love of order and propriety. Temporarily, he seems to have succumbed to the doctrine that the end justifies the means but long before the war was over he was warning the Congress that "the necessity of the case has in all ages and nations of the world been a fruitful, though dangerous, source of power. . . . The whole history of mankind bears testimony against the propriety of considering this principle as the parent of civil rights; and a people jealous of their liberties will ever reprobate it."[7]

His activities in connection with the non-importation agreement were only the beginning of Jay's transformation. He was a member of the second Continental Congress but soon hastened home to join in the organization of a revolutionary government in New York. For a while the revolutionary state government was run by a body called the Provincial Congress. It operated largely through committees and Jay was always a member, and frequently chairman, of the more important of them. It was his work on these

---

[7] Quoted in JAY, I at 45.

committees which first won him the esteem of Washington who was then preparing to defend New York City. Jay's work was very far removed from that of the conscientious lawyer he had been two years previously. It was expected, and expected correctly, that New York would bear the brunt of the British attack. Instead of arguing writs of attachment and writs of replevin he employed spies, rushed around getting cannon and shot for the troops and, to crown all, recommended a method of defense so severe that it is scarcely credible. He urged that the City of New York be destroyed and that all the state below the Catskills be desolated. His idea was then to fortify the army strongly in those mountains and shallow the Hudson below there so that the British fleet could not get up that far.[8] This scheme, it is needless to say, was not adopted.

But what must have been the strangest work for one of his naturally judicial temperament was that which he performed on the Committee of Safety. He was chairman of this body which had been formed to suppress the activities of those opposed to the revolutionary cause. This committee was by no means idle. When Howe captured New York City there were twenty-seven of its prisoners in the city hall and forty-three, including the mayor, in the "new jail." Fishkill then became the seat of the Committee of Safety and, in effect, the capital of the state. Day after day batches of prisoners of both sexes and all ages were examined there. Some were convicted of receiving protection from the enemy, others of corresponding with the enemy and others simply of disaffection to the cause. Strange as it may seem this tribunal, presided over by a future Chief Justice, even convicted Peter Van Schaack, Jay's close friend and at one time a leader of those opposed to the measures of the home government, of having "long maintained an equivocal neutrality in the present struggles" and of being "in general supposed unfriendly to the American cause."[9] Van Schaack

[8] Letter from Jay to Robert Morris, JOHNSTON, I at 85.
[9] VAN SCHAACK, at 70.

and his brother, who was convicted with him, were sent to Boston under guard but "at their own expense." Another prisoner, James McLaughlin, was convicted of being "notoriously disaffected" and was ordered sent to Captain Hodges of the ship of war *Montgomery*. The Captain, in turn, was ordered "to keep him aboard the said ship, put him to such labor as he may be fit for, and pay him as much as he may earn."[10] The crimes for which these people were convicted scarcely sound as though they would hold water in any court of justice, but the punishments were doubly remarkable as emanating from a revolutionary tribunal and as happening in the eighteenth century when, under the common law, practically everything was a hanging offense. There was plenty of sentiment among the New York Whigs in favor of hanging, drawing and quartering and the humanity of these punishments was brought about only by Jay's utmost exertions.

At an early age he had lost faith in the widespread belief that the best method of increasing the observance of the criminal law is to increase the penalties. His busy life left him little opportunity to advocate reforms in the criminal law and it was not until he became governor of New York that he was able to write some of his convictions into statutes. He was not only in favor of less severe penalties but was among the first to believe that prisons should be reformatories rather than merely places of punishment. The order to "put him to such labor as he may be fit for, and pay him as much as he may earn" was very radical penology in the eighteenth century.

Shortly after the adoption of the Declaration of Independence Jay had been appointed a member of a committee to draft a constitution for the newborn state. By this time his reputation as a draftsman was so well established that the other members of the committee practically left the task to him. The British invasion and his work on the Committee

---

[10] PELLEW, at 69.

of Safety kept him from getting at it for some time although he did not forget that, as he wrote, "we have a government, you know, to form, and God knows what it will resemble." He finally found time to shut himself up in the country to do the job. He started with the premise that, for the new government to be stable, it must copy the old colonial government as closely as possible but aside from this he had few precedents to guide him. The property qualifications for voters of every class were taken over almost bodily from the old government. The legislature was divided into two chambers, largely in imitation of the English constitution. The executive, as in the case of all draftsmen of early American constitutions, gave Jay the most difficulty. He decided to retain the office of governor but the difference between an elected governor and a royal governor was no clearer to him than to his contemporaries. The doctrine that an elected executive could do no wrong was then unknown and Jay was certain that any office which carried substantial executive power with it would sooner or later be occupied by a tyrant. To guard against this he provided in his constitution that the governor should share his power of appointment with a Council of Appointment and his veto power with a Council of Revision.

The latter of these was Jay's answer to the constitutional problem which the English revolutions of the previous century had left unsolved. Conflicts in constitutional interpretation between the people of New York and the various departments of their state government, and conflicts of power among those departments, were not to be decided on the battlefield but in the Council of Revision. This Council was composed of the chief executive and judicial officers of the state and exercised its power through a sort of veto on the acts of the legislature. It thus differed fundamentally from the ultimate American doctrine of judicial review. The Council was not exercising a true judicial function as that function is understood in American constitutional law. In practice it wrote opinions explaining its vetoes and such of these opinions as were written by Jay, who was a member of the Council during the first few years of its existence, indicate that his intention had been that the Council should pass only on the constitutional aspects of legislation. It was in the manner in which it did this that it deviated from the theory of constitutional law which was ultimately worked out. That theory goes back to the common law cases of a sheriff exceeding his authority. In those cases the question of authority was determined incidentally, in private litigation in which the question of the sheriff's authority happened to become important. Jay's Council, on the other hand, was to act on its own initiative and without waiting for a private citizen to raise the constitutional point. There is nothing in Jay's career to indicate that he ever thoroughly grasped the difference. The sole instance in which, as Chief Justice of the United States, he might be said to have held an Act of Congress unconstitutional[11] certainly does not so indicate.

As Chief Justice of the United States Jay was to decline to do various things on the ground that they were not judicial in character. He was thus in a sense the founder of that distinction between judicial and non-judicial functions which, in the history of American law, has been drawn with ever increasing refinement. He may have originated the doctrine but he had certainly never thought out its ramifications for his life is strewn with instances in which he seems to us of the present day to have mingled judicial and non-judicial functions. A striking instance is his objection to the action of the constitutional convention in changing his draft constitution so as to give the courts the power to admit their own attorneys and appoint their own clerks. His attitude in this instance may have been partly mere conservatism, for his own certificate of admission to the bar was signed not by a judge but by the acting royal governor. But certainly his belief that the courts should not have control of their own clerks cannot be considered conservatism.

---

[11] *Hayburn's Case*, 2 Dall. 409, 1 L. Ed. 436 (1792).

It is precisely the type of provision which, when it is found
in state constitutions today, is regarded as stemming directly
from Jefferson and Jackson.   This modern attitude is a
result of an oversimplification of our early history. Jefferson
himself sometimes deviated far from the modern concept
of a democrat while Jay, as Chief Justice of the United
States, charged a jury that it was the final judge of the law
as well as of the facts.[12]   When Jay became a revolutionary leader he adopted the doctrine of the sovereignty
of the people. He occasionally made strange applications of
that doctrine.

The Council of Revision was Jay's most original contribution to political science. It aroused a great deal of discussion in that constitution-making age and may have had
some influence on the presidential veto which was later
embodied in the federal constitution. Both the President
and the Council of Revision were expected to exercise their
power over legislation in a quasi-judicial manner. Both
actually did so for a time but the Council's later history is
such that its final demise, half a century after its introduction, was greeted with general satisfaction.

Jay had early found it impossible to reconcile the American demand for freedom with the continued existence of
human slavery. A few years after this period he wrote that
so long as that institution was tolerated the American
"prayers to Heaven for liberty will be impious. This is a
strong expression but it is just . . . . I believe God governs
this world, and I believe it to be a maxim in His as in our
court, that those who ask for equity ought to do it."[13]
Slavery had always existed in New York and Jay knew that
he could not get rid of it simply by including a provision to
that effect in his draft constitution. Indeed, the institution
was so far from being unpopular in the state that when he
later ran for governor one of his opponents' chief battle

---

[12] *State of Georgia* v. *Brailsford*, 3 Dall. 1, 1 L. Ed. 483 (1794).
[13] Letter from Jay to Benson, September 17, 1780. JOHNSTON, I
at 406.

cries was that, if elected, he would "rob every Dutchman of his slaves." At this time he hoped, however, that in the general wave of reform which the Revolution had engendered he might be able to get such a provision adopted if he introduced it from the floor. Unfortunately he was called away from the convention during the debate on the constitution by the illness and subsequent death of his mother. It was not until he became governor that he finally succeeded in getting slavery abolished.

He was not entirely satisfied, either, with the religious provisions of the constitution. He himself was naturally of a tolerant disposition, a tolerance which increased with age and which applied to those who differed from him politically as well as to those who differed from him religiously. He was a man of strong and active piety but, perhaps because of his political association with the Presbyterians, he early learned the art of keeping his particular religious beliefs to himself. The most perfect harmony prevailed between him and his Presbyterian father-in-law but there was never the slightest suggestion that Jay's own Episcopalianism was in doubt. This man-of-the-world attitude covered all but one element of his religious beliefs. That element was a strong dislike and distrust of the Church of Rome. It was a relic of the sad day when the Jays had fled from the Dragonnades, imbibed as an infant from his father and increased by his own reading. As a young statesman Jay had been anxious to play up the unpopular Quebec Act, the Act which restored the rights of the Roman Church among the French Canadians, as one of the reasons for the Revolution. His argument was that the King's signature of that Act was a violation of his coronation oath against Popery. It is interesting that George III himself later took the position that his ministers, in asking him to sign a bill removing some of the Catholic disabilities in England, were asking him to violate his coronation oath. Jay was not so bigoted as the King. He did not favor any active political steps to suppress Popery. His belief that every man is

entitled to think as he pleases was real but he felt strongly
that the authority of the Pope over his followers was a
danger to the state. His objection was not to Roman Catholics but to Papists. The obsolete word alone is capable of
expressing his precise attitude. If he could have drawn the
New York constitution entirely to suit himself it would have
required, as a preliminary to any participation in the government, the taking of an oath denying the authority of
"every foreign King, Prince, Potentate and State, in all
matters *ecclesiastical* as well as civil."[14] The quotation is
from the constitution for, while it did not go to the extent
that Jay would have liked, it did include a provision requiring such an oath as a preliminary to naturalization. As the
number of Roman Catholics in the state at the time of the
adoption of the constitution was negligible the effect should
have been the same. But Jay, with his own strong religious
feelings, overrated the importance of oaths.

His fear of ecclesiastical interference in political matters
was not confined to interference by the Church of Rome.
Perhaps this enlargement of his ideas was due to the fact
that he himself was opposed politically by almost all the
clergy of his own church. In any event his draft of the
constitution contained a provision, which was adopted, forbidding the holding of any civil or military office by any
minister or priest of any denomination.

Upon the organization of the new state government, Jay
became Chief Justice. His early ambition for a judicial
office had been fulfilled but it was the irony of his life that
both times that he sat on a bench he found the duties distasteful. Both times he blamed his disappointment on the
peculiar circumstances surrounding the office he held. It
is more probable that it is due to the fact that he had overcome the shyness that had once made him look to the bench
as a refuge. In his first judicial office his chief complaint
was that his work consisted mostly in the trial of criminal

---

[14] First New York Constitution, Art. XLII.

cases. The usually well-concealed sensitiveness of his nature and, it is probable, the inherent pettiness of trial work, made him rapidly develop a dislike for his new duties. So much of the state was in the hands of the British that the court never sat *en banc* and civil litigation was almost non-existent.

The only thing he enjoyed about his new position was his ex officio right to sit in the Council of Revision. The sessions of this body were secret and if it disapproved of a bill it sent it back to the legislature with a sort of *per curiam* opinion setting forth its reasons for so doing. However, the minutes indicate which member actually wrote the opinion which was adopted as that of the Council. It appears from these minutes that in the case of every bill which was objected to at a meeting at which Jay was present he was the member that raised the objection. His reasoning in so doing was always judicial. Thus, one bill was objected to because it referred to the Committee of Safety "as if it had been a body constitutionally instituted and known to the law of the land"[15] and another because "to punish men for acts by laws made subsequent to the commission of such acts" is "arbitrary and unjust."[16]

Jay did not preside at criminal trials long. A little more than a year after he had taken office as Chief Justice of the state the legislature decided that he could temporarily perform a more valuable function by representing the state in the Continental Congress than by staying at home and writing veto messages. The central governing body of the incipient nation was, at that time, almost a congress in the diplomatic sense for the states sent and withdrew delegates at will. The New York legislature's decision, however, to strengthen that state's representation had nothing to do with the need, which was great, for abler men in the Congress. It was governed purely by local motives. The inhabitants of Vermont, which New York then claimed as part of its

[15] STREET, at 205.
[16] STREET, at 211.

territory, had decided to have a little Fourth of July of their own and had organized themselves into the State of Vermont. This struck the New Yorkers as very heinous conduct and Jay, without resigning his office as Chief Justice, was sent to Philadelphia to get the help of the central council of the revolted colonies to bring home to the Vermonters the enormity of revolting from their lawful sovereign.

Jay himself had little sympathy with the rather absurd attitude of the New York state government. Instead of obtaining a detachment from Washington's already too scanty army for use against the Vermonters he worked out a plan which called for the recognition of Vermont as an independent state and the creation of a mixed commission, always a favorite device with him, to determine the boundary. Both these propositions were indignantly rejected by the New Yorkers who instead, and regardless of the war with the King, raised troops to coerce the Vermonters. Massachusetts and New Hampshire did likewise for they both claimed parts of the territory that went to make up the state which the rebels had set up. Washington's personal interference prevented bloodshed but it was not until after the adoption of the federal constitution that the status of Vermont was finally determined.

Perhaps it was the lack of sectional interest which he had displayed in the Vermont affair but Jay had not been at the Congress long when, on a vacancy occurring in the office of president of that body he was elected to fill it. He accepted, and resigned his judgeship. He had, while still under forty, attained what his wife correctly described as "the first office on the Continent." The Congress might be a weak body but it was still the only government that the United States as a whole had.

It is likely that Jay, in accepting the office, planned to hold it for a short time and then to retire from public life. The office was in no sense a permanent one and Jay, while he probably enjoyed the dignity that went with that office, never evidenced any intense political ambition. Essentially he was still the Huguenot bourgeois who believed in minding his own affairs, taking care of his family, paying his bills and generally doing his duty as he saw it in a quiet way. Once drawn into public service his sense of duty, together with a gradually increasing feeling that no one was quite as capable of handling public business as he was, had kept him there. But the war had played havoc with his private business affairs. Even as a member of the first Continental Congress he had complained that his small *per diem* allowance of four or five dollars was not sufficient. While he had received some sort of pay during most of the time he had given to the revolutionary cause the general poverty of the governmental bodies he served and the terrible currency situation made his remuneration constantly less satisfactory. There was little chance, it is true, of practicing law in New York City while it remained in the hands of the British but Jay had inherited a considerable quantity of farming property. His increasingly frequent expressions of a desire to retire from public life were governed by a desire to live on this property with his wife. She had been spending most of the time at her father's home in New Jersey since the British invasion had driven them from New York City.

It was to be a good many years before he settled down on a farm. He had not been President long when the Congress decided that there was a possibility of obtaining help from Spain. The anxiety with which the fathers looked all over Europe for help was a relic of their colonialism. This was so strong that, even after the peace, college presidents would go to Europe when they were endeavoring to increase their endowments. It had already led to the appointment of nearly all the ablest American civilians to diplomatic posts. Jay's turn was next and he rather reluctantly accepted the appointment of minister to Spain.

He knew it would probably be several years before he returned, for in those days a journey across the Atlantic was not undertaken lightly, so his wife accompanied him. His mission was hopeless from the start, for Spain had no sympathy for the Americans. Its Prime Minister, Florida Blanca, recognized clearly that an independent power in the Americas was a constant threat to the Spanish colonial empire. The Spanish scheme was to take advantage of England's distress and regain Gibraltar. The very elements seem to have intended to teach Jay the uselessness of his mission for it took him, counting a lengthy stay in Martinique which was due to the damage which the ship in which he originally sailed had suffered in a storm, a little over three months to reach Cadiz. He spent the next two years in Spain and they were the most unhappy in his life. The Spanish government never even recognized his official status. The chief communications he received from America were drafts which the Congress drew on him in the blithe expectation that he would succeed in borrowing money from the Spanish government with which to meet them. Jay did succeed in raising a little money but it was a herculean effort. Spain, which still pretended to be a great power, had little enough money for its own use. Jay hated his duties and he hated the country. He found living there both expensive and very unpleasant. His dissatisfaction reacted on his character. He quarreled with his secretary of legation, a former congressman from Maryland named Carmichael. He quarreled even more violently with his private secretary, his brother-in-law, Brockholst Livingston. Jay accused the two of conspiring against him, of incompetence and of treachery of all sorts. As, after Jay left Spain, Carmichael established an excellent reputation as the American diplomatic representative there and as Joseph Story, who subsequently sat on the Supreme Court of the United States with Brockholst Livingston for many years, speaks of the latter as "accessible and easy," it is impossible to assume that Jay was without fault in these difficulties.

The only good things Jay found in Spain were the wines and the cigars. He had already set up as a connoisseur of wines and throughout the time he spent in Europe he made it a point to sample every possible brand. The smoking of cigars was at that time an almost exclusively Spanish custom. Jay was an inveterate smoker throughout life but up to this time he had smoked only pipes, particularly the long clay variety known as churchwardens. After his sojourn in Spain his idea of a smoke was a good Havana.

Nothing in his life ever gave Jay greater pleasure than to learn that he had been appointed one of the commissioners to negotiate peace with Great Britain. It meant that he could leave Spain. The French were very anxious to keep those negotiations under their thumb as they had no desire that the United States should develop into anything but footballs for European politics. Originally the Congress had chosen John Adams alone to negotiate peace terms. But Adams' well-known independence and pugnacity made this choice by no means acceptable to Luzerne, the French minister in Philadelphia. By means which did not always redound to the honor of the delegates, French influence had become very strong in the Congress and that body hastened to rectify its error by instructing Adams that, in negotiating peace, he was "to make the most candid and confidential communications upon all subjects to the ministers of our generous ally, the King of France; to undertake nothing in the negotiations for peace or truce without their knowledge or concurrence; and ultimately to govern yourself by their advice and opinion."[17] Even then Luzerne was not satisfied and insisted that additional commissioners be appointed to help keep Adams in line. The Congress readily complied and appointed Jay, Franklin, Jefferson and Laurens. Paris was fixed as the place where the commissioners should meet.

Franklin was already in Paris. Jay arrived there in June of 1782 and Adams in October. Jefferson and Laurens, the latter of whom was a prisoner in the Tower, never reached France. Jay arrived with a pretty thorough conviction that

---

[17] Quoted in PELLEW, at 162-163.

there was a secret treaty between France and Spain which was designed, among other things, to keep the United States from spreading to the Mississippi and from enjoying the right to fish on the Newfoundland Banks, which latter occupation was one of the chief sources of livelihood for the New Englanders. He had come to this conclusion from his negotiations with the Spanish court in the course of which he had attempted to obtain a recognition of the Mississippi as the western boundary of the United States even though the Congress ordered him to yield that point. His letters indicate how short-sighted he thought this course was.

However, partly because of what he did in Spain, pursuant to the instructions of the Congress, the belief became general in the South and West that he was a provincial Easterner who could not see that the nation was manifestly destined to expand. Nothing is further from the truth. It can be stated categorically that if Jay had been among the absent commissioners when the treaty of peace was negotiated the original boundaries of the United States would have been smaller. In his negotiations with the Spaniards he had from time to time expressed a willingness to make temporary concessions for the purpose of receiving the aid which was so badly needed, but there was no statesman in the United States who was more certain than he that the new nation would ultimately fill the Mississippi valley. It was fortunate for this country that Lord Shelburne happened to be in charge of the British side of the negotiations leading to the treaty of peace for it was because of his sympathetic attitude that Jay was able to obtain far better terms than the United States were entitled to in view of the military situation.

Franklin, whose long residence in France had made him very friendly to the French authorities, was by no means certain that Jay's surmise was correct but he allowed Jay to go ahead and deal directly with the British agents in Paris, without bringing the French diplomats into the negotiations.

When Adams arrived he approved everything that Jay had done and Franklin finally agreed that there probably was such a secret understanding and that they were therefore justified in breaking their instructions. Lord North's ministry had fallen and the British were as anxious to obtain peace as the Americans. With a few interruptions the negotiations proceeded smoothly and in a comparatively short time the terms had been agreed upon. The Americans obtained more than they could reasonably expect and, as Jay told one of the British envoys, the treaty was such that "it should not be in the interest of either party to violate it."[18] That conception of the object of a peace treaty is still beyond the capacity of most statesmen.

Jay took a vacation of a few months after the signing of the treaty. One of the British commissioners had complained, during the negotiations, that Jay, "although he has lived till now as an English subject," was "as much alienated from any particular regard for England as if he had never heard of it in his life"[19] but the first place he now went to was England. The high point of his enmity for that country had been reached and passed. He was received everywhere with that regard which he valued and he made a host of friends. The experience was to be repeated on his subsequent visit and he developed a liking for the mother country which was by no means an advantage to him politically in America. Perhaps his willingness to forgive and forget was enhanced by the fact that he could boast, like Theodore Roosevelt, that he did not have a drop of English blood in his veins. As a young man he had once so boasted in the presence of an English official who had acidly remarked that if that was the fact it was as well to conceal it. But the situation was different in the case of a leader of a successful revolution from that of a young colonial.

He liked England but he refused to remain as the American minister. The things which Europe had to offer and

[18] PELLEW, at 177.
[19] PELLEW, at 177-178.

which could not then be obtained in America, notably theaters and music, had little appeal for Jay. He had done his duty to the public; now he was going to attend to his own affairs. He had taken this vacation in Europe partly to avoid a winter crossing for he was throughout life extremely susceptible to seasickness. But with the return of spring he returned to New York "like," wrote John Adams, "a bee to his hive, with both legs loaded with merit and honor." His mind was made up to go back to arguing writs of attachment until such time as he, like his father, should retire to his estate in Westchester.

He was welcomed on his arrival in New York with the freedom of the city in a gold box and the news that the Congress had already defeated his intention of retiring to private practice by electing him Secretary for Foreign Affairs. This office had been established about three years before when it finally became clear, even to the Congress, that all the executive work of the government could not be performed through committees. The nationalism of the period was so feeble that, for a time, the Secretary for Foreign Affairs handled not only the correspondence with foreign countries but also that with the various states of the Confederation. The first Secretary had been Jay's former partner, Robert R. Livingston, but after two years of wrangling with the incompetent Congress he had returned to his chancellorship. For the next year the government got along without any minister of foreign affairs. The diplomatic correspondence was addressed to the President of the Congress and most of it went unanswered. When a reply was absolutely essential, the correspondence would be referred to the Congress, which would in turn refer it to a committee which would then draft an answer. A year of this was enough for everybody and when it was suggested that the vacant office be filled by electing Jay to it, there was no opposition. He refused to accept the position until he was certain that New York was to be the seat of the Congress.

It is doubtful if he could have found any position in
which he would have been happier. He had talked a great
deal about returning to the practice of the law but he must
have realized that if he did so he was likely to find his duties
irksome. The law in those days consisted chiefly of litigation and it is difficult to imagine Jay enjoying it. Perhaps
he had done so as a young man but he had now spent a
decade in work which was much more congenial. As Secretary for Foreign Affairs he was located in his home town
and had an opportunity to look after the substantial family
property which consisted largely of mortgages on New York
real estate and notes of New York merchants. The salary
which he received as Secretary was four thousand dollars a
year, which was later, on account of the increasing insolvency of the Confederation, reduced to thirty-five hundred.
It was likely at all times to get into arrears and, when paid,
to be paid in depreciated money. Jay seems to have been
able to get along very well on his salary and his own private
income. America was then a poor country and was suffering
from a severe post-war depression. He built a house, which
soon became a great social center, just below Wall Street.
His wines were well known and his cook was famous. His
wife became the town's first social leader. Their children
spent much of their time at Liberty Hall for Jay, like many
men whose complexions are naturally colorless and who
seem to themselves to be overly susceptible to illness, was
extremely anxious that his children should grow up in the
country and become ruddy and athletic. But Elizabeth was
not far away and the separation was never for long. If the
government of the Confederation had had a little more
power his position would have been perfect.

What little power the Congress had was soon in his
hands. It came to him naturally, by right of merit, and
without intrigue or struggle. He was what the central government had long needed, a man of ability and integrity who
was willing to work. Whether people liked or disliked him
personally they knew that if he was taking care of a matter

it would be handled promptly and with common sense. The Congress was a constantly changing body. The delegates came and went and sometimes it was difficult to obtain a quorum. For the most part the membership was poor in quality. Everybody was glad to leave matters in the hands of Secretary Jay. Soon the French minister wrote his government that "it is as difficult to obtain anything without the cooperation of that minister," Jay, "as to bring about the rejection of a measure proposed by him."[20]

He performed his duties in a modest office of two rooms. He sat in one of these while his two clerks and his visitors sat in the other. He spent long hours here for the new member of the concert of powers had plenty of diplomatic troubles. Most of them were due to its own wretched constitution.

Jay soon found, if he doubted it before, that, while the Congress might be willing to give him most of the power that it had, it had no real power to give. The most important questions which he was supposed to settle as Secretary were with England, Spain and the Barbary pirates. In none of these cases could he arrive at a satisfactory solution and always for the same reason, the total want of power in the Confederation. The English refused to give up the posts they still retained in the territory they had ceded and had a plausible excuse in the failure of the United States to perform their obligations under the treaty of peace. So long as Jay was unable to give them any real assurance that the Confederation would perform its obligations he, of course, was not in a very strong position from which to insist that the British evacuate the posts. The same thing was true when it came to a commercial treaty with Great Britain. American commerce had grown up under the protection of the British navigation laws and now found that it could not thrive outside that protection. Jay wished to get American commerce back inside the navigation laws by restoring the

[20] Quoted in PELLEW, at 232.

British to their old favored position in America. But they thought, and rightly, that since, as a matter of practice, every state did as it pleased in managing foreign commerce, they would regain their old position without giving up anything in return. The Spanish, likewise, refused absolutely to let the Americans navigate the Mississippi. It was clear that the only way the Americans would ever gain that right was by force and the Confederation had no force. But the most humiliating negotiation was with the Barbary pirates. The navies of the great powers protected their own nationals but those powers purposely refrained from crushing the pirates, as they thought the Berbers performed a service in rendering the Mediterranean too dangerous for any but the merchantmen of the great naval states. At that time the United States had one of the largest merchant marines in the world but no navy and no money. The consequence was that the Secretary for Foreign Affairs could neither threaten the pirates nor ransom the Americans that were made slaves. The views of the latter in regard to the evils of centralized government were probably considerably different from those of Patrick Henry.

Nor was the condition of the Confederation improving. On the contrary, it was obviously steadily falling to pieces. A graceful method of retirement presented itself to Jay before long. When the New York state government was organized George Clinton had, to the surprise and chagrin of people like General Schuyler, been elected governor. He was an Ulster County Presbyterian and by no means a rabid democrat but their complaint was, to quote the General, that "his family and connections do not entitle him to so distinguished a predominance." Jay himself seems to have taken Clinton's election with that broad-minded tolerance which was one of his strongest characteristics. Clinton was constantly re-elected but his strength was always upstate. Due to the fact that New York City had never been captured by the Americans but had been peaceably surrendered by treaty many members of the old Anglican-Tory party re-

mained there. These naturally became anti-Clintonians.
Now that Jay was living at home again he was drifting back
into his old associations. It was the basis for those charges
of Toryism which were to be leveled against him in the
coming years with increasing frequency. The anti-
Clintonians of all sorts now decided to make Jay their candidate for governor. But he could not be persuaded. He
was happy where he was. "A servant," he told them, "should
not leave a good old master for the sake of a little more pay
or a prettier livery," and he had no stomach for the vituperation with which he knew that the campaign would be
conducted.

But he was already too closely identified in local politics
with the anti-Clintonians for the governor to permit his
election to the federal constitutional convention. His influence on the drafting of the constitution was therefore less
than that of either of his two immediate successors as Chief
Justice, Rutledge and Ellsworth. His own unique contribution to the art of constitution-making, the Council of Revision, was debated in the constitutional convention and
rejected. His work lay nearer home.

Even the delegates to the convention were not very
enthusiastic over the result. They had all had to compromise too much. The only reason the constitution was finally
ratified was that the wiser men of the nation knew that
things could not go on as they were. But they also knew
that ratification could only be accomplished through an intense campaign of education. The newspapers of the day
were rather sorry affairs and modern methods of propaganda
had not been invented. The best means known, a barrage
of pamphlets and speeches, was employed. Jay himself
would have preferred a much stronger central government
than that provided for in the proposed constitution. He
had less state loyalty than almost any of our early statesmen, except Hamilton, and would cheerfully have made the
states mere administrative districts. But he strongly favored

ratification of the proposed constitution as the best plan available. After he had written a few pamphlets and newspaper letters in its support, he and Hamilton determined to produce a thorough exposition of the proposed new government. Later Madison joined them. Jay was the oldest and, at the time, by far the most distinguished of the trio, but as he was ill during most of the time that *The Federalist* was being written and published he wrote very little of it.

His most important work in connection with the adoption of the constitution was in the New York convention. He was the leader of the Federalists there with the able assistance of his old partner, Chancellor Livingston, and of Hamilton. It was the last time Jay was to act politically with his wife's family. William Livingston died shortly after the adoption of the constitution and the Chancellor became an ally of the Clintonians. New York politics was gradually taking on its pre-revolutionary shape and Jay was returning to the group in which he was born. To the end he retained his broad tolerance and his belief that the victory of those opposed to him politically did not necessarily mean the end of the world but he was becoming more and more conservative, more and more a member of that group which the Jeffersonians later labeled Tories.

After the necessary number of states had ratified the constitution, a President and Vice-President and members of the new Congress were elected. The old Confederation was never formally dissolved. It simply died a natural death by the absence of all the members of the Congress. Jay was virtually the government of the United States in the interregnum. He buried the old government and supervised the birth of the new. It was to him that Washington turned for advice on the organization of the government. The esteem which the President had acquired for Jay when the latter was a young revolutionary leader in New York had increased and had ripened into friendship. Washington admired the sense of duty which had kept Jay in the service of the Congress during the lean years and it was generally believed that he offered the latter the choice of positions in the new administration. In any event when in September of 1789, on the same day on which he signed the Judiciary Act, the President sent the names of his nominees for the Supreme Court to the Senate, Jay's name headed the list as Chief Justice. Perhaps Jay would have been happier if he had chosen the state department. If he had done so the Federalist administration would probably have lasted longer for he had political qualities, notably his balance, which Hamilton totally lacked. But the Chief Justiceship was a much greater office and Jay had always wanted to be a judge.

The Court sat for the first time at the February Term, 1790, but naturally there were no cases on its docket. The commissions of the judges were read and they were sworn into office. The question of procedure had to be settled and it was decided that the best solution was simply to provide that the rules of the English courts should be followed whenever applicable unless, in a particular instance, a definite rule to the contrary should be adopted. The Court also provided that all process should be in the name of the President of the United States and that "counsellors shall not practice as attorneys nor attorneys as counsellors in this court."[21]

The lack of cases to come before the Court did not mean that the judges had nothing to do. The Judiciary Act had divided the country into three circuits and had provided that two Supreme Court judges should ride each of the circuits twice a year. As the Supreme Court consisted of the Chief Justice and five associate justices this meant that each individual on the Court had to ride through one-third of the United States twice a year, either on horseback or by stage, or occasionally by boat, as well as come to the seat of government twice a year for the sittings of the Court. It was this intensive traveling that had made Washington

---

[21] 2 Dall. 399, 1 L. Ed. 432.

purposely avoid appointing elderly men to the Court and
that prompted Gouverneur Morris later to remark that he
was "not quite convinced that riding rapidly from one end of
this country to another is the best way to study law. I am
inclined to believe that knowledge may be more conveniently
acquired in the closet than in the high road."[22]   This circuit-
riding feature of the Act was partly copied from the English
assize system but it was also designed to help cement the
states together. It was thought that the constant visits of the
judges of the Supreme Court to the various communities of
the country would tend to break down the widespread feeling that the central government was something remote and
foreign with which the average man had nothing to do.
It was undoubtedly intended that the traveling judges, by
means of charges to grand juries, should attempt to explain
the nature of the new government throughout the land. Jay
was to travel about and to prop up the shaky government by
bringing home its existence and nature to the people.

He liked his function as a public relations man for the
new government very well. He was usually greeted at the
various towns to which he went on circuit with some sort
of ceremony. The grand juries which he addressed generally consisted of men prominent locally and his charges
were heard with interest and received wide publicity. But
he soon found that while a system of traveling courts
might work in a small country like England the distances
in the United States were greater and the roads were worse.
He soon came to regret his old life as Secretary for Foreign
Affairs and to complain that "the judiciary" was not "on its
proper footing."

He seems to have had little realization of the importance
his Court was to obtain as the arbiter between the federal
government and the states and between all government and
the individuals composing the nation. This seems to have
been due to a belief that the conflicts would be few and far

[22] Quoted in FRANKFURTER and LANDIS, at 17.

between and would be settled privately, by letters and conference, rather than publicly by formal judicial decisions. The first one to come before him arose out of an Act of Congress providing for pensions for veterans of the Continental Army. Under the act in question the various federal judges were to determine those eligible for pensions. As their decisions were subject to review by the Secretary of War, it was, under the American doctrine of the separation of powers as later worked out, clearly unconstitutional but as this conclusion involves some rather subtle reasoning it would not have been surprising if Jay, with his rather vague ideas on the subject, had performed the duties assigned to him by the act. This he did not do. Instead, when, on circuit, he received the first application for a pension, he stated his opinion that he had no authority to pass on the application in his judicial capacity, and then adjourned court and heard the application as if, in his capacity as a private citizen, he had been appointed a commissioner for that purpose.[23] All the circuit courts seem to have come to much the same conclusion independently but in no case was their decision expressed in exactly the form in which we would expect it. The exact technique of the new constitutional law had yet to be worked out.

That technique was not worked out until after Jay had left the bench. His contribution to the development of the position of the Court was less subtle. It was in discouraging Washington's tendency to treat him as a member of the administration. Jay took part in political decisions to an extent which would now be deemed scandalous but he drew the line when the President asked for a written opinion on the law involved in a case which was then in the courts. Instead of an opinion Washington received a letter pointing out the division of functions between the executive and the judiciary. This letter had far more importance on the development of the American constitutional system than any judicial decision which Jay ever rendered. His con-

---

[23] Note to *Hayburn's Case*, 2 Dall. 409, 1 L. Ed. 436 (1792).

tribution was in character and prestige rather than in legal opinions.

Jay wrote only one important opinion[24] as Chief Justice and it is chiefly important because of the insight it gives us into his ways of thought and because it first brought to light that curious doctrine of state sovereignty which was to culminate in the Civil War. Nearly all the few cases which were filed in the Court during his brief administration arose out of the various state confiscatory acts. All the states had tried to seize all the Tory property they could and, naturally, in the case of intangible property this sometimes led to conflicts between the states. The first state[25] to take advantage of the new machinery was Georgia and the insistence with which it pressed its rather flimsy legal position gave the Court a great deal of trouble. But the shoe was soon on the other foot. The same clause of the constitution under which Georgia had brought its action, the clause which defines the judicial power as extending to all cases "between a State and Citizens of another State," was now used by one Chisholm to bring an action against that state. Georgia refused in any way to admit the jurisdiction of the Court. To a dispassionate observer its position would seem to have been answered completely in Jay's opinion. He satisfied himself that the case fell within the express provision of the constitution and then analyzed the position of Georgia in language whose logic would seem to be irrefutable although it is still in advance of the law. He saw no reason why the feudal idea that a prince was not amenable to suit should be applied to an American state. The sovereignty of a feudal lord and the sovereignty of a government instituted by the consent of the governed were essentially different. His discussion of the nature of the new type of sovereignty which existed in America had a thoroughly democratic tinge and culminated in the expres-

---

[24] *Chisholm* v. *Georgia*, 2 Dall. 419, 1 L. Ed. 440 (1793).
[25] *The State of Georgia* v. *Brailsford*, 2 Dall. 402, 1 L. Ed. 433 (1792).

sion of a desire which certainly was in line with the aspirations of the Revolution. "I wish," he wrote, "the state of
society was so far improved, and the science of government
advanced to such a degree of perfection, as that the whole
nation could in the peaceable course of law, be compelled
to do justice, and be sued by individual citizens."

His wish was in vain, for those who exercised the powers
of government in the name of the people were as disinclined
to submit themselves to justice as feudal princes. The
reaction from the idealism of the Revolution took place in
both the parties which were soon to divide American politics. The decision of the Court in the *Chisholm Case* was
promptly reversed by a constitutional amendment yet Jay's
question remains. Why is the City of Philadelphia suable
but not the State of Delaware? Why, in a democracy, should
a mail truck be allowed to run over a citizen with impunity?
In the first conflict between a state and the Court, it was
the state which based its position on the outworn concepts
of feudalism. Jay had found that the representatives of the
people, when vested with power, were as disinclined to do
justice as those who claimed to rule by divine right. The
experience contributed to his growing feeling of disappointment not only with his own position as Chief Justice but
with the entire results of the Revolution. But his sane outlook always prevented his disappointment from reaching
the ridiculous extreme which was found in the notorious
Essex Junto and even from that admiration of the English
constitution which Hamilton so freely avowed. To the end
of his life Jay remained a republican.

The rebuff Washington had once received had not taught
him the sharpness of the distinction between the branches
of government. There was as yet no strong feeling either
on or off the bench that the judges should stay out of politics.
That feeling grew out of the later attacks on the judiciary.
So when the increasing rifts with Great Britain threatened
war the President did not hesitate to ask the Chief Justice

to go to England as a special envoy. Jay saw no more reason why the office he held should prevent him from complying with the President's wishes than, more than a century later, in another crisis, Lord Reading saw any reason why his office of Chief Justice of England prevented him from acting as special envoy to the United States. The crisis which faced the American government in the eighteenth century was as severe as the crisis which faced the British government in the twentieth.

Jay cannot be accused of ambition in accepting the embassy. The American military position was so weak that he knew he would have to yield to nearly all the British demands. The very idea of attempting to make a treaty was denounced by a great many Americans. He would make far more enemies than friends by going, while if he remained in America and rested quietly on his laurels he stood a reasonable chance of gaining the Presidency. It was not ambition, but self-satisfaction, which determined his decision. He knew that it was essential that some sort of understanding be arrived at with Great Britain and that no man was likely to gain any popularity by representing the United States in the negotiations. He himself had already negotiated one treaty with the British very successfully and he felt that no one could handle the present situation better than he. It was clear to him that duty called.

He arrived in London with few instructions to fetter him, for in those days of difficult communication an ambassador necessarily had to have wide discretion. The negotiations were conducted with the Foreign Minister, Lord Grenville, personally. The latter had received a very shrewd analysis of Jay's character from the British minister in America in which the Chief Justice was described as one who could "bear opposition to what he advocates provided regard is shown to his ability." "Almost every man," the report further read, "has a weak spot and Mr. Jay's weak spot is Mr. Jay."[26] He received the utmost respect in England.

---

[26] Quoted in BEMIS, at 205.

The King was gracious to him; the ministers treated him as a man of great importance, and he was invited everywhere. His love of farming led to a friendship with Sir John Sinclair, the head of the Royal Agricultural Society, and their mutual hatred of slavery drew him and Wilberforce together. In both cases the friendships were continued for years by correspondence.

Jay had little to trade with in the negotiations other than Grenville's fear that America might join with the Baltic powers in an armed neutrality. But Hamilton, with the indiscretion which sometimes characterized him, confided to the British minister in Philadelphia that the United States would never adopt this course. This information was promptly transmitted to London and destroyed Jay's only trading position. It was typical of the entire negotiation for the efficient and widespread diplomatic service behind Lord Grenville always put him in the position of a man who can see more of the cards than his opponent. Jay himself gave away little information for he was so discreet that he once confided to a diary that he had heard a number of excellent anecdotes that day but did not think it advisable to write them down for fear the diary should fall into the hands of the wrong person. Despite Hamilton's indiscretion Jay did, after an extended negotiation, succeed in making a treaty, which itself was an achievement, but on less favorable terms than anyone in America expected. As is well known, the treaty was signed most reluctantly by Washington and ratified by the narrowest of margins. It evoked a storm of popular protest which destroyed any possibility that Jay might ever become President.

The Chief Justice was never to return to the bench. He was again asked to stay in London as minister. This he refused but on his return to New York he found, as on his previous trip, that he had been elected to office in his absence. This time it was the governorship of New York. The anti-Clintonians had long been endeavoring to induce him to run for he was the one member of their group who stood any chance of being elected. He had always shown himself indifferent to political popularity but he was widely known and universally respected. Clinton had been governor too long and the natural swing of the political pendulum was against him. Jay's dislike of the rough and tumble of an election had prevented him from entering actively into his friends' plans but he had allowed them to campaign on his behalf in 1792. Apparently no one saw any impropriety in this and he was, in fact, elected governor. By means of some very fancy political jugglery the Clintonian returning board counted him out. By doing so they made certain of his election in 1795. So on his return he found himself elected governor, when he did not even know he was a candidate.

The most widely known fact about Jay is that he resigned the Chief Justiceship to become governor. This is commonly cited to prove the unimportance of the Court at the time. Others have explained his action as due to his dislike of circuit-riding. The governorship, as Mr. Justice Cushing wrote him, would be more for his "ease and comfort, than rambling in the Carolina woods in June."[27] The discomfort of circuit-riding certainly is not the whole explanation. Jay was a sedentary man with rather bad health but he certainly knew just what he was getting into when he accepted the Chief Justiceship. The Judiciary Act had already been passed and he was well acquainted with traveling conditions in eighteenth-century America. He disliked being separated from his wife but as governor he had to spend a good deal of time away from her. When the state capital was transferred to Albany he could not take her with him, since it was only with great difficulty that he obtained two rooms for his own use, one of which he used as a bedroom and the other as an office.

He undoubtedly was disappointed with the position of the Court. It is not clear just what he had expected that position to be. That the Court was the "keystone of our polit-

[27] Letter to Jay, dated June 18, 1795. JOHNSTON, IV at 176.

ical fabric" he knew. But he did not see how it was going to perform its function as such. The readiness with which the eleventh amendment, overruling his decision in the *Chisholm Case*, was being ratified by one state after another made him believe the Court never would be allowed to become important. But above all, he had found that judicial duties were irksome to him. His judicial aspirations were a carry over from his youthful days. Men thought of him as a judge because of his integrity, his active conscience and his broad-minded tolerance. But he had been out of touch with the law too long. His tastes were now executive rather than judicial.

The governorship gave him the opportunity to carry out two favorite projects. One was the abolition of slavery in New York and the other was the reform of the criminal law. He was temperamentally opposed to severe punishment and was among the first to believe that one of the objects of punishment was to reform the criminal. He endeavored to avoid party politics and on the whole gave the state an excellent administration. Among the judicial appointments which he made was that of James Kent to the state supreme court.

At the end of two terms of three years each he had had enough. He was never driven by intense ambition and his self-esteem was amply satisfied by his long and distinguished record, culminating in the governorship of his native state. The political needs of the Federalists could not deter him from retiring for he was free from that partisanship which identifies the opposite party with the powers of darkness. Some years later he once even went so far as to vote for a Jeffersonian candidate for the legislature when he thought the Federalist candidate to be a man of bad character.

On his retirement he expected that he would at last be able to live the life of a country gentleman. So he settled down on a farm of about eight hundred acres which he had inherited from his mother and which was located near Bedford in Westchester County. He lived here for the next

twenty-eight years but one of the pleasures he had expected
was denied him for his wife died shortly after his retirement. They had had a large family of whom two sons and
five daughters reached maturity. Only one of the latter
married, so Jay's house was not lonesome after the death
of his wife. Both the sons, Peter Augustus and William,
were men of some distinction and both were remarkably
like their father. Both were men of unblemished character
who acquired their chief fame as anti-slavery advocates.
The family resemblance can even be traced in the next
generation. One of the grandsons, again named John Jay,
was an anti-slavery advocate, an early Republican, minister
to Austria and a leader in civil service reform.[28]

Jay himself kept up his anti-slavery activities after his
retirement. He also spent much of his time in the study of
theology. He refused to take any active part in politics and
the only offices he accepted were those of president, first of
the Westchester Bible Society and later of the American
Bible Society. But his main interest was in his farm. He
experimented with different breeds of live stock and different kinds of crops. He planted shade trees for his descendants and he corresponded with his extensive circle of
acquaintances on both sides of the Atlantic about the
products of their regions.

One serious attempt was made, just as he was retiring,
to bring him back into public life. When Ellsworth resigned
the Chief Justiceship, President Adams, without consulting
Jay, nominated him to fill the vacancy. The nomination was
promptly confirmed but Jay refused to accept the position.
If he had made a different decision John Marshall would,
in all probability, never have been Chief Justice.

Jay outlived almost all his contemporaries and it is difficult to realize that when this erstwhile member of the De
Lancy faction in colonial New York died, Andrew Jackson
had already been inaugurated President. Jay died May 17,
1829 and was buried in the family cemetery at Rye.

---

[28] Peter Augustus, William and John, Jr., were all of sufficient
importance so that articles on them may be found in the Dictionary of
American Biography.

Chapter II.

JOHN RUTLEDGE

Important Dates

Born, at or near Charleston, S. C., September 1739.

Barrister-at-law, Middle Temple, London, 1760.

Elected to Commons House of Assembly, S. C., 1761.

Married Elizabeth Grimke, 1763.

Delegate to Stamp Act Congress, 1765.

Delegate to First Continental Congress, 1774.

Delegate to Second Continental Congress, 1775.

President of South Carolina, 1776-1778.

Governor of South Carolina, 1779-1782.

Delegate to Continental Congress, 1782-1783.

Judge of Court of Chancery of South Carolina, 1784-1791.

Delegate to Constitutional Convention of 1787.

Associate Justice, Supreme Court of the United States, 1789-1791.

Chief Justice of the Court of Common Pleas and Sessions of South Carolina, 1791-1795.

Chief Justice of the United States, appointed July 1, 1795, nomination rejected December 15, 1795.

Died July 18, 1800.

JOHN RUTLEDGE

From the portrait miniature
by John Trumbull

Jay's resignation did not convince Washington, at least, that the position of Chief Justice was not of great importance. His first choice for the vacancy was the man whom he undoubtedly regarded as the country's ablest statesman. But Hamilton seems to have shared Jay's opinion and declined the appointment.

While the President was wondering to whom next to offer the position he received an application for it from John Rutledge of South Carolina. Rutledge, whom John Marshall later described as "a gentleman of great talents and decision," had been the undisputed leader of his state during the Revolution and a leading member of the federal constitutional convention. When the new government went into operation he had fully expected the Chief Justiceship to be offered to him for, as he now wrote Washington, he believed his "pretensions to the office of Chief Justice were at least equal to Mr. Jay's in point of law knowledge." Washington had much the same opinion for he appointed him an Associate Justice and took care to date his commission in such a manner that he ranked next to the Chief Justice. This, however, struck Rutledge as almost an insult and he now took occasion to point out that he "certainly would not have taken the commission" as Association Justice if it had not been for Washington's "very friendly and polite letter which accompanied it." Despite his acceptance Rutledge had never attended a session of the Court, although he sat a few times on circuit, and, when the Chief Justiceship of South Carolina was offered to him, he took it as an opportunity to resign from Jay's court. Apparently he was afraid that Washington would construe this previous conduct as evidencing a preference for the service of his native state over that of the national government and for that reason he thought it necessary to let the President know that he would accept the

Chief Justiceship, if offered, "tho more arduous and trouble-
some than my present station, because more respectable and
honorable," and because of "the duty which I owe to my
children."[1]

Rutledge had gauged Washington's thoughts correctly
and, on the receipt of this letter, the South Carolinian was
immediately given a recess appointment as Chief Justice
under which he took his seat at the head of the Court at the
August term, 1795.

The speed with which the President acted indicates how
glad he was to receive this application. During the latter
years of his administration he had great difficulty in inducing men of first-rate importance to accept even the greatest
offices of the government. He did his best to fill offices on
merit alone yet he was forced to descend in the State Department from Jefferson to Randolph to Pickering and in the
Treasury from Hamilton to Wolcott. Rutledge has been so
completely forgotten, except possibly in his native state, that
it is difficult for us to realize his stature among his contemporaries. At this time his reputation was probably equal to
that of Jefferson—who had still some distance to cover
before he became President—or Jay. He had played a more
active, executive part in the war than either of them. He
was admired and trusted in his own state to an extent to
which no other American, except Washington, was admired
and trusted by his native section. In devotion to the cause
he antedated all the great men of Washington's administration, for he had been an influential member of the Stamp
Act Congress. He had followed this by membership in the
first and second Continental Congresses and it was only the
accident that he had returned to South Carolina to organize
and head the first rebellious state government there which
prevented him from signing the Declaration of Independence. He had been an important member of the constitutional convention and his influence in South Carolina was

[1] Quoted in WARREN, I at 127.

such that he had had little trouble in inducing that state to ratify the work of the convention. And to top his other formal qualifications there have been few Chief Justices whose previous judicial experience equaled his.

Yet he remains one of the most shadowy of that rather statuesque group of patricians who fathered the world's greatest democracy. There are various reasons for this. One is the circumstance of his Chief Justiceship, for he is the only Chief Justice who has actually sat under an interim appointment and has subsequently failed to be confirmed. Very few of his letters have been preserved and the few that have been tell us very little about him. He is not credited with the preparation of any of the numerous important state papers of the period. He contributed little to the theory of the Revolution. Patrick Henry thought him the leading orator of the first Continental Congress yet not one of his speeches has been preserved. Nor do any of the fragments of his speeches which have come down to us contain any phrases with the universal appeal of those few phrases on which Henry's own fame is based.

There are even more important reasons. He was a very able practical statesman but not a man of very enlarged ideas. He was no believer in political democracy yet in the federal convention he opposed any property restrictions on the right to vote for representatives, purely on practical political considerations. He feared the growth of the west yet he favored a stronger central government, again for the practical reason that he saw that the loose union of the Confederation was leading to disaster for all. He did not advocate any humanitarian reforms as Jay did in his opposition to slavery and in his endeavors to reform the criminal law. At a time when statesmen from slave states, such as Jefferson and George Mason, were searching earnestly for some means of getting rid of that institution, Rutledge was advocating the importation of additional slaves. His reasoning was simple. First, the people of his state needed more

slaves, and, secondly, if the proposed constitution prevented
them from getting more slaves they would never ratify it.
His administration of justice in his own state inclined to
over-severity. He was one of the first American statesmen
to discover the importance of the "interests" he represented.
In the first Continental Congress he succeeded in having rice
exempted from the list of articles which were not to be
exported. Yet his politics were truly practical and not moti-
vated solely by narrow provincial interests for, except on
one occasion, he never forgot that unless the rebels hung
together they were in great danger of hanging separately.

His practicality was the source of his strength and also
the mark of his limitations. His common-sense observations
were appreciated. His insistence on the interests of his own
state made him popular at home and made the nation at
large regard his name as almost synonymous for South
Carolina. It was his own state, rather than the nation as a
whole, which he loved and served. He habitually referred
to it, both before and after the Revolution, not as his province or his state but as his country. Indeed, this mode of
expression seems to have been so common that in one of the
books on which this study is based, published in Charleston
half a century after his death, it is used and Philadelphia is
referred to as being "abroad."

This habit of looking on South Carolina as their country
was well established among its inhabitants long before the
Revolution. The intensity of the feeling is somewhat odd, for
South Carolina was the most colonial of all the colonies. Its
natural resources fitted better into the British system of
colonial imperialism than did those of any other colony
along the North American seaboard. Rice and indigo were
articles which were needed in England, which could not be
raised there and which could be raised in South Carolina.
A small body of capitalistic planters managed their production and the labor was supplied by negroes, indentured
whites and convicts sentenced to transportation. Upon gain-

ing their freedom the members of the latter two classes usually entered a definitely low social class in the lowlands or became small farmers in the interior uplands. In either event they were of small importance politically, socially or economically.

The only part of the population which Rutledge, at least until the British occupation somewhat enlarged his views, regarded as of any importance was the planter aristocracy which centered around Charleston. It was a very small group. In the years immediately following the Revolution a few dozen families owned and ruled the state. The same surnames occur over and over again in the public records. The meager reports which record Rutledge's judicial labors in the state courts reveal that the judges, the counsel and, in any cases involving substantial property rights, the parties were all closely related. This group did not have the long tradition behind it which is usually associated with the concept of an aristocracy but what it lacked in age it made up in exclusiveness. Even as late as Washington's administration the Charleston merchants were rigorously excluded from its social functions and, consequently, organized various social clubs of their own to which they commonly gave more or less humorous names. In many respects the little colony of South Carolina with its all-important capital city, its inter-related aristocracy, its despised merchants, and its large slave population bore a close resemblance to the city states of antiquity. It was perhaps not without reason that its early historians were so fond of comparing their heroes to the heroes of Plutarch.

In return for its rice and indigo South Carolina imported everything it needed, in the nature of a manufactured article, from the mother country, including its professional men. Among the latter were two brothers of the name of Rutledge, of whom one, Andrew, was a lawyer and the other, John, was a physician who arrived in Charleston about the time of the birth of George Washington. They came, not directly from England, but from that Ireland whose social system has been compared by one of the most brilliant of modern English writers to that of South Carolina. The transition from the governing caste of Englishmen in Ireland to the governing caste of Englishmen in Charleston was easy. Andrew, the first to arrive, speedily married a wealthy widow and rose, before his death, to be Speaker of the Commons House of Assembly. Mrs. Andrew had a daughter, Sarah Hext, by her first husband who was the heiress of her father's substantial estate. The Rutledge brothers had no intention of allowing this fortune to pass out of their hands and when Sarah was of the mature age of fourteen she married Dr. John, who thereupon, in the words of an early writer, "abandoned the service of Esculapius and resigned himself to the superior charms of uninterrupted domestic life."[2] The future Chief Justice was born the next year, in September of 1739, either in or near Charleston.

John Rutledge never seems to have attended any regular school. At first his father taught him, but his father died when he was quite young and his mother then sent him to various private teachers the most important of whom, David Rhind, is supposed to have been "an excellent classical scholar, and one of the most successful of the early instructors of youth in Carolina." When not quite sixteen his general education stopped and he spent the next two years studying in the office of James Parsons, a barrister who had left the Irish for the Carolina bar. This seems to have been merely a stop-gap adopted by Mrs. Rutledge because she regarded John as still too young to be sent to England. That, of course, was where he would be sent ultimately, as were the sons of all the big planters. This was so usual that in the days of the Revolution five of Rutledge's colleagues on the committee which drew up the South Carolina constitution were members of the inns of court. Rutledge's already quoted and rather sneering remark that his "pretensions to

---

[2] FLANDERS, I at 433.

the office of Chief Justice were at least equal to Mr. Jay's in point of law knowledge" probably reflects the opinion which these Carolina Templars had of their colonially trained brethren.

The idea that the two years which John spent with Parsons might more profitably have been spent in William and Mary or some other of the small colleges which already existed in the more northerly colonies seems never to have occurred to the Rutledges. Indeed, there was so little communication with the other colonies that Rutledge seems to have been unaware of the existence of a college in America prior to his attendance at the Stamp Act Congress. Even at that late date no educational institution worthy of the name existed in South Carolina and on his return from the meeting of the Congress he endeavored to induce the legislature to remedy the defect by calling their attention particularly to the fact that Virginia had a college.

Rutledge's education was never hampered by financial difficulties for his mother, who had been left a widow while still in her twenties, proved herself a very capable manager of her large property. So at the end of his two years with Parsons, John sailed for England where he entered the Middle Temple. There were few requirements for admission to the English bar in those days other than the eating of the necessary number of dinners within the environs of the inns of court and the ability to pay the substantial prices which were charged for that privilege, but, while the requirements may have been few, the fact that that bar produced such lawyers as Mansfield and Eldon indicates that the opportunities must have been many.

The only evidence we have as to the amount of law Rutledge absorbed here is to be found in the very meager reports covering his later judicial labors. Only two cases were decided during his brief term as Chief Justice of the United States but there are a number of his opinions in the early South Carolina reports. These opinions indicate a

decided dislike of the practice of writing a voluminous legal
essay on every petty case which came up for decision but,
in the few instances where Rutledge did discuss the authorities, he shows a thorough understanding of what he was
doing. While these decisions and the impression which he
made on the many able lawyers with whom he later came
into contact indicate that he studied in the Middle Temple to
some purpose, his chief interest undoubtedly was in acquiring the art of public speaking. For that purpose he haunted
both houses of Parliament for, as he wrote his younger
brother Edward when the latter in turn went to London to
study law, "reading lectures upon oratory will never make
you an orator."

The desire to be a great orator was Rutledge's one intellectual ambition and the success with which he pursued it
is evident from the extremely laudatory terms in which all
the Carolinians contemporary with him speak of his eloquence. He had the necessary physical characteristics. He
was a large man with an impressive voice and, at least in
his later years, a rather stern and dignified appearance
which was enhanced by a broad forehead and flashing black
eyes. The adjective most frequently used by those who
heard him, in describing his manner of speaking, is "torren-
tial." Their emphasis on his energetic manner and on his
ability to move his audience and, in appearance at least,
himself emotionally is so great that the first impression one
receives is of a man who was governed more by his emotions
than by his intellect. The facts of his life do not bear out
this first impression. With the exception of a few sudden
outbursts of temper, his actions were governed by definite
logical reasons. Emotional oratory was a fount which he
could turn on or off at will. It was a faculty which he had
acquired by study because of its practical value, not an inherent characteristic. When it could serve no useful purpose, as in the federal constitutional convention, his style of
speech was terse and logical.

After three years in London he was admitted as a barrister-at-law and returned to Charleston in the same year, 1760, in which another young man of almost the same age, George III, ascended the throne.

This return to South Carolina requires explanation. The most he could hope for in his native country was to make a reasonably good living and to hold some minor governmental offices. The colonial system did not contemplate the existence of colonials of great ambition or ability. Even the judges in South Carolina were appointed from England and were of such a quality that it was commonly reported of one of them, Skinner, who held the Chief Justiceship of the colony in the 1760s, that the first time he had opened a lawbook was on his voyage out to Charleston. On the other hand, the freest scope for ambition to be found in eighteenth-century England was at the bar. The social distinction between a solicitor and a barrister was, it is true, sharp and it was difficult for any but members of the aristocracy or of the upper middle classes to become barristers. But when this hurdle had been surmounted there seems to have been a reasonably fair field for ability. Lord Eldon and Lord Stowell, who were brothers, were men of no family. Lord Chief Justice Tenterden, in the next generation, was the son of a barber. Nor was English birth essential, for an American by birth, John Singleton Copley, the son of the painter of that name, became Lord Chancellor under the name of Lord Lyndhurst. There was probably much more prejudice against Scotchmen than there was against Americans and yet both Lord Chief Justice Mansfield and Lord Chancellor Loughborough were Scotchmen by birth.

In the circumstances it would appear that the logical course for a young man in Rutledge's position was to stay in England. He already was a barrister, he had money enough to finance himself, at least until he got started, and he undoubtedly had ability. If his ambitions were political rather than professional the English rotten borough system was made for a man in his position. At the time of the reform bill the defense of the conservative position was based on the fact that the great eighteenth century statesmen, men like Burke and Fox and even the elder Pitt, had not sat in Parliament as the freely chosen representatives of the people, but as the protegés of great lords who owned seats. Somewhat later, Gladstone entered parliament as a member for a rotten borough whose owner, a duke, wanted to add to his party's oratorical strength and was impressed by Gladstone's record in the Oxford Union. With a reasonable share of luck Rutledge could have entered Parliament in a few years. Yet he returned to South Carolina, not for a visit, but permanently. After the Revolution he followed much the same course. He never seems to have cared to be a member of the Continental Congress any longer than was necessary to complete some specific task. During the government of the Articles of Confederation he declined an appointment as minister to the Netherlands and an appointment as a commissioner to adjudicate some boundary disputes among Massachusetts, Connecticut and New York. Rutledge did not even, after his admission as a barrister, follow the custom among law students from Carolina and travel one of the English circuits before his return.

This apparent lack of ambition was not due to lack of energy or to a philosophic disdain for the things of this world. The quality which impressed all his contemporaries was his extreme energy and his entire career stamps him as a practical man with a flair for administration rather than as a philosophic thinker. Unlike Washington, he was not content to be a prosperous plantation owner. He undoubtedly worked hard at his law practice in Charleston and he held public office practically all his life. After the Revolution, when he had twice held the highest office in the state and might reasonably be supposed to be content, he sat first in the Court of Chancery and later in the law courts, although these positions did not pay salaries which made them desirable to him for that object alone. Clearly he was ambitious but his ambition was of the kind that demanded precedence among the people with whom he had grown up rather than far away from home.

He seems never to have looked upon himself as an Englishman who happened to be born in one of the out-lying possessions of the empire. His habitual reference to South Carolina as his "country" was meant in a very real sense. While that colony had less self-government than the colonies to the north of it the planter aristocracy early developed a strong local patriotism. Perhaps this was due to the fact that so few of them had come from England, for a substantial number of the planters were of Huguenot or, like the Rutledges, English-Irish extraction. In any event John Rutledge shared to the full in the local patriotism of the class in which he was born. He seems never even to have thought of trying his fortunes in the capital of the empire.

There was a numerous body of Carolinians studying in the Middle Temple with Rutledge, and their letters home had given him such a reputation that he had no difficulty in establishing a practice. Upon his return clients were so anxious to retain him that before his ship had anchored a defendant in a breach-of-promise suit went down the harbor in a small boat, met the ship and retained Rutledge. Admission to the local bar was a mere formality which he speedily went through. Upon the completion of the ceremony he rushed home and handed all the money in his pockets to his mother so that, as he explained to her, he might be able to say that he had started his professional career without a guinea in his pocket. His poverty did not last long for his fee in the breach-of-promise case was a hundred guineas.

In the fourteen years between Rutledge's return and the opening of the Revolution he became the undisputed leader of the South Carolina bar. The competition was small. The class system effectively kept down the number of practitioners and there were only about twenty lawyers in the entire province. Justice was administered on the same incredibly expensive scale as in eighteenth-century England and, in spite of the small population, Rutledge's annual earnings are supposed to have run around twenty thousand dollars. The excellence of the system was not fully appreciated in the more remote parts of the province and there justice was administered by a sort of vigilantes known as regulators. But there is nothing to indicate that Rutledge was a leader in law reform.

He had become a member of the Assembly shortly after his return from England. Relations between that body and the governor were strained over a number of local issues. Rutledge immediately joined in the fray on the Assembly's side. His doing so can be ascribed only to conviction for the ample patronage in the hands of the governor would have made it very much worth his while to have taken the other side. Such conflicts were perennial in all the colonies except the two that were so fortunate as to elect their own governors but, while this dispute was at its height, the passage of the Stamp Act furnished a further source of irritation. Then came the call by Massachusetts for a congress of the colonies to determine what should be done. The reaction in South Carolina to this proposal was not so unanimous as might have been expected. England had frequently done things which had irritated her colonies but precedent had not yet established the practice of calling a congress about it. In addition, South Carolina was located far from the colonial center of population and did not think of itself as having much in common with Yankee fishermen and Dutch patroons.

Rutledge aligned himself without much hesitation with what might be prematurely called the nationalists. It was his practical turn of mind that brought him to this position. He realized that any opposition to the royal measures which was to be effective would have to be unanimous. His eloquence was an important factor in causing the Assembly to send delegates to the Stamp Act Congress, and he was one of the delegates. That Congress was the scene of no world-renowned actions but it was the first national meeting of the embryo nation and Rutledge was there. This is probably the first time he had been in any part of America outside his own colony and, like most of the other delegates, this was his first opportunity to get acquainted with men from colonies other than his own. The impression he made on the other delegates was such that, although the youngest member of the Congress, he was made chairman of the committee to prepare a memorial and petition to the House of Lords which was then a more important branch of Parliament than it is now. Meanwhile the people of Charleston expressed their opinion of the obnoxious act by seizing a load of stamped paper and sending it back to England; by breaking open the homes of suspected citizens to search for stamps, and by compelling Chief Justice Skinner to drink "damnation to the Stamp Act."

During the decade after the Stamp Act Congress Rutledge lived the life of a successful South Carolina lawyer and planter. He had risen as high as was possible in his native province. Although still a young man all he could look forward to was maintaining his position; a position which was of importance only so long as he stayed within a colony whose total population was less than that of many present-day American counties. One wonders whether he did not regret giving up the opportunity to start practice in London. But there is nothing to indicate that he was not entirely satisfied with his position as a leader in the small governing class in the small colony in which he was born.

Rutledge's career as the leader of the Carolina bar was interrupted by the renewal of the debate between the Crown and its loyal subjects overseas. The tax on tea was imposed and was followed by the Boston Port Bill. In Charleston as in the other colonial centers the Whigs soon held a public meeting to determine what should be done. Already at this meeting one of the leaders, Gadsden, was advocating independence but Rutledge threw all the weight of his eloquence against this as well as against a proposal that the colonials, as a retaliatory measure, refuse to import British goods. He was, however, much in favor of sending delegates to the proposed Continental Congress, although he strongly opposed a motion to restrict their scope of action with specific instructions. After the delegates were elected, among them Rutledge, his younger brother Edward, and Gadsden, he shouted down an inquiry from the floor as to what was to be done if the delegates did not properly represent the views of the meeting in the Congress with a vigorous "Hang them! Hang them!"

Rutledge had married Elizabeth Grimke, a woman of his own class, shortly after he started to practice. Almost nothing is known about her except that he seems to have been very much attached to her. She and their eldest son now accompanied him to Philadelphia where the work of the Congress was relieved by an almost continual social round. One of the first of these, an "elegant supper," which all the delegates attended and where they "drank sentiments till eleven o'clock" was sufficient to convince the rather testy and suspicious John Adams that "the two Rutledges," John and his brother Edward, "are good lawyers."

The chief work of the Congress was the preparation of addresses and other state papers in which the American position in regard to the limitations on the powers of Parliament were set forth. Many reputations were made in the drafting of these documents. Rutledge never used a pen freely and one suspects that he had no great scholarly interest in the theory of government. His greatest contribution was his trenchant practical comments on the floor. These began with a remark at the first session in opposition to a motion to appoint a committee to formulate rules for the conduct of business that "doubtless the usage of the House of Commons would be adopted . . . and . . . as every gentleman was acquainted with that usage, it would be a waste of time to appoint a committee on this subject."

He soon had a reputation in the Congress for vehement and forceful speaking which almost equalled that which he had in South Carolina. His vehemence was more apparent than real, for he chose his words so warily that, on the one side, John Adams, the leader of those who were already thinking of independence, could refer to him as one of his "able coadjutors" and, on the other, Joseph Galloway, the chief Tory in the Congress and one who was to die in England a pensioner of the Crown, could report that Rutledge "is a gentleman of an amiable character, has looked into the arguments on both sides more fully than any I have met with, and seems to be aware of all the consequences which may attend rash and imprudent measures."

On his return from Philadelphia, the rebels in South Carolina proceeded to organize themselves by electing a body called a provincial congress of which, naturally, Rutledge was again a member. This body did not purport to supersede the royal government but confined its activities to enforcing the non-importation agreements, by more or less peaceable means, and to electing delegates to the second Continental Congress. Rutledge was again among the delegates but when it became apparent that it was necessary to set up rebellious governments in each of the colonies he decided, quite wisely, that he could be of more use at home. He had already become the undoubted leader of the Whig cause in his native province and, when the new provincial government was organized, he was elected its head with the title of His Excellency the President. The surprisingly large salary of nine thousand pounds a year was attached to this office.

He had been largely instrumental in drafting the new constitution which was conservative in tone and designed to keep control in the hands of the planter aristocracy. As many features as possible of the colonial government, including the establishment of the Episcopalian church, were retained. Rutledge himself was, throughout his life, a member of that church although his religion seems to have been of that temperate variety which kept him from ever being accused of impiety or praised for excessive piety.

The royal government made no serious attempt to interfere with the Carolinians. One attack was made on Charleston which was easily repulsed and the province then entered an era of unexampled prosperity. Rutledge, however, did not continue to hold the office of President. The news of the Declaration of Independence arrived in Charleston shortly after the repulse of the British attack and the Assembly took the occasion of the transformation of the province into a state to revamp the constitution substantially. This action Rutledge strenuously opposed on the peculiarly American doctrine that the power of the legislature was limited as provided in the constitution under which it was elected and that the sole power to modify that instrument remained in the people. The doctrine that legislatures, specifically Parliament, are limited in power was the fundamental principle on which the Revolution was based but despite this and his own prestige, for Rutledge was undoubtedly the state's leading citizen, he was unable to sway the legislature from its purpose. He was true to his principles, however, and declined to hold office under the new constitution adopted by the legislature. He therefore resigned as President of the state but was re-elected governor, which was now the title of the chief executive officer, in 1779, when the state was again threatened by the British.

The attack this time came overland and was more serious. It was led by General Prevost who had already subdued the almost uninhabited state of Georgia. When Prevost had advanced to within a few miles of Charleston something happened whose true story has been hidden, except for its main outline, by the efforts of the patriotic historians who wrote the story of the Revolution in the years immediately succeeding the war. All that is certain is that a message was sent to Prevost by the governor and council of South Carolina, on behalf of the state, offering to remain neutral through the remainder of the war and to allow the fate of South Carolina to be settled by that of the other colonies. If there was any blame connected with the sending of this message, Rutledge must shoulder a good part of it. It is inconceivable that it could have been sent against his opposition and unlikely that it was sent without his active cooperation.

Like most of the revolutionary statesmen he had been driven to advocate independence by the stupidity of the imperial government rather than by his own desires. He was perfectly willing to allow questions affecting the whole empire to be settled in London so long as the colonies were allowed to manage their internal affairs themselves. By now it was fairly plain that this result would be obtained even if the British government won the war in a military sense. While he himself had more sense of American nationality than was usual in South Carolina, he shared in a degree the feeling that that state was in a separate category. It was far away from the colonial centers of population; its social and economic organization was different from that of the other colonies, and its background was certainly more closely akin to that of Barbadoes than to that of Pennsylvania. These feelings were intensified in the present situation. The state's large slave population meant that its own military resources in man power were weak while its commonest and most valuable form of property, slaves, was of a kind most likely to disappear during an invasion. Rutledge was a nationalist in the sense that he usually saw the practical advantages in acting with the other states readily enough but his country was still South Carolina, not the United States.

In any event the British general preferred a free course

of rapine to the subjugation of the state by statesmanlike means and declined to continue the negotiations on this basis. No equally favorable opportunity was ever again offered to a royal officer. The offer expired when the feeble national government sent an army under General Lincoln which compelled Prevost to retire to Savannah.

The next year the British, this time under Cornwallis, returned to the attack with such success that Lincoln who, because of the insistence of the Carolinians that Charleston be defended, had allowed himself to be shut up in that town, surrendered with his whole army. Soon the entire state was in the possession of the British. The conquerors exercised their power with a barbarity which made it utterly impossible that another offer, such as that which Prevost had received, would ever be made.

The British success resulted in an unexampled mark of confidence in Rutledge for, just before the overthrow of the state government, the Assembly voted to delegate "till ten days after their next session, to the Governor, John Rutledge, Esquire, and such of his Council as he could conveniently consult, a power to do everything necessary for the public good, except the taking away the life of a citizen without a legal trial."[3] There is no record that he abused this power. He might be haughty but he was just. On rare occasions his temper might get the better of him but he could be relied on to make restitution. Such an instance had occurred during the siege of Charleston. He had been so irritated at the negligence of a militia sentinel that he had struck the latter with his riding whip. The next day Rutledge "rode back again to the same place, and addressed those who were on the station; stated, with much dignity and propriety, that in his extreme anxiety for the public welfare, he had hastily struck a citizen at that station ... and had come publicly to express his regret

[3] Quoted in FLANDERS, I at 567.

for having done so, and to hope that nothing more might be thought of it."[4]

A governor without a government he now went to beg for help from North Carolina, Virginia and the Continental Congress. With what he obtained, he gave such assistance as he could to Marion, Sumter and the other guerrilla chiefs. But while always ready to help he had no patience with cruelty and injustice even if indulged in with the highest ends in view. The war in South Carolina at this period was conducted with a ferocity and cruelty unequalled in any other Anglo-Saxon civil war. While Rutledge cooperated fully with the patriotic guerrilla chiefs he did not adopt the attitude that all their acts were justified. He allowed them to take certain articles of private property for the public good but he had occasion to write to one of them, Horry, "if I ever hear another complaint of the abuse of the press-warrant, which, confiding in your discreet exercise of it, I gave you, I will instantly revoke it, and never let you have another."[5] Even Marion, who was famous for his fairness, was warned by Rutledge to spare plow horses when making impressments. But the highest tribute to Rutledge is that when the state was finally cleared of the British and he laid down his dictatorial authority, no complaints were made of the manner in which he had exercised it. Indeed, the only complaint seems to have been that he had been too generous in his treatment of the Tories.

The most important effect that this experience had on Rutledge was to change him from a Carolinian into an American. Among the very few letters of his which have been preserved are some that he wrote at this time to the South Carolina delegates in Congress. From one of them it would seem that he intended, in the event the British retained possession permanently of part or all of South Carolina, to throw in his lot with the new nation rather

[4] Quoted in FLANDERS, I at 560.
[5] Quoted in FLANDERS, I at 583 note.

than what he had, up to then, called his country. "I still hope," he wrote, "tho' I have no hope of regaining Charleston, except by treaty, that the Country will be preserved, and North and South Carolina, and even Georgia, retained, in the Union."[6] The height which his new found nationalism reached borders on the ridiculous for his youngest son, born in 1783, was compelled to bear the cacophonous name of "States Rutledge."

Rutledge's term of office as governor expired shortly after he laid down his dictatorial authority. Under the constitution then in force, he was not eligible for re-election. He then served for a short time in the Congress but he was anxious to return to his native state. His desire was soon gratified for in 1784 he was elected one of the three judges of the newly created court of chancery in South Carolina.

This was the first real equity court in the state and, while its decisions were reported by Desaussure, one of Rutledge's successors as chancellor, to use the word by which the judges were popularly called, these reports unfortunately contain none of his opinions. Even if his habitual dislike of pen work kept Rutledge from creating the customary judicial record, his administrative efficiency enabled him to leave a rarer one. Chancellor Desaussure states that "it hath repeatedly happened that on the rising of the court . . . not one case has been left undecided—a circumstance which certainly is rare in any country, and it is probable has never occurred in the court of chancery in England since the days of Sir Francis Bacon."

When the federal constitutional convention assembled in 1787 Rutledge was there for the same reason that other men of affairs were there. He came because he realized that it was impossible for conditions to continue as they were. It was simply a question of time until the Americans would be either the vassals or the subjects of some European

---

[6] Letter dated May 24, 1780 published in *South Carolina Historical and Genealogical Magazine*, October 1916.

power and would be looking back with envy to the comparative freedom they had enjoyed as British subjects. It was becoming increasingly clear that while there may have been objections to the manner in which the imperial government had exercised its powers, the answer did not lie in the destruction of those powers. They had to be vested somewhere. The navigation laws may have been irritating but at least while they existed there was some American commerce. It is frequently forgotten that those laws were designed to protect not only the British manufacturer but the Virginian tobacco planter and the South Carolinian rice and indigo planter. In return for the protection which British manufactures enjoyed in America, American agricultural products were given favored treatment in Great Britain. Being taxed to support the British navy might be abhorrent but at least when that navy protected the New England merchantmen Americans were not sold as slaves in Algiers.

Rutledge soon became one of the leaders of the convention and Oliver Ellsworth, his successor as Chief Justice, claimed in after years that the constitution had been "drawn by himself and five others, viz., General Alexander Hamilton, Gorham of Mass., deceased, James Wilson of Pennsylvania, Rutledge of South Carolina and Madison of Virginia."[7] Rutledge's chief service was in advocating a strong and single executive for he seems to have had little of the fear, customary at the time, of such an executive although he wished the power to appoint judges to be in the Congress rather than in the executive. A suggestion that the power of the President be limited by a revisionary counsel, as in the constitution Jay had drawn for New York, met with his unqualified disapprobation on the very lawyer-like ground that "the Judges ought never to give their opinion on a law till [sic] it comes before them."[8] He recog-

[7] FARRAND, III at 397.
[8] FARRAND, II at 80.

nized that the only feasible basis of authority for the new government was the will of the people, but he favored a system of indirect elections and checks and balances which would prevent its administration from being swayed by those temporary gusts of popular passion which he, in common with nearly all our early statesmen, greatly feared. In support of his plea for the indirect election of the President and both branches of the Congress, he took occasion to point out, what was undoubtedly true, that "if this Convention had been chosen by the people in districts it is not to be supposed that such proper characters would have been preferred."[9]

The fact that, on the organization of the new government, he was not offered the position of Chief Justice was so great a disappointment to him that he thereafter took little interest in the doings of that government. He scarcely condescended to notice his appointment as an Associate Justice of the Supreme Court. He never attended a single session of that Court and definitely resigned in 1791 when he was appointed to the newly created office of Chief Justice of the Court of Common Pleas and Sessions in South Carolina. He seems to have made no attempt to gain a senatorship or other non-judicial office, although the ease with which he could have done so is shown by the fact that he received the South Carolina vote for Vice-President. Once on the bench he evidently intended to spend his life there. Neither the salary—as chancellor he had received five hundred pounds a year—nor his apparent lack of scholarly interests explain this. Perhaps the explanation is found in the hint which is occasionally dropped that in his later years his natural pride more and more became great haughtiness. This trait reached such an extreme that he once kept a grand jury waiting for an hour and, when on his ultimate appearance that body indicted him for being late, instead of turning the matter off with an apology or

[9] FARRAND, I at 359.

a joke, announced, "Mr. Clerk, hand me the presentment," and, on receiving it, put it in his pocket and continued, "Gentlemen, I would have you to know that it is never ten o'clock till I am in Court."[10]

His wife had died in 1792, the year following his appointment as Chief Justice of the state. They had a large family, who in turn had numerous descendants, and from what little is known of their married life they seem to have gotten along together excellently, so excellently that a short time after her death it began to be whispered among his friends that her loss had affected his mind. His mother, to whom he was always closely attached, died about the same time and this may also have been a factor in his mental ailment.

Subsequent events undoubtedly show that his mind was losing its balance but his reported decisions in the Court of Common Pleas do not indicate it and the derangement could not have been very apparent or news of it would have become public. This was so far from being true that when three years after his wife's death Washington appointed him Chief Justice of the United States the appointment was generally received, throughout the nation, with satisfaction. But the Charleston papers which reached the North shortly after the announcement contained strange news.

From them it appeared that just prior to his appointment Rutledge had made a speech violently denouncing Jay's treaty. According to a prominent Federalist newspaper in Boston Rutledge had made it "mounted upon the head of a hogshead, haranguing a mob assembled to reprobate the treaty and insult the Executive of the Union . . . insinuating that Mr. Jay and the Senate were fools or knaves, duped by British sophistry or bribed by British gold . . . prostituting the dearest rights of free men and laying them at the feet of royalty."[11] The intemperance of the language and the public attack on Washington's administration may

[10] O'NEALL, I at 27.
[11] Quoted in WARREN, I at 130.

have been due to Rutledge's mental affliction, the precise nature of which is unknown, but his opposition to the treaty probably reflected his real views.

Although he had been reluctant to sever the political ties with Great Britain he had become, in his later years, bitterly anti-British. In this, as in most of his actions, he reflected the sentiment of his environment. The barbarity of the British troops in the Carolinas is almost beyond belief. Rutledge himself had suffered severely. Most of his then ample property had been destroyed and his mother, who was a vigorous patriot, was taken into custody by a British commander. The fact that a large proportion of the population was of Huguenot, rather than British, extraction, a proportion which was increased after the war when a great number of refugees from the servile revolt in Hayti came to Charleston, may also have contributed to the anti-British sentiment. His own ancestry was not such as to give him any special feeling of loyalty for in the eighteenth century most of the opposition to British rule in Ireland came not from the Celtic Irish but from the Anglo-Irish. If Rutledge had been in close touch with national affairs his sense of practicality would probably have caused him to support the treaty, however reluctantly. It was necessity that had caused Washington to sign the treaty but in those days of poor communication, Rutledge was not fully aware of that necessity. It was the penalty he paid for his isolation and his preoccupation with local interests. His dislike of the treaty may have been helped in part by his feeling that the Chief Justiceship should have been given to him, instead of Jay, on the organization of the government and by the fact that, in going to England, Jay had superseded another South Carolinian, Pinckney, the regular minister. This attack on Jay's treaty certainly indicated no settled dislike of the general course of the national administration on the part of Rutledge and his friends for the planter aristocracy of South Carolina long remained a Federalist island in an almost solidly Jeffersonian South.

The Federalists of the North allowed for none of these factors. Rutledge's friends tried to excuse his conduct by stating that after the death of his wife his mind had been slightly deranged but that since the date of the obnoxious speech he had fully recovered. This was making matters worse. One of the defects of the constitution is that it makes no provision for the insanity of any officer of the government. From this it would seem that if Rutledge was once confirmed and then became insane again the seat of the Chief Justice would have to remain vacant until he died. This was probably the determining factor in the rejection of his nomination although the only opinion which he wrote as Chief Justice[12] does not indicate any derangement. Nor did anyone find anything wrong with his demeanor on the bench of the Court except a certain haughtiness. Certainly no man whose sanity is in doubt should hold judicial office, but the Federalists had started urging his rejection because of his opposition to the treaty. As a consequence, the Anti-Federalists treated the rejection of the nomination, when it took place, as, in the words of Jefferson, "a declaration that they will receive none but Tories hereafter into any Department of the Government."[13]

After his rejection, Rutledge had another violent attack of insanity but recovered to such an extent that, when Mr. Justice Iredell visited Charleston in traveling the Southern circuit a few years later, he wrote his wife that Rutledge "is perfectly recovered, and in such high spirits that he, and another gentleman, and myself, outsat all the rest of the company at a friend's house."[14] Despite his optimistic appearance at that time, Rutledge had other recurrent attacks of insanity until, in 1800, he died at the home of an Episcopal bishop.

---

[12] *Talbot* v. *Jansen*, 3 Dall. 133, 1 L. Ed. 540 (1795). Rutledge also announced the conclusion of the court in *United States* v. *Judge Peters*, 3 Dall. 121, 1 L. Ed. 535 (1795).

[13] Letter dated Dec. 31, 1795 from Jefferson to William Branch Giles. P. L. FORD, VII at 44.

[14] Letter dated May 11, 1798 printed in McREE.

In view of the doubt as to Rutledge's sanity, a doubt which subsequent events prove to have been amply justified, it is difficult to see how the Senate could have done anything but reject the nomination. In making the nomination Washington had followed the same conception of the functions of the Chief Justice as he had in appointing Jay and as he subsequently followed in his appointment of Ellsworth. In all three instances the appointee was an able and respected statesman who also had a reputation as a lawyer. On the facts known in the capital city, Rutledge clearly met Washington's qualifications. His fits of mental instability were a closely guarded secret. To the President, Rutledge was the wise and able leader of South Carolina during the war. If he had been the same man in 1795 there is no reason to doubt that his administration of the Supreme Court would have been able and successful.

Chapter III

OLIVER ELLSWORTH

Born, Windsor, Conn., April 29, 1745.

Attended Yale, 1762-1764.

Graduated, Princeton, 1766.

Studied theology, 1766-1767.

Studied law, 1767-1771.

Married Abigail Wolcott, 1772.

Deputy to General Assembly from Windsor, 1773-1775.

Elected to the Committee of the Pay Table, 1775.

State's Attorney for Hartford County, 1777-1785.

Delegate to Continental Congress, 1777-1783 (intermittently).

Member, Governor's Council, 1780-1784.

Judge of Superior Court, 1784-1789.

Delegate to Constitutional Convention of 1787.

United States Senator, 1789-1796.

Chief Justice of the United States, 1796-1800.

Special Envoy to France, 1799-1800.

Died, November 26, 1807.

OLIVER ELLSWORTH

From the portrait miniature by John Trumbull

There is an appealing Americanism about the Connecticut Yankee who next sat at the head of the Supreme Court. Jay's broad and philosophic outlook would have made him seem somewhat of an exotic anywhere. Rutledge was the product of an environment which was to remain an undigested element in the nation. Ellsworth reflected his background as completely as did the South Carolinian but Ellsworth's background was one in which those democratic ideals which Jefferson preached were put into practice to an extent which has never since been equaled. The fact that, as a young man, Ellsworth had for several years rented a farm which he tilled himself, without the help of slaves or servants, marks the immeasurable difference between him and his immediate predecessor.

Ellsworth had neither Jay's brilliance nor Rutledge's eloquence and power of leadership. His rise had been slow, unspectacular, and based on the painstaking doing of detailed and uninteresting work. Many of his contemporaries remarked on the scantiness of his reading in political theory yet his influence in the organization of the government had been greater than that of either Jay or Rutledge. He was the first member of the constitutional convention to grasp the precise significance of what was going on; the first to speak of the new government as "partly national; partly federal." He arrived at this conclusion not through abstract reasoning but through the inexorable logic of facts. He insisted that the states had to be retained for purposes of local government, for he was very much alive to the diversity of conditions in different sections of the country. But his years as a hard-working and modest member of the old Congress had destroyed his belief in the efficacy of a confederation of states. He had not arrived readily at the solution which permitted both the continued existence of the

81

states and the creation of a strong central government. At the conclusion of the war there had been a full debate in the Congress on the defects in the organization of the government. Hamilton and Madison were full of suggestions. Ellsworth admitted the defects; admitted that it was absolutely necessary that something be done but was not at all clear what that something should be. But his strongest faculty was his power of continuous mental growth. All his contemporaries remark on his surprising intellectual development during his six years as a senator. And so it was that, amid the angry clash of conflicting proposals and the earnest debate of the constitutional convention, he first grasped the principle of a government "partly national; partly federal."

He had arrived at this conclusion through a very practical consideration of how the central government was to enforce its authority. Under the Articles of Confederation the answer to this problem had been simple. The authority of the central government had not been enforced. If the new government was to be purely federal—for to Ellsworth and his colleagues the words federal and confederate meant the same thing—that authority could be enforced only through the use of military power. There is no other way to apply compulsion to a state for it cannot be arrested by the sheriff and thrown into jail. But the use of military power against a delinquent state means in practice the waging of a war against it. That was the argument of those in favor of a purely national government and it cannot be answered. Ellsworth's concept of a government "partly national; partly federal" supplied a solution. "How necessary for the Union," he told the Connecticut ratifying convention, "is a coercive principle. No man pretends the contrary; we all see and feel this necessity. The only question is, Shall it be a coercion of law, or a coercion of arms? . . . I am for coercion by law—that coercion which acts only upon delinquent individuals. This constitution does not attempt to coerce sovereign bodies, states, in their political capacity. No coercion is applicable to such bodies, but that of an armed force. . . . But this legal coercion singles out the guilty individual and punishes him for breaking the laws of the Union."[1]

Events proved that he had not advanced a theoretical solution for a theoretical difficulty. The method of enforcing federal authority which he outlined to the Connecticut convention is precisely the method which is now in use. The most common method today of testing the constitutionality of a state statute is to bring a proceeding in the federal courts to enjoin the state official who threatens to put it into force. If the statute violates the federal constitution no action is taken against the state which passed it. The action is against the state official, the "guilty individual."

Since the beginning of Washington's administration, Ellsworth had been the leader of the Senate. His leadership was very real. Adams later blamed the difficulties of his own administration on the fact that Ellsworth was no longer in the Senate and, in the middle of the next century, new senators were still told stories of the way he had dominated that body.[2] But for the most part his leadership was of that secondary kind which carries out the decisions of others intelligently and effectively with labor, patience and skill. If Hamilton suggested and Washington agreed Ellsworth got the bills through the Senate with only such changes of detail as were necessary to make the basic idea workable. He was so useful where he was that it is surprising that he was ever offered another position. Nor was the secondary type of leadership which he had displayed up to then altogether in line with Washington's conception of the type of man who should head the Court.

These considerations weighed with the President for Ellsworth was not his first choice. The number of first-rate

---

[1] Speech by Ellsworth printed in BROWN, appendix, at 359-360.
[2] HOAR, II at 45.

men was limited. Hamilton had already refused the position. Jefferson would seem to have been the logical choice
but Hamilton's faction had gained too much influence with
the President to permit this. One can only regret the failure
to appoint Jefferson. Our history would have run a much
smoother course if the Alien and Sedition Laws had been
held unconstitutional by the Supreme Court rather than
been proclaimed unconstitutional by a state legislature.
Jefferson followed the latter procedure only after he came
to believe that the Court was incapable of performing that
balancing function which had been designed for it.

His Hamiltonian advisers could not prevent the President
from considering his old friend, Patrick Henry. When Henry
indicated that he would not accept, Washington seems to
have given up in despair. Without consulting the appointee,
the President sent the nomination of Cushing, the senior
associate justice, to the Senate where it was immediately
confirmed. The appointment can only be justified on the
basis of seniority for there were abler men on the Court than
Cushing. He was a typical Vicar of Bray; a man whose sole
object in life was to hold his job and keep out of trouble.
He was so successful at this that he had been appointed a
judge in Massachusetts by the royal government and had
succeeded in retaining his position when that government
was overthrown. His chief claim to fame is that he was the
last American judge to wear a full-bottomed wig; a practice
which he was forced to give up by the gibes of the New York
street urchins. Cushing's appointment was readily confirmed but he realized that the Chief Justiceship would place
him in a very conspicuous position; a position so conspicuous that he might be compelled to depart from that safe and
colorless anonymity which he had valued all his life. He
declined the appointment after a week's consideration but
continued to sit as an Associate Justice for many years.

Cushing was by birth a member of the old office-holding
Massachusetts aristocracy. Ellsworth's background was very

different. His great-grandfather had been among the first
settlers in Connecticut, the colony which had been founded
as a democratic refuge from the Massachusetts oligarchy.
His grandfather had been a storekeeper and his father a
farmer. The family had always lived in the town of Windsor, one of the oldest settlements in the state, and there
Oliver Ellsworth was born, April 29, 1745, the second child
and second son of Captain David Ellsworth of the Connecticut militia.

The Chief Justice never disowned his background. In his
boyhood there was only one carriage in Windsor and the
people ate off wooden trenchers; in his retirement, when he
was one of the state's wealthiest citizens, he always walked
the mile or so to church and dressed "like a respectable
farmer." When away from home he was noted for being
rather particular in his dress but when one of his neighbors
suggested that he could afford a better sleigh than the one
he had, his reply was, "Well, well, Mr. H——, I suppose I
might; but if I should get a new sleigh perhaps Mr. H's
family would think they needed a better one than they have;
and if you get one, some other neighbor will want one;
everybody in town will want a new sleigh."[3] He did not
give his children allowances; he paid them for the doing of
chores. He set up two of his sons as storekeepers in Windsor. His sole display of riches was in a rather more elaborate house than most of his neighbors.

Ellsworth had not always been so contented with the
ways of Windsor. In his old age he was convinced that of
all the countries in the world he liked the United States the
best and of all the United States he liked Connecticut the
best but in his youth there were signs of rebellion. His
father wished him to become a minister of the established
Congregational or, as he would have called it, Presbyterian
church. At the age of sixteen Oliver went, dutifully enough,
as a sort of apprentice to the pastor of a neighboring village.

[3] BROWN, at 338.

The next year he entered Yale where he rapidly fell from grace. His scholarship record was poor and he was frequently disciplined for violations of the college rules. His first offense was in joining with ten others "to scrape and clean the college yard" in the evening although the record does not indicate why the faculty was so opposed to cleanliness. His next offense was in "having a treat or entertainment last winter" and still another was that he, with others, "presently after Evening Prayers on Thursday last put on their hats and ran and hallooed in the College Yard in contempt of the Law of College." These offenses were during his freshman year but his most serious offense was during his sophomore year when he was fined four shillings for joining in "a general treat or compotation of wine both common and spiced in and by the Sophomore class."[4]

At the end of two years his career at Yale terminated, although it is not entirely clear whether he quit or whether he was expelled. His father was a substantial farmer but by no means a wealthy man. He had supported his son at Yale but it would not have been surprising if he had now ceased to do so. From the difficulty which Ellsworth afterwards had in starting a practice in his native town it would seem that the Yale episode reflected severely on his local reputation. But his father was still determined to make him a minister. So the next year young Ellsworth entered Princeton. Here, too, he established no great reputation for scholarship but was long remembered for his skill in college politics which then consisted in the management of literary and debating societies. Princeton drew its students from more diverse backgrounds than did any other colonial college and his experience there should have somewhat broadened him. If it did the effect soon wore off. When he first appears on the national scene he was as thoroughly a product of Connecticut as Rutledge was of South Carolina. It was Ellsworth's services in the Continental Congress which

[4] BROWN, at 15-16.

first gave him his national outlook. His development in this respect can be measured by two incidents. One of his first acts on entering the Continental Congress had been to support a resolution blaming the ills of the country on the low morality of the people as indicated by the prevalence of play-going, gaming and horse racing. That was when he was still a simon-pure Yankee. Later, one of the reasons he gave for ratifying the federal constitution was the need to set up a government strong enough to obtain the navigation of the Mississippi. It was not a reason which appealed to early New England. That jealousy of the growth of the west which Rutledge displayed was, as is well known, so strong in the northeastern states that it led at one time to serious consideration of the idea of breaking away from the Union.

When Ellsworth was graduated from Princeton at the age of twenty-one he still intended to carry out his father's wishes and enter the ministry. He spent the next year studying with a minister in New Britain but Ellsworth had not lost the independence of spirit which had caused his departure from Yale. The causes of his dislike of the ministry are not clear. They could not have been entirely pecuniary for the bar in colonial Connecticut was not a very lucrative occupation and, in fact, was just beginning to be recognized as a profession. The ministers were still supported by taxes, not voluntary contributions, which was to their advantage both financially and socially. It could not have been due to theological difficulties for he had not yet displayed enough intellectuality of any kind to make it likely that he had found such difficulties. If it was due to skepticism, the skepticism was not of long duration for as he grew older he became very religious and, after his retirement from the Chief Justiceship, spent the major portion of his time in the study of theology. His early biographers attributed his desire to enter the law to his argumentative disposition but there should certainly have been ample scope for that in a church of which Jonathan Edwards was the leading light.

The advantage which Ellsworth sought at the bar seems to have been a greater personal freedom than was available in the ministry. There was no place in a parsonage for that tendency to violate the minor conventions of respectability which had been responsible for his difficulties at Yale. He was to find that there was scarcely more room for it at the Connecticut bar. But in a few years this tendency in his character disappeared. Its sole manifestation in after life was in his power of intellectual growth.

After a year's study in New Britain his mind was made up. He was determined, despite the opposition of his father, to study law. The opportunities for doing this in colonial Connecticut were even less than in colonial New York or South Carolina. Those colonies at least tried to administer the common law but there were a great many people in Connecticut who claimed that the common law was not in force in that province. As one of the men in whose office Ellsworth studied, Jesse Root, phrased it in the preface to his reports, one of the first American law books, the common law was only "adapted to a people grown old in the habits of vice"[5] while the law which the courts of Connecticut administered "was derived from the law of nature and of revelation."[6] It was very difficult to advise a client of his rights under the "law of nature and of revelation," particularly since there were no reported decisions under that law, and, as Kirby, the first Connecticut reporter, phrases it, "the rules of property became uncertain, and litigation proportionately increased."[7] There were no local reports until after the Revolution so Ellsworth, even though he studied in Root's office, was compelled, so far as he studied any books at all other than the local statute books, to study books which taught the law of a people "grown old in the habits of vice." Even so, his studies seem to have been confined to two volumes. Bacon's *Abridgement* and Jacob's *Law Dictionary*. As

---

[5] I Root's Conn. Reports, preface, at iii.
[6] II Root's Conn. Reports, preface at iv.
[7] Kirby's Conn. Reports, preface, at iii.

the former of these was already a century and a half old
Ellsworth certainly did not acquire much knowledge of those
numerous branches of the common law, such as the law of
contracts, which had grown up in the interval. His study
of these books did not even give him a very thorough knowledge of the old established portions of the common law. His
ignorance comes to light in a curious anecdote. When he
was in England as Chief Justice he visited Westminster Hall
where an eminent barrister asked him, "Pray, Chief Justice,
in what cases do the half blood in America take by descent?"
Related by the half blood was a technical expression refer-
ring to those, for example, who were descended from different wives of a common male ancestor. The rules of
inheritance, under strict common law, between relatives by
the half blood were truly astonishing. Ellsworth seems to
have been so ignorant on the subject that he did not even
understand what his questioner was driving at for he repeated the story on his return as an illustration of the common European belief that the Americans are a race of half-
breeds.

Naturally the study of two books did not occupy Ellsworth for the entire four years during which he studied law.
He attended all the sessions of court that he could and made
up for the lack of local reports by observing the law in
action. His father had given Ellsworth up in disgust after
his abandonment of the ministry and the latter had now to
make his own living. There is a vague tradition that for a
time he taught school but, if so, it was not for very long. His
chief source of income was the chopping of wood which he
hauled to Hartford and sold by the cord. He was well fitted
for such work. His build was that of the traditional American. He was six feet two with broad shoulders, blue eyes
and a high forehead. He had worked on a farm as a boy
and he now developed the possibilities of his physique
further. The mature Ellsworth was a big, strong and erect
man but his friends frequently remarked on "the charac-

teristic plainness of his face." Curiously enough, however, in view of the popular belief that gout is a disease confined to those who have been underworked and overfed for several generations, he suffered greatly from this disease in the latter part of his life. It was not until he was broken down by the gout that people spoke of his appearance as distinguished.

After his admission to the bar clients did not flock to him as they had to Jay and Rutledge. So he continued his wood chopping for a year and then increased his responsibilities by marrying Abigail Wolcott, who was sixteen at the time. So far as so democratic a community as Windsor can be said to have had a leading family the Wolcotts were it. But the democracy of the town was so real that Ellsworth's poverty was not regarded as an objection. Nor was his connection with the Wolcotts of any material assistance to him.

Mrs. Ellsworth did not grow with her husband. She remained throughout life a typical Windsor housewife. After her husband's political career was fairly launched he spent a good deal of time away from home but she seems never to have accompanied him. Her interests were centered in the management of the household and the raising of the children. Home was a place where he came for rest and relaxation. He played with the children but she had to punish them.

Ellsworth's love of children was one of his strongest characteristics and in it he found his means of relaxation. There is no record that he ever played games of any kind except with children. When he had solved some difficult problem he would look around for children to play with, with his own when he could, when they were not available then with other people's. When he was in Hartford as a member of the Council, a contemporary tells us, "a little lad, by the name of John Bull, who lived in the neighborhood of Mr. Ellsworth's lodgings, found out that he was a very amusing playmate at a certain hour of the day, and therefore regularly made his appearance at the door, to have a romping with his jocose companion."[8]

Ellsworth's immediate problem after getting married was to find a source of livelihood. During the first three years after his admission to the bar his professional earnings totaled nine pounds, Connecticut money, which was scarcely enough even in that simple community. He solved the problem temporarily by renting a farm from his father. It was not a very elaborate place. There was not even a horse on it and apparently it was largely unfenced when Ellsworth took it over. He lived here for several years, walking the ten miles to Hartford whenever court was in session. He had to be present not only to keep up and increase his knowledge but because counsel were frequently retained on the spur of the moment from among those present.

The Ellsworth that emerged from this period of poverty differed considerably from the carefree student who had been a problem to the Yale authorities. The easy-going casualness was gone. Ellsworth himself was well aware of the change. "After I left college," he told one who later asked the secret of his success, "I took a deliberate survey of my understanding. I felt that it was weak—that I had no imagination and but little knowledge or culture. I then resolved on this course of study: to take up but a single subject at a time and to cling to that with an attention so undivided that if a cannon were fired in my ears I should still cling to my subject. That, sir, is all my secret."[9]

It was bitter enough to find himself, a college graduate in a day when college graduates were rare, making a living chopping wood. The neighbors added to the bitterness, for there must have been many a farmer who talked of the way Captain Ellsworth had wasted his money on the education of his son. To keep his self-respect in his home community Ellsworth had to be a success and he set about his end de-

[8] Quoted in FLANDERS, II at 117.
[9] BROWN, at 26n.

liberately. His method was to force himself to concentrate
and he trained himself so thoroughly in that method that in
after life he was famous for his fits of absent-mindedness.
He would stand for hours looking out the window or would
come to the table and eat a meal without saying a word.
When engaged in intense thought he would sometimes
audibly mutter. An underlying nervousness appears in his
habit of consuming great quantities of snuff when thinking.
Indeed, his family would measure the intensity of his
thought by the depth and frequency of the piles of snuff
around him. He could not think without snuff. He once
tried to reduce his consumption by leaving his snuff-box in
the attic so that it would be necessary for him to climb two
flights of stairs to get at it. It was in vain. However deep
his concentration he always found himself climbing the attic
stairs and he soon abandoned the experiment.

As his neighbors began to notice the change in his character his prospects looked up. He was still without clients
but the year after his marriage he was elected to the legislature. The following year he was retained in a case which
established his professional reputation. From then on his
rise was not only steady but so rapid that Noah Webster,
who studied law with him in 1779, reports that at that time
Ellsworth was handling from a thousand to fifteen hundred cases.

The number of cases Ellsworth handled indicates their
quality. The commerce of the state was for the most part
in the hands of the foreigners of Rhode Island and New
York. The later sentiment in Connecticut in favor of a
stronger union arose largely out of this foreign control of
its commerce. That state was itself almost entirely agricultural; Ellsworth thought that the country as a whole would
remain so "for centuries." There was a very equal distribution of wealth and so, while the people might be litigious,
they could not afford very expensive law suits. It was a
system in which counsel were not expected to be very well

prepared. Elaborate briefs could not be demanded on "the law of nature and of revelation." The judges were scarcely more learned than the juries and the simple issues usually involved were settled by common-sense arguments backed, perhaps, by a few scraps of biblical quotation.

When he was about thirty he left his farm and moved to Hartford. This meant that he could no longer represent Windsor in the legislature but at the same time that body elected him a member of the Committee of the Pay Table. This was a sort of commission of finance which had been set up originally at the time of the French and Indian wars and which was now to handle the colony's finances in the revolutionary war which was just breaking out. The canny Yankees knew what they were doing when they entrusted Ellsworth with their money. He had hardly begun to earn a good income before he evidenced a remarkable ability to handle it. In all probability his income at no time came anywhere near equaling what Rutledge earned but Ellsworth spent very little of what he made. Even in Connecticut he had a reputation for being thrifty and overly fond of a shrewd bargain. His most successful personal business venture seems to have been in the building of houses in Hartford for rent. Ellsworth in many respects was typical of that class of small-town and semi-rural capitalists which is still found in this country. He had the strong financial honesty of the class and he had, in an exaggerated degree, its secretiveness. There have been few men who have believed as thoroughly as the mature Ellsworth that the less other people knew about his business the better off he was. He would take elaborate precautions to keep all knowledge of his own business transactions even from his family and his attitude was the same in regard to public business. One of his first actions on the national scene was to oppose a resolution, offered by Hamilton, to open the sessions of the Continental Congress to the public. His attitude in the Senate was the same and he was one of the last members of that body to admit that no great harm could come from allowing the public admission to some of its sessions.

If he was as secretive with public business as with private he was likewise as close with public money as he was with his own. His care of the public finances was the foundation of his political success.

Two years after his appointment to the Pay Table he became State's Attorney of Hartford County. His duties in this position interfered neither with his law practice nor with his subsequent membership in the Continental Congress. He first became a member of that body in 1777 and was a member intermittently until 1783. Connecticut treated its members of the Congress like a diplomatic delegation. The individuals composing it were constantly coming and going so that none of them would have to be away from home for too long a stretch at a time. The delegation sent constant written reports to the Governor and a special messenger was retained by the state for the purpose of carrying communications back and forth. No record was kept of who actually wrote these reports and they were always signed by all the Connecticut delegates present. They are the dryest and most matter-of-fact letters in the world. It is not certain how many of these letters Ellsworth himself wrote but the same general criticism applies to nearly all his correspondence. He hated to write so intensely that the brevity of one letter to his wife makes it almost witty. The entire letter read,

> "One week and then
> Oliver Ellsworth."[10]

In view of Ellsworth's subsequent appointment as Chief Justice, the most interesting service he performed as a delegate to the Congress was as a member of the Committee of Appeals. This body was in a sense a forerunner of the Supreme Court. One of the first military steps taken by the

---

[10] BROWN, at 237.

Congress had been the commissioning of privateers and as soon as they began to bring in prizes it was necessary to set up some system of courts. The law of the sea required that some court adjudicate the captured ship to be a prize and, in addition, there were numerous disputes over the distribution of the prize money. State courts of admiralty were set up but this was the one branch of government which the states agreed properly belonged to the central government. Appeals from the state admiralty courts soon began to come in. At first these were heard by the Congress as a whole. This proved so unsatisfactory that about the time Ellsworth was elected a delegate a standing committee of appeals was set up. The constant changes in the membership of the Congress and thus in that of the committee made this scarcely more satisfactory. Finally a Court of Appeals, with a membership of three permanent commissioners, was created.[11]

Ellsworth's activities as a member of the Committee of Appeals were unimportant. Maritime law was a totally new field to him and he did not think his duties to the State of Connecticut required him to master it. It was not until he was appointed Chief Justice that he regretted his neglect of his opportunities on the Committee. In its early years the Supreme Court had more to do with admiralty than any other branch of the law. Ellsworth hesitated somewhat before accepting his appointment as Chief Justice and the main reason for his hesitation was his total lack of knowledge of maritime law. Contemporaneously with his acceptance he started a course of study in admiralty.

A much more congenial part of his congressional services were his duties as a member of a number of financial committees. Such appointments were not sought, for any financial committee of the government of the Confederation was distinctly a committee on the lack of money. But Ellsworth

[11] The decisions of the Court of Appeals under the Confederation are to be found in Dallas.

gladly participated in this work. His thrifty soul was shocked by the high cost of government and he did not conceal his opinion that the expense was due to the extravagance of those in charge. During the course of his political career his ideas changed to such an extent that toward the close of that career he complained that "our country pays badly." In the beginning his attitude was that of the typical farmer and he blamed the extravagance of the government on the fact that the capital was in a large city. It was essential, he wrote, that the Congress "should remove to a place of less expense, less avocation, and less influence, than are to be expected in a commercial and opulent city."[12]

Experience changed his ideas. In the course of his duties he gradually learned that the real difficulty was not in the extravagance with which the Congress spent an irredeemable paper currency but in the lack of revenue which made that currency worthless. The inability of the Congress to pay its debts horrified him. Financial integrity was to him a cardinal virtue. He felt the flagrant insolvency of the government of his country as a blemish on his own character. Even after he left the Congress he constantly harped on the defaults in the payment of interest on the foreign debts of the United States. Provincial as was his general outlook, or perhaps because of his provinciality, he regarded a default in the foreign debt as much worse than a default in the domestic debt.

The simplicity of his financial morality was more than equaled by the simplicity of his knowledge of economics. As a member of the Congress he enthusiastically supported a proposal to restore the value of the currency by fixing the prices of commodities by law. He learned slowly but, and this is the most important aspect of his character, he learned. He next supported a proposal to set aside a specific source of revenue for the central government. When he left the

---

[12] FLANDERS, II at 111.

Congress at the conclusion of the war he still hoped that this last proposal would prove workable.

He did not leave a great reputation behind him. He was respected for his sincerity and his willingness to work but he had not developed a great reputation for ability. He was of the same age as Jay but, while Jay had established an international reputation by the manner in which he had handled the peace negotiations, Ellsworth was still in the adolescence of his statesmanship.

The next few years, during which he sat in the Superior Court of Connecticut, witnessed a remarkable development of his talents. When he arrived at the Constitutional Convention he was no longer the Windsor farmer. He had become the statesman whom Washington was to consider worthy of the Chief Justiceship. He had spent many pinches of snuff on the problem presented by the breakdown of the Articles of Confederation and he had come to some definite conclusions. He was convinced of the necessity for a thorough overhauling of the central government. But he was equally determined that the states should not lose their identity. It is chiefly owing to him that the states have equal representation in the Senate—a system utterly indefensible at the present day. When he had once gained equal representation for the states in one branch of Congress he was very liberal in assigning powers to the federal government.

His influence in the convention was not all gained on the floor. He again had a reputation, like the one he had gained at Princeton, for ability to manage men. In particular, the acceptance of the idea of representation by states in one chamber and by population in the other seems to have been due largely to his work outside the convention hall.

Part of his influence arose from his willingness to accommodate the particular desires of other members. It was in this manner that he gained the support of Rutledge and the other South Carolina delegates. The South Carolinians had

a hard time gaining allies for their proposal that the new
government be expressly prohibited from interfering with
the slave trade. To Ellsworth the question of whether South
Carolina imported more slaves was distinctly a local question to be settled by that state alone. He did not see why
Virginia, whose delegates were the chief opponents of the
slave trade, should be allowed to impose its moral ideas on
South Carolina. It was this willingness to recognize the
peculiar interests of others which was largely responsible for
the influence he gained, first in the convention and later in
the Senate.

His willingness to accommodate Rutledge was not based
on any love of slavery. Ellsworth had never owned a slave
and had had little experience with the institution. He never
showed any abolitionist tendencies but he had occasional
qualms of conscience on the subject. Once he "met a little
colored girl and patted it on its head and said, 'Just as happy
as any child in the neighborhood now, but bye and bye'—
then shook his head and passed on."[13] He would not own
slaves himself but he regarded any attempt to interfere with
the institution by political means as an unwarranted intru-
sion in his neighbors' affairs. It was the existence of just
such peculiar local interests that had made him so insistent
that the states be retained. His attitude on the question of
the slave trade caused Calhoun, many years later, to deliver
a eulogy on Ellsworth in the Senate.

The reputation that Ellsworth had gained in the convention was so great that when the Senate of the new government met—for he had been elected a senator—he seems almost automatically to have become its leader. That body was
peculiarly adapted to his talents for managing men. There
were only twenty-six members, so small a number that on a
cold day they would all leave their seats and gather around
the fireplace. The sessions were secret. There were a number of able men in the Senate and most of them were Feder-

---

[13] Quoted in BROWN, at 236n.

alists. But in a very short while Ellsworth was the recognized administration spokesman. It was due not only to his talent in management but to his willingness to spend long hours hammering out the dry details of a bill. If the Senate had been larger, or if its proceedings had been public, he would not have gained his hold nearly so easily. In that event oratory and the ability to appeal to the public would have been more important. While Ellsworth was famous for his ability to convince Connecticut juries his reputation as a speaker never extended much beyond that.

The most important work he performed in the Senate was the drafting of the Judiciary Act of 1789. "This vile bill," wrote one of his colleagues, "is a child," of Ellsworth's, "and he defends it with the care of a parent, even with wrath and anger."[14] No part of the constitution is more vague than that which relates to the judiciary and many features of this Act are by now as firmly imbedded in our governmental system as if they were parts of the constitution. The most striking feature of the Act is its provision for a double system of courts.

We are so accustomed to a double system of courts that we think it a feature inseparable from a federal government. As there are two governments over each man, the state and the federal, it seems obvious that, as each of these governments has its own officials and departments, each should have its own courts. Yet the world is full of federations in which the states have their own officials and departments, yet in none of them do the states and the federal government each have its own system of courts. The constitution of Australia was modeled on that of the United States, yet Australia does not have a separate system of federal courts. Its constitution gives Parliament power to create "other federal courts" besides the High Court, but this power has never been exercised. Canada is a federation and is our closest neighbor but has no separate system of federal courts. Many

---

[14] MACLAY, at 89.

features of the constitution of the Union of South Africa were
taken from that of the United States but there are no inferior
federal courts. In all these dominions the same courts administer state and federal law with a superimposed federal
supreme court to harmonize their decisions and act as the
final interpreter of the supreme organic law. It is clearly a
case of everybody being out of step but Jim.

This peculiarity of our federal system is not based on any
mistake on Ellsworth's part. Like all Ellsworth's political
opinions at this period it is directly traceable to experience
under the Articles of Confederation. At that time the states
were all willing to concede that admiralty and maritime matters were properly within the jurisdiction of the central government. Yet the Committee of Appeals and the later Court
of Appeals found the utmost difficulty in getting their decisions in prize cases accepted by the state courts. In one case
in which the decision of the national court had been ignored
by the Pennsylvania courts that decision was subsequently
confirmed by the Supreme Court in Marshall's time.[15] Yet
even at that late date the Governor of Pennsylvania actually
called out the militia in the endeavor to defeat the process of
the federal courts.

The Act contained another striking provision and one
whose value was at least questionable. This was the provision for three grades of courts, the supreme court, the circuit
courts and the district courts, but only two grades of judges.
The Supreme Court consisted of six members, including the
Chief Justice. The country was divided into three circuits
with a circuit court for each. These courts actually circulated
and sat in the various cities in their territories. The membership of a circuit court was three judges but no such position as "circuit court judge" was created. The membership
of those courts was to be a combination of the judges of the
other two grades of courts. Every time a circuit court was

---

[15] See *United States* v. *Judge Peters*, 5 Cranch 115, 3 L. Ed. 53
(1809).

called to order, whether in Charleston, South Carolina or
Boston, Massachusetts, two justices of the Supreme Court of
the United States were to be sitting. The full membership
was to be made up by having a local federal district judge
sit with them. The circuit courts were not, like our present
circuit courts of appeals, purely appellate. Both the circuit
courts and the district courts were courts of original jurisdiction, although in different kinds of cases, and the circuit
courts had, in addition, a limited appellate jurisdiction over
the district courts. As there were two terms a year of the
circuit courts, each Supreme Court justice had to ride through
one-third of the United States on horseback twice a year in
addition to riding to the capital and back for the sessions of
his own court. This was partly copied from the English
assize system but undoubtedly the main idea was that it was
better for the courts to travel than to compel the litigants to
do so as even the Court of Appeals for prize cases of the Confederation had been ambulatory.

The circuit court features of the Act began to break down
almost as soon as they were put into operation. Yet such
was the popularity of the idea that even today each member
of the Supreme Court is in theory assigned to a particular
circuit.

Ellsworth's work on the Judiciary Act had far more influence on the development of the Supreme Court than any
judicial decision he ever rendered. The very foundation of
the Court's subsequent power over state legislation is found
in the provision of that Act which provided for appeals to
the Supreme Court in cases where the constitutionality,
under the federal constitution, of a state statute had been
drawn into question and the highest court of the state had
decided in favor of the validity of the statute. The debate
over the Act had been long and acrimonious but this provision was generally accepted. The objections to the Act were,
as one of its opponents expressed it, that it "certainly is a

vile law system, calculated for expense." [16]   The early fears
of that group which afterwards denounced Marshall's decisions were not of the power of the Court over legislation.
Their fear was rather that the Court would be the willing
tool of a usurping Congress and President.

Ellsworth's mental stature and public reputation increased immensely during his six years as senator. He
worked closely with that little group of Boston Federalists
which revolved around Secretary of State Pickering but his
practical good sense and, perhaps, his democratic background, kept him from going to the extremes to which they
went. The anti-Federalists recognized the difference. Very
little of the vituperation which they poured out on the Federalists was directed at Ellsworth. Even Senator Maclay,
whose opinion that the Judiciary Act was "a vile law system"
has already been quoted, confided to his diary that "Ellsworth has credit with me."   Ellsworth's political balance
showed particularly on Jefferson's election. His opposition
to Jefferson was strong and inevitable for it was based on
fundamental differences in temperament. To him the chief
objection to the Virginian was that he was "a visionary
man." Jefferson's opposition to state support of any religion
would alone have been sufficient to stamp him as "visionary"
in Ellsworth's mind. To the latter a state church stood in the
same category as a state school system or a state judicial
system. In a report to the Connecticut legislature on the
subject he added "nor is any individual allowed to refuse his
contribution, because he has no children to be instructed, no
injuries to be redressed, or because he conscientiously believes those institutions useless. On the same principle of
general utility . . . the legislature may aid the maintenance
of that religion whose benign influence on morals is universally acknowledged." But his dislike of Jefferson did not
cause him to approve the plan to throw the Presidency to
Burr. Nor was he implicated in any of Pickering's subsequent, and more or less treasonable, schemes.

[16] MACLAY, at 114.

The nation as a whole was well satisfied with his appointment as Chief Justice. The only dissatisfaction was among the Associate Justices who did not think that a training in "the law of nature and of revelation" was equal to a training in the common law. His judicial career is too short to determine whether they were right. He wrote, all told, less than a dozen opinions for the Supreme Court and none of these was in an important case. Only three cases were decided during Ellsworth's term of office which were of importance in the development of constitutional law and he took part in the decision of none of them. The first of these[17] was the first case in which the Court was asked, at the suit of a private citizen, to declare an act of Congress unconstitutional. The second[18] involved the question of whether the provisions of the peace treaty with Great Britain which provided that no impediment was to be placed on the recovery by British subjects of debts due to them from Americans overrode a Virginian statute sequestering such debts. The third[19] was an appeal from a state court of last resort based on the claim that the state statute which that court had upheld violated the provision in the federal constitution prohibiting the passage of *ex post facto* laws by any state. The first two had been argued, but not decided, before Ellsworth took his seat. The decision in the first had been in favor of the validity of the act of Congress which was called into question and the decision in the second had been against the validity of the Virginian statute. It is not quite clear why he took no part in the decision of the third although, since the appeal was from Connecticut, he may well have considered himself disqualified on account of some previous connection with the case. The most interesting aspect both of the case in which the constitutionality of a federal statute was called into question and of the case in which the constitutionality of the Connecticut statute was called into question is that

---

[17] *Hylton* v. *United States*, 3 Dall. 171, 1 L. Ed. 556 (1796).
[18] *Ware* v. *Hylton*, 3 Dall. 199, 1 L. Ed. 568 (1796).
[19] *Calder* v. *Bull*, 3 Dall. 386, 1 L. Ed. 648 (August Term, 1798).

everyone seemed to take it for granted that it was the proper
function of the Court to determine these questions. If it was
not, there was no method of determining such questions except by diplomatic negotiation between the states and the
federal government. That method necessarily makes force,
war, the ultimate arbiter. To use Ellsworth's words, it involves a "coercion of arms" rather than "a coercion of law."

The question of whether the peace treaty overrode the
various state acts confiscating or sequestering debts due to
British subjects aroused far more popular feeling. The Virginians were the ones particularly interested. Prior to the
war most of the Virginian planters had habitually been in
debt to British tobacco merchants. The Virginian statute had
provided for the payment of these debts into the state treasury which later returned the money. But as the repayment
was made in the depreciated continental currency the debtors
were practically in the position of having to pay the same
debt twice. It was a situation which was to trouble the
Supreme Court many times.

Ellsworth was to pass on it once but it was on circuit in
a case in which the North Carolina statute which confiscated,
rather than merely sequestered, such debts was called into
question.[20] He held that the statute was no longer in force
but he did not put his decision squarely on the constitutional
provision making treaties the supreme law of the land. Nor
did he place it simply on the precedent established in the
Virginian case which had already been passed on by the
Court. He treated the state statute and the treaty as if they
were intrinsically statutes of equal force and then based his
decision on the rule that if there is a conflict between two
statutes the one which was passed later prevails. On this
reasoning the state could easily have gotten rid of the treaty
provision by repassing the confiscatory statute. Ellsworth
must have realized this but there is nothing to indicate

---

[20] This decision was not reported at the time but Ellsworth's
opinion is printed in FLANDERS, II at 197-202.

whether his opinion was based on the assumption that it was as well not to go the whole distance at once or whether he did not himself clearly understand the principle involved.

Unlike Jay, Ellsworth thoroughly enjoyed his judicial duties, even the circuit riding. His health was already beginning to break down but he was still well enough to do the necessary traveling. He had never been very far from home and he enjoyed the opportunity to tour the United States. He had no fine sensibilities which were wounded by the necessity of sentencing criminals. The foundation of his own career had been laid in the trial, both at the bar and on the bench, of petty cases. They did not bore him even in Connecticut and now, when from the dignity of the bench he came into contact with strange local customs and ways of life, they had a piquancy which had then been lacking. He did not share the opinion of his old teacher, Root, that the common law was fit only for a people "grown old in the habits of vice." He increased his knowledge of that law by study and, as was to be expected with a man who was attempting to administer a system which he did not thoroughly understand, he followed the English precedents slavishly. The most conspicuous instance was a case[21] on circuit in which he held that the English doctrine that if a man had been born a British subject he could never change his allegiance applied to an American citizen. In the case in question it meant that since the individual involved had been born in Connecticut it was impossible for him to make himself a French citizen. It is impossible to conceive of Jay arriving at such a conclusion. The English doctrine was based on feudal notions of allegiance and in rendering his decision Ellsworth completely ignored those differences between feudal sovereignty and republican sovereignty which Jay had so carefully pointed out in the *Chisholm Case.*

Nor did Ellsworth appreciate the limits between the dif-

---

[21] *Isaac Williams Case,* reported in note at 2 Cranch 82, 2 L. Ed. 214.

ferent branches of government so completely as Jay. In contrast to the latter's refusal to give Washington a legal opinion, Ellsworth, after he had assumed the Chief Justiceship, gave the President an opinion that the House of Representatives was not entitled to demand a copy of the instructions which had been given to Jay when he was sent to London.

His action in this instance and his decision in the North Carolina case indicate his chief weakness. He had never been accustomed to long-range, abstract thinking. His attitude had always been to decide the concrete point without too much consideration of its theoretical ramifications. That attitude had served admirably in both the Constitutional Convention and the Senate for in both cases he had been working with men who did an ample share of abstract thinking. But in the Court it was different. If either of the instances referred to had been decisions of the full Court the influence of his colleagues might have caused a somewhat different result. But his relations with the Associate Justices were not very cordial and he probably consulted them as little as possible.

As in the case of one of his successors whose appointment was resented by the Associate Justices, Ellsworth soon succeeded in establishing his position as the head of the Court. An anecdote will illustrate the method. Shortly after his appointment he and Samuel Chase, one of the associates, were sitting together in a circuit court in Philadelphia where Jared Ingersoll appeared for one of the litigants. As soon as he opened his argument, Chase interrupted with the statement that the court did not care to listen to argument on the point. He tried a second point and then a third point and each time was interrupted by Chase. Ingersoll then sat down and the Chief Justice calmly took out his snuff-box, tapped it on the side with his finger, as was his custom before taking a pinch, and said: "The Court has expressed no opinion, sir, upon these points, and when it does you will hear it from the proper organ of the Court. You will proceed, sir."[22]

The story may not seem altogether in keeping with Ellsworth's general reputation for extreme affability. That reputation rests on too much testimony for it to be put in question by this single story. But for many years now Ellsworth had been treated with general respect and when so treated showed himself open and affable. The at best slightly concealed opinion of Justices Wilson, Paterson and Chase that they had been insulted by his appointment was a different matter.

Ellsworth's judicial services, like Jay's, ended with a diplomatic appointment. Like Jay, too, Ellsworth reaped more abuse than glory from his diplomatic labors. The circumstances were similar. Both England and France went out of their way to insult the new nation. Jay's treaty had deferred the war with England but France had refused to make any treaty unless the United States agreed to pay tribute—the XYZ affair. The consequence was that the United States waged an informal war with France for about two years. Then the latter country intimated that it would like to discuss a settlement of the difficulty. The Federalists were, if possible, more opposed to making a treaty with Jacobin France than the anti-Federalists had been to making a treaty with monarchical England. But President Adams was convinced that both were equally wise. He followed a bad precedent by selecting Ellsworth to head the mission. There had been some excuse in Jay's record for taking him from the bench for such a purpose but there was none in Ellsworth's. He had neither diplomatic knowledge nor experience. His insight into the politics of Europe appeared when, shortly before sailing, he called on Adams and, much to the latter's amusement, suggested that the mission be deferred because of the imminence of a Bourbon restoration. The main reason for selecting him was that he was the only New

---

[22] FLANDERS, II at 187-188.

England Federalist temperate enough to be trusted to make a real effort to come to an understanding with France. His reason for taking the appointment was his general attitude that it was his duty to take orders. As had already appeared when he gave Washington a legal opinion, he seems to have had little conception of the independence of the judiciary. He regarded himself in his capacity as Chief Justice as responsible generally to the President.

Ellsworth did not enjoy his diplomatic experience. The voyage was stormy; he was seasick; he developed what the eighteenth century called gravel in his kidneys, and his gout took a severe form which it retained from then on. Paris did not seem to him comparable to Connecticut. He knew no French except what he had learned on the way over and while in France, for he had entered on his strange duties with the thoroughness which always characterized him. The intellectual pleasures of Europe did not appeal to him. He was not interested in looking at pictures or statues, in attending theatres or operas, or in becoming acquainted with the latest books. In Connecticut he had by this time acquired a great reputation as a conversationalist but there was little interest in Paris in the narrow fields of Congregational theology and American politics to which intellectual conversation in New England was confined.

The Connecticut Yankee at Napoleon's court wrote his opinions of the strange land to his twin boys, Harry and Billy, aged eight, in rhyme:

"The men in France are lazy creatures,
    And work the women and great dogs,
The ladies are enormous eaters,
    And like the best toadstools and frogs.

The little boys are pretty spry
    And bow when Daddy's paid them,
But don't think they shall ever die,
    Nor can they tell who made them.

But Daddy's boys are not such fools,
    And are not learned so bad,
For they have Mamma and good schools,
    And that makes Daddy glad.

Daddy won't forget them pistols."[23]

_____

[23] BROWN, at 301-302.

His lack of knowledge of the ways of diplomacy led him to make some tactical blunders in the negotiations but he finally succeeded in concluding a convention which temporarily patched up relations between the two countries. The anti-Federalists were satisfied but it did not add to his reputation with the Federalists. "I can account for it," wrote his intimate friend and fellow Connecticut Yankee, Wolcott, "only on the supposition that the vigor of Mr. Ellsworth's mind has been enfeebled by sickness."[24] Ellsworth heard such comments while still in Europe and wrote King, the American minister in London, "I am very sorry to hear that his Majesty has been deranged [George III had had one of his fits of insanity], and still more so to learn that I am supposed to be in the same predicament."[25]

Ellsworth had sent his resignation to the United States along with the convention. His kidney trouble and his gout gave no indication of improving and he did not think that he would ever again be able to ride circuit. His intention was to pass a winter in the south of France, for the convention had been signed in the fall, but first he went to England to try the effect of the waters of Bath. He liked the country so well that he stayed there until his return to America in the spring.

Sometime after he had begun to accumulate means he had acquired a substantial white frame house in Windsor of the kind which still gives charm to many New England towns. He had named it Elmwood and there he spent the remainder of his life. His time was largely taken up by the study of theology and by a series of notes on agriculture which he wrote for the *Connecticut Courant*. American farming was then completely unscientific and those notes were based on his discovery, while in England, of the works of Arthur Young. Ellsworth always hated to use a pen but he had the assistance of Noah Webster in the preparation

[24] Quoted in FLANDERS, II at 249.
[25] Letter dated Feb. 26, 1801, printed in FLANDERS, II at 262.

of these notes. Even so, they were regarded with an amused cynicism by most of the Connecticut farmers to whom they were addressed. They had more influence in his own family. Of his twin sons, Harry, after being the first Commissioner of Patents, became a great developer of Western lands and promoter of the use of agricultural machinery. The other twin was at one time governor of Connecticut. An elder son, Oliver, Jr., who had accompanied his father to Europe and for whom Ellsworth had great hopes, died shortly after their return.

During his retirement, Ellsworth also served, more or less nominally, in the Council of Connecticut and was offered the Chief Justiceship of the state supreme court on the creation of that office. He accepted but before he actually took his seat decided that his health would not permit him to sit. Shortly after he died, on November 26, 1807.

Chapter IV

JOHN MARSHALL

Born near Germantown, Fauquier County, Virginia, September 24, 1755.

Lieutenant in the Culpeper Minute Men, 1775-1776.

Lieutenant and Captain, Continental Army, 1776-1779. (Not actually discharged until 1781).

Attended William and Mary College, 1780.

Admitted to bar, August 28, 1780.

Elected to House of Delegates of Virginia from Fauquier County, 1782, 1784.

Elected to Council of State of Virginia, 1782.

Married Maria Ambler, January 3, 1783.

Elected to House of Delegates from Henrico County, 1787.

Member, Virginian Convention to ratify Federal Constitution, 1788.

Elected to House of Delegates from Henrico County, 1789, 1795, 1796.

Special Envoy to France, 1797-1798.

Member of Congress, 1799-1800.

Secretary of State, 1800-1801.

Appointed Chief Justice, January 20, 1801; confirmed January 27, 1801.

Died, at Philadelphia, July 6, 1835.

JOHN MARSHALL

From a portrait by Chester Harding

With the appointment of John Marshall as Chief Justice and the election of Thomas Jefferson as President the Supreme Court stepped out of swaddling clothes. For the first twelve years of its existence the central government had been in the possession of a small group, many of whose members were able, nearly all of whose members were conscientious, but all of whom, as a group, believed most thoroughly that they, and they alone, stood between the country and chaos. They had not concealed their opinion that they were the only people capable of running the government successfully. That opinion had not added to their popularity, which was never very great. It had contributed materially to the growth of an opposition party. This unpopularity had increased the feeling of isolation which the governing group had had from the beginning; it had added to the feeling among the members of that group that they could not afford to allow any quarrels to arise between the different branches of the government. It was the duty of all to see to it that nothing was done which might rock the ship of state. If Chief Justice Jay felt that the Pension Act as drawn was unconstitutional, the thing to do was to amend that act so that it would meet his scruples. In turn, the judges expressed their constitutional views in private conversation with the other officers of the government rather than in public judicial pronouncements. The Chief Justice was almost as intimately associated with the President as if he were a member of the cabinet.

It was a situation which could not last. A system of checks and balances assumes a certain antagonism among the men entrusted with the various powers of government; it assumes that a man entrusted with one of the powers of government will use it to check and balance the exercise by the men entrusted with the other powers of government of

113

the powers entrusted to them. The constitution was drawn
on the assumption that political parties would never arise;
there is no place under it for an official or semi-official
Opposition. The concentration of the powers of the executive branch of the government in the hands of one man
prevents even that outlet for the minority which is found in
parliamentary governments where the executive power is
lodged in a committee, a cabinet, whose members, while in
general working together, almost necessarily represent vary-
ing shades of opinion. The members of the constitutional
convention had assumed that the chief antagonism would be
between the executive and legislative branches; between the
President and the Congress. But the first change of party
showed that Congress and the President were much more
likely to work together than to oppose one another.

The Supreme Court remained. It was the sole branch of
the government in the hands of the opposition. In theory
the judiciary was an independent branch of the government;
the occasion was now arising for determining whether it was
so in fact. Could a Chief Justice who belonged to a dis-
credited political party hold his seat against a victorious
political party in absolute possession of the other two
branches of the government? Could he, under those circumstances, enforce those guarantees of personal freedom
which were written in the constitution? Above all, could the
Court, without physical power at its command, exercise its
function of drawing the limits on the powers of Congress
and of the states? If so, the problem raised by the series of
three Anglo-American revolutions, the problem of how to
make limitations on power effective, had been answered. It
was up to Marshall to make Washington's hope that the
Court would be "the keystone of our political fabric" a
reality.

*   *   *   *   *   *

That conception of the functions of a judiciary was
peculiarly American and the man who was called upon to

breathe life into that conception was equally peculiarly an
American product. John Marshall was by birth a frontiersman, the first man with that background to reach high federal office. The power and independence of the judiciary
were not to be established by colonial aristocrats like Jay and
Rutledge or conservative New Englanders like Ellsworth but
by the precursor of Jackson and Lincoln.

Marshall's grandfather had been a small farmer in tidewater Virginia; the owner of two hundred acres of poor land
in a country in which people of importance measured their
estates in terms of thousands and tens of thousands of acres.
The next head of the family, Thomas Marshall, the father of
the Chief Justice and, according to the latter, "a far abler
man than any of his sons,"[1] was determined to rise in the
world. He began by improving his social status through
marriage. His wife was a daughter of a clergyman named
Keith, a scion of the family of that name which had been for
centuries hereditary Earls Marischal of Scotland. This
Keith had been mixed up in the Jacobite rebellion of 1715
and, when he learned that the British preferred a king who
could not speak English to one who was guilty of the heinous
sin of popery, had fled to Virginia. There he had married
Mary Isham Randolph, a first cousin of Jefferson's mother.
Thomas Marshall does not seem to have acquired, with his
wife, any of the Randolph or Isham wealth and, shortly after
his marriage, he determined to seek his fortune in the
wilderness.

The frontier was not contemporary with the founding of
the first settlements. It had taken a century and a half to
fill up the narrow strip of tidewater land of which the first
settlers had taken possession. It was not until the middle of
the eighteenth century that the surplus population from the
small independent farms of Virginia and Pennsylvania, re-
cent immigrants, many of them Germans, and adventurers
from everywhere began to push their way into freshwater

[1] Discourse by Joseph Story, DILLON, III at 327, 330.

Virginia. Thomas Marshall took his wife, a few farm animals and the two slaves he had inherited from his father
and went along. He built his first home near a place called
Germantown in what is now Fauquier County, Virginia.
Here John, the eldest of the Marshalls' fifteen children, was
born in 1755, a few weeks after Braddock's defeat.

The Marshalls were distinctly a superior family on the
frontier. Thomas Marshall had had little formal schooling
but he had succeeded in acquiring some education for himself. There were no schools for women in colonial Virginia
but his wife had acquired from her father, who was a man
of considerable culture and of extremely fine sensibilities,
what was a very superior education for a colonial dame.
The Marshalls always managed to have a few books around
them which was truly a rare thing in the wilderness.

Thomas Marshall did not have to depend for a living, like
the majority of his neighbors, entirely on his hunting and
farming. Like so many of the frontier leaders he had some-
how acquired a knowledge of surveying. The taming of the
wilderness furnished plenty of work for surveyors and before long his profession brought him a job which was to
have a profound influence on his son's career.

Thomas Marshall and George Washington had known
each other as boys. The latter was the surveyor of the huge
Fairfax estate, with its millions of acres, and he now employed his boyhood acquaintance as his assistant. The
longer Thomas Marshall knew George Washington the more
he admired him. The latter became his model in everything.
Long before the country as a whole knew Lord Fairfax's
surveyor as anything but an able frontier soldier he was
being pointed out to John Marshall as the perfect example
of all that a man should be. With that upbringing John
could never join with the majority in the Virginian legislature, on Washington's retirement, in denying formally that
the public career of the father of his country had displayed

"wisdom, valor and patriotism."[2] It helps explain why Marshall was to be the last important Federalist in his native state.

The Marshall home near Germantown was the usual wilderness cabin but after a few years there Thomas Marshall had become sufficiently prosperous to live in greater comfort. He had acquired an interest in some land about thirty miles west of Germantown, in a small valley in the Blue Ridge mountains know as the Hollow. Here he built what was a mansion for the frontier. It was not built of logs but of whip-sawed uprights and boards and contained two rooms, a veritable luxury in the backwoods. In addition, there were two half-story lofts over the two rooms, a stone "meat house," a one-room log cabin for the negroes, and a log stable. Here John lived until he was eighteen and, one of his later contemporaries informs us, "he ever recurred with fondness to that primitive mode of life, when he partook with a keen relish of balm tea and mush; and when the females used thorns for pins."[3] The chief food of the family consisted of bear meat, venison and fish, for game was much more plentiful than domestic animals. About the only thing the farm produced was maize and that was largely consumed at home after having been turned into corn meal or whisky.

The Marshalls moved to the Hollow some time before John was ten. His boyhood was lonely. The neighborhood was still too unsettled for him to find any playmates of his own age except among his father's slaves. John's amusements were chiefly hunting and fishing for, like all children of the frontier, he learned to shoot as soon as he was strong enough to hold a gun. It was here that he developed the magnificent physique which enabled him to ride circuit until he was eighty. He came of a virile family. In an age when infant mortality was taken for granted all the fifteen chil-

[2] BEVERIDGE, II at 160.
[3] Quoted in BEVERIDGE, I at 39n.

dren of Thomas and Máry Marshall lived to be married.
John grew big and strong in his frontier home. When he
left to fight the British he was a powerful backwoodsman,
over six feet tall, with a dark complexion, thick black hair
and almost black eyes. His eyes alone, which seem to have
been peculiarly expressive of his deeply emotional nature,
distinguished him from the horde of burly roughnecks whom
the frontier produced. Otherwise his low receding forehead
and general coarseness of appearance seem, throughout his
career, to have left an unfavorable first impression on most
people with whom he came in contact.

His early schooling was derived largely from his parents.
His mother taught him to read the few books available. The
most important of these were the Bible and the works of
Pope. The latter caught his fancy early. Throughout his
life Marshall loved to read poetry and it was one of the
causes of the close friendship between him and Story, the
latter of whom is probably the only member of the Supreme
Court who has ever published a volume of his own verse.
Marshall later related that before he was twelve he was
thoroughly acquainted with the *Essay on Man* and it is not
impossible to find a prose Pope in Marshall's great constitutional opinions. Pope may be the least poetic of poets, but
his poetry, like the constitution of the United States, con-
templates an orderly rather than a chaotic world.

Thomas Marshall had become a member of the House of
Burgesses when John was four years old and sheriff of
Fauquier County a few years later. The latter was the most
powerful local office in colonial Virginia and, because of the
fees and perquisites, by far the most lucrative. These offices,
together with his connection with George Washington and
Lord Fairfax, whose home at Greenway Lodge, near Win-
chester, was not very far away, kept Thomas Marshall in
contact with the world outside the frontier. With his eager
desire to improve himself he learned all that he could from
the men with whom he came into contact. An unusual pro-

portion of what he thus learned was transmitted to John, for the relation between Thomas Marshall and his eldest son was one of remarkable intimacy.

When that son was fourteen his home in the Hollow was included in a parish of the Church of England. The rector lived for a time with Thomas Marshall who was one of the vestrymen. At night the clergyman slept in the loft with the Marshall children and in the daytime he taught them. Under him John "commenced reading Horace and Livy."[4] This teaching did not last long but John continued the study of the classics by himself with sufficient success so that, in his old age, he was careful to point out the advantages of "proficiency in Greek and Latin" to his grandson.[5] Some years later, when he was nearly twenty, John had another fragment of formal education when he attended for a few months an academy in Westmoreland County kept by a Scotch parson named Campbell, an uncle of the poet.

When John was eighteen his father was ready to move again but this time he was not going further west. Instead he purchased seventeen hundred acres in the same county for "nine hundred and twelve pounds ten shillings current money of Virginia."[6] His new estate was named Oak Hill and here he built a house with no less than seven rooms, four below and three above.

Thomas Marshall was not ambitious for himself alone. He had come a long way but his seventeen hundred acres in the backwoods still did not compare, for example, with the ten thousand acres and two hundred slaves which Thomas Jefferson had on the banks of the James. The Marshalls now had a good start on the road to success but Thomas Marshall expected the clan to rise a good deal further. His ambitions demanded a lawyer in the family for the law was the occupation of those members of the aristocracy who

[4] STORY, MISC., at 185.
[5] Letter dated Nov. 7, 1834 from Marshall, OSTER, at 55.
[6] Quoted in BEVERIDGE, I at 55.

were not content merely to be planters. His eldest son from his "infancy," to quote John's own words, had been "destined for the bar."[7]

Thomas Marshall's first active step in this direction was to purchase a copy of Blackstone when, shortly before the outbreak of the Revolution, that book was republished in America. This his son was expected to read before entering the office of some lawyer in the eastern counties where he would receive such legal education as was then available in Virginia. John did not find Blackstone—one of the most readable textbooks ever written—very enticing reading and before he could claim to have mastered it the Revolution interrupted the career which his father had planned for him.

There was no question in the Marshall household as to the right and wrong of the revolt. The frontiersmen, unlike many members of the classes from which Jay and Rutledge came, did not think of themselves as Englishmen who happened to live on the western side of the ocean. The representatives from the backwoods were the most radical members of the House of Burgesses and, in the case of the Marshalls, any possible doubt was removed by the conduct of George Washington. It was a cardinal principle with Thomas Marshall, as it was later with his son, that the master of Mount Vernon could do no wrong.

When the news of Concord and Lexington reached the backwoods the frontiersmen organized themselves into a regiment. Thomas Marshall was a major and John, doubtless through his father's influence for he was not quite twenty, was a lieutenant.

The frontiersmen had not drilled for long when the call to action came. Patrick Henry sent an express over the wilderness to warn them that the royal governor, Lord Dunmore, was making hostile preparations. The regiment marched over the hills to Williamsburg clad in "strong

---

[7] Autobiography, OSTER, at 197.

brown linen hunting shirts dyed with leaves" and with the
words "Liberty or Death" worked on each breast.[8] There
was a bucktail in each hat and the weapons of the frontier,
a tomahawk and a scalping knife, in each man's belt. They
took part in the battle of Great Bridge, the skirmish which
ushered in the war in Virginia, and were disbanded in March
of 1776. Four months later John was commissioned a lieutenant in the Third Virginia regiment, in which his father
was again a major, and entered the regular Continental
Army where he remained for the next few years.

When Marshall joined the Continental Army it had just
lost the city of New York to the British and was fighting
desperately to keep from losing the city of Philadelphia as
well, with all the territory in between. All winter they cam-
paigned through New Jersey although the troops were "without blankets; many of them barefooted."[9] The wretched
government of the Confederation had no money and no
power to raise any by taxation. Its only resources were the
issue of a paper money that depreciated every day and requests to the states for contributions which were seldom
given. Both the state and central governments had the ortho-
dox Whig fear of a regular army and hoped to fight the British with militia. But the militia "come in, you cannot tell
how; go, you cannot tell when; and act, you cannot tell
where" and "consume your provisions, exhaust your stores,
and leave you at last in a critical moment."[10] Provisions,
of course, were always lacking and, while Washington usually succeeded in getting some kind of ammunition for his
men, the muskets they had were so defectively made that
there was always trouble in fitting the cartridges. All these
difficulties were not due to the enemy but to the American
lack of organization. In fact, the cause of independence appeared to be falling rapidly of its own weight and there was
a rush on the part of the people to return to the allegiance of

[8] BEVERIDGE, I at 74.
[9] MARSHALL, II at 554.
[10] Washington, quoted in MARSHALL, II at 538.

the King. A large part of Washington's small army had to be kept constantly in Philadelphia to prevent that city from throwing off the American yoke and Marshall himself was of the opinion that "had the conduct of the British army been such as to cherish the expectation, that security to . . . persons and property was attainable by submission, it is not easy to say what limits could have been set to the anti-American spirit."[11]

Shortly after the battle of Trenton, Marshall was raised to the rank of captain-lieutenant and, at the battle of Brandywine in the following summer, he was part of the light infantry which was sent out in front to annoy the enemy. The loss of that battle was followed by the loss of Philadelphia and, at the end of that year's campaign, Marshall, along with what was left of Washington's army, retired to Valley Forge for the winter. Shortly after their arrival here he was appointed a deputy judge advocate. The duties of the position must have been fairly arduous for desertions were frequent and were kept down as much as possible by severe punishments. He did not treat his power lightly but usually gave his decision only after mature deliberation and frequently explained it by a written opinion.

If Marshall was disgusted with the inefficiency of the government the previous winter, his disgust doubled in his second winter with the army of the Revolution. There was nothing at Valley Forge when the army arrived there except a group of wooded ravines and the men who were, according to von Steuben, "literally naked, some of them in the fullest extent of the word,"[12] had, at first, to sleep with such shelter as the trees gave them. They were tolled off in parties of twelve to build huts but it was more than a month before all of these were erected and, when they were, twelve soldiers had to live in each fourteen by sixteen hut. Food became scarcer and scarcer. Raiding parties did what they could to

---

[11] MARSHALL, III at 64.
[12] BEVERIDGE, I at 111n.

remedy this, but sometimes there was nothing in the camp to eat. Deaths from starvation and exposure were frequent.

It was at Valley Forge that Marshall first won Washington's esteem on his own account and not merely because he was his father's son. The ragged and starved soldiers deserted at every opportunity; the commander-in-chief was harassed by officers anxious to obtain their dismissal. The Congress complained about the lack of victories and many of its members entered into an intrigue to make Gates commander-in-chief. The farmers of the vicinity, except those of German descent,[13] refused to furnish supplies to the Americans and rushed to the British with any military information they obtained. There were few people who gave Washington any help, but Marshall was among those few. The frontier captain, according to one of his brother officers, "was the best tempered man I ever knew" and "enlivened" "the gloomy hours" with "his inexhaustible fund of anecdote."[14] He was extremely popular with the common soldiers; a popularity which foreshadowed the day when he was to be the only Federalist who could get elected to office in an otherwise solidly Jeffersonian Virginia. This popularity was increased by his athletic skill. When the weather became warmer the army tried to forget its troubles in the playing of various kinds of games. Marshall distinguished himself in the pitching of horseshoes, in running and by jumping over a pole "laid on the heads of two men as high as himself."[15] The social ease and gift for popularity which Marshall seems always to have had is all the more remarkable when one remembers his solitary boyhood. It is true he had had the society of his brothers and sisters and of the children among his father's slaves but neither the position of eldest child nor that of young master is likely to develop social ease with equals.

---

[13] BEVERIDGE, I at 110.
[14] BEVERIDGE, I at 118.
[15] Conversation reported by President Quincy of Harvard, THAYER at 12.

The terms of enlistment of the soldiers in the Continental Army were always short and in the latter part of 1779 Marshall returned home since the soldiers he had been commanding had served their terms and there were none to replace them. Later he visited his father who was now in command of the state artillery with headquarters at Yorktown.

The girls of Yorktown had heard of the handsome and brilliant young captain and a ball was arranged to welcome him. The competition at the ball was expected to be keen but when the girls saw the sloppy appearance of their hero it disappeared. He struck them as more of a plowboy than a cavalier. Only one, Maria Ambler, who was then only fourteen years old, still took an interest in him and he soon returned the interest. Before the war the Amblers had been reckoned wealthy in Yorktown, a city which was regarded as quite a center of wealth and luxury, but the war, which had destroyed the commerce of the state, had ruined them. They had lost their great mansion and now lived in a "small, retired tenement." Captain Marshall was soon a constant visitor here for, as the troops he was supposed to command never appeared, he had plenty of time on his hands. He soon overcame the unfavorable first impression. The Ambler girls decided before long that so far from being an uncouth frontiersman he was a person of quite superior culture. Much of his courtship consisted in the reading of poetry to the family and, one of the elder daughters relates, he "thereby gave us a taste for books which probably we might never otherwise have had."[16]

It was fitting that the love of John Marshall and Maria Ambler should develop in an atmosphere of poetry for to the end their relationship had a remarkably poetic quality. She does not seem to have been in any way an exceptional woman but Marshall had an inherent romantic sentimentality that endowed her in his mind with all the remarkable

[16] *An Old Virginia Correspondence.*

qualities which other people were unable to see. For much of their married life she was an invalid; she never accompanied him to Washington for any of the sessions of the Supreme Court, and she mixed a definite querulousness in her affection for him. The faults which other people saw in his wife only increased his tenderness for her. Her death when he was in his seventies so affected him that he "rarely," Story wrote his own wife, "goes through a night without weeping over" her. "I think," added the New Englander, "he is the most extraordinary man I ever saw, for the depth and tenderness of his feelings."[17]

Neither family raised objections to the match but the Captain appreciated that he had nothing on which to get married. Even in those primitive times a man was not expected to marry with no other occupation than a commission in an army in which there was no pay day. He turned naturally to the law which he had always expected to enter and which was not then a profession which required years of study and announced his intention to take it up to the girl's family.

They were pleased, and he succeeded in tearing himself away from Yorktown long enough to enroll at William and Mary College where George Wythe, afterwards chancellor of Virginia, had started a sort of law school. Marshall was here less than two months in all and during that time did not give the study of the law by any means his entire attention. In fact, he probably confined his studying largely to being physically present at Wythe's lectures for his note-book is full of learned notes reading, "Miss Maria Ambler," "Miss M. Ambler," "Miss M. Ambler-John Marshall," "John Marshall, Miss Polly Am.," "John, Maria," "John Marshall, Miss Maria" and "Molly Ambler."[18] It is possible that, despite the superior interest of his love affairs, he might have succeeded in finishing the course if Molly's family had not decided to

---

[17] Letter dated March 4, 1832, STORY, II at 86.
[18] BEVERIDGE, I at 159-160.

move to Richmond. On the way they stopped for two days
at Williamsburg where the college was located and this
ended his studies completely. After those two days Wythe's
lectures were too dull to be endured and Marshall abandoned them to follow the Amblers to Richmond. He never
returned to school. Upon his arrival in Richmond he obtained a license to practice law from his cousin, Thomas
Jefferson, who was then governor. Marshall's legal ambitions at the moment did not extend beyond a desire to make
enough money to support a wife, so, after obtaining this
license, he returned to Fauquier County where he was
admitted to the bar at a meeting of the county court. About
this time he also resigned the commission which he still held
as a captain in the Continental Army.

In his first year at the bar Marshall had no clients, for
Rutledge's unique experience was not to be repeated. The
young lawyer spent his time helping run his father's plantation and visiting Richmond where Molly Ambler was. His
only other journey was to Philadelphia. It evidenced the
seriousness of his intentions, for the object of the trip was to
obtain vaccination against small-pox. That disease was the
scourge of the eighteenth century but, although the means
of obtaining inoculation against it had been known for some
time, vaccination was still regarded by a large proportion of
the population as a new and dangerous thing; so much so
that there was a statute in Virginia which made vaccination
practically impossible. The trip to Philadelphia was not
easy for the war had made horses of all kinds extremely
scarce and Marshall found it necessary to walk both ways.
His appearance on his arrival in the city was so disreputable
that he was refused admission to a tavern.

A year after his admission to the bar he was elected to
the House of Delegates from Fauquier County. The personal popularity which he always built up so readily, his
war record and his father's influence made the office easy
for him to obtain. As the House of Delegates met in Rich-

mond his election had more than business advantages for him. Now that he was steadily in Richmond he made much faster progress in his suit and, within two months after the legislature met, he was married. After Marshall had paid the minister he "had but one solitary guinea left."[19] His father gave him one negro and three horses and that, with his salary as a member of the legislature, constituted his fortune.

One finds in the life of nearly every famous judge a period during which he studied intensely; a period during which he built up a solid store of learning on which his later career was based. Such a period is absent in the life of Marshall. During his early years at the bar he did not entirely neglect the study of law but it is clear, both from the reputation he established as a pleasant and convivial companion and from the record which he kept of his purchases of books, that his studying does not deserve the adjective "intense." This record may not be complete for it was kept in the careless manner which was characteristic of him. It contains extremely miscellaneous items ranging from his losses at cards to the price of his wife's new hat but it does not indicate what books he borrowed nor how thoroughly he read those which he purchased. Among the latter were Mason's Poems, Blackstone's Commentaries, Blair's Lectures, Kaim's Principles of Equity, Montesquieu, Dionysius Longinus on the Sublime, Machiavelli's Works, The History and Proceedings of the House of Lords, Churchill's Poems and a sort of digest of commercial law called Lex Mercatoria Rediviva. But the bar at which he practiced was more brilliant than learned; so much so that in the biographies of the judges which are included in one of the early Virginian reports it is recorded of one judge, Tyler, that "he disliked law books and particularly those of England."[20] Marshall

[19] Quoted in BEVERIDGE, I at 166.
[20] 4 Call (Va.) xxiii.

would hardly overcome his natural laziness in such surroundings.

That laziness was largely confined to the acquisition of
book learning. It cannot be called a dislike for reading for
his sister-in-law's statement that he first gave her family a
love of books has already been quoted and to his extreme old
age he retained a fondness for novels and poetry. Nor were
his laziness and his love of society insuperable difficulties to
his acquisition of knowledge. He had much of his father's
ambition and, if he had felt a real need to do so, his character was certainly strong enough to have overcome these
obstacles. He had in an extraordinary degree two faculties
which kept him from feeling that need. One of these was
his flair for the acquisition of oral information; his ability to
extract the utmost from every set speech or casual conversation which he happened to hear. The other was his even
more remarkable ability to analyze and digest any information which he acquired in any manner. It was these two
faculties which lay at the basis of his judicial success. As a
judge he was never known to object to the length of time
counsel talked and in some important constitutional cases
they literally talked for days. But the opinion which he
would finally write would not be a mere résumé of the
speeches of counsel. It indicated a thorough grasp and
analysis of their arguments.

Marshall's fame undoubtedly owes a great deal to the
brilliance of the bar which practiced before him, and in the
Richmond of his younger days the opportunities for listening
to unusual men were almost equally great. It was the heyday
of Virginia; the period in which Richmond was frequented
by men such as Washington, Jefferson, Madison, Patrick
Henry and George Mason in addition to the men, such as
Wythe and Edmund Randolph, whose fame is chiefly professional. The town was small and Marshall was a member
of the legislature, which was the center of social life, so he
must have had some contact with each of these men but he

does not seem to have made any special effort to mix with the leaders.

For a time he lived in a house of two rooms, one of which he used as an office. He associated largely with the other backwoods members and engaged heartily in all their activities, including the consumption of corn liquor. He made no effort to appear the dignified lawyer. At a somewhat later period a prospective client who had been advised to retain Marshall failed to do so after seeing the latter "strolling through the streets of Richmond attired in a plain linen roundabout and shorts, with his hat under his arm, from which he was eating cherries." [21]

Marshall's willingness to take a drink with anybody, his ability to beat nearly anybody in any of the popular sports and his general good nature soon made him the favorite of the backwoods members of the legislature. They were not long in expressing their preference. He had been a member for less than a fortnight when, by a sort of spontaneous movement among this element of the legislature, he was elected to the Council of State. This body shared the governor's power and owed its origin to that fear of a strong executive which was common to all the states. Marshall's election horrified the bigwigs of Virginian politics. They looked upon membership in the Council of State as something reserved exclusively for tried and distinguished veterans. The judges undertook, and undertook successfully, to teach Marshall the all-important rights of seniority. They used their power to make things unpleasant for the struggling young lawyer so successfully that he soon resigned from the Council. It is the first indication of that trait in his character which always made him prefer professional success to political distinction.

The reasonableness which he showed in this matter helped him professionally and his career was soon progressing swimmingly. His personal popularity brought him clients

---

[21] Quoted by THAYER, at 29; also in Thayer's speech in DICKINSON, at 33.

and his professional learning was ample to enable him to handle their cases successfully. The law was still in a formative stage. There was no universal agreement that the law of England as it existed at the time of the Declaration of Independence was now the law of the United States. The feeling that the common law was "fit only for a people grown old in the habits of vice" and that America should have a system of law based on that "of nature and of revelation" was not confined to Connecticut. Change was in the air and it was still within the realm of possibility that America would adopt the civil rather than the common law.[22] No great effort was required to master the small body of local precedent and statute. That Marshall did merely through attending the sessions of the courts and of the legislature. There was small danger that a lawyer who could analyze a problem and solve it by reasoning from general premises would be embarrassed by a freak statute, an unanticipated departmental ruling or an illogical precedent.

Marshall's career prior to his appointment as Chief Justice is marked by one characteristic which distinguishes it from those of nearly all his contemporaries. He was without political ambition. His desire, rather, was to become successful in what has come to be the conventional American meaning of that term. The habit of looking on political success as the highest form of success was a colonialism; a derivative from a Europe in which a man's importance in the eyes of the populace was determined by his importance at the court of his king. Marshall had the most valuable of political faculties, a phenomenal gift for popularity. But he preferred to use it to obtain clients rather than to obtain office. He sat in the House of Delegates for two terms but as soon as his practice was firmly established he declined to run again for election. His action was not due to the fact that he no longer lived in Fauquier County. He had not done so the

---

[22] See Pound, *The Place of Judge Story in the Making of American Law.*

second time he was elected and he was now the owner of eight hundred acres of the Oak Hill estate which his father, who had moved to Kentucky, had deeded to him. His ownership removed any objection which might otherwise have been made to the fact that he spent most of his time in Richmond for localism had not yet reached its heights in American politics. His allegiance to his home county was amply demonstrated by the fact that he invested his first surplus earnings in the purchase of another tract of Fauquier land.

It was only the beginning of his speculation in land. Law was to him originally only a means of making a living and of obtaining some capital which, through shrewd investment, he hoped to develop into a substantial landed estate. He had been raised in an atmosphere of land trading and land speculation. It was the chief business of both George Washington and Thomas Marshall and, towards the end of the war, the former suspected the latter of trying to inveigle him into purchasing the Oak Hill estate at an excessive price. Both of them had carved the foundations of their fortunes out of the Fairfax estate and, shortly after the adoption of the constitution, John Marshall headed a syndicate which purchased, from his lordship's heirs, the unsold remainder of that estate, consisting of about one hundred and sixty thousand acres. It ended his purchases, for the syndicate was not adequately financed, and for the twenty years after this transaction Marshall had constant difficulty in meeting the obligations he had assumed. These difficulties increased his natural inclination to devote his time to his own business and, if it had not been for pressure from outside sources, he would probably have died a popular, successful and prosperous Virginian lawyer and plantation owner..

His indifference to political success was itself one of the chief factors which thrust him forward politically. The legislature in which Marshall sat was largely dominated by that element in American politics which is most conveniently described as Populism. Before the Revolution Virginia had been a province of debtors. The great planters, mighty men at home, were in many instances mere appendages of English commercial houses who bought their tobacco and to whom they were habitually in debt. The Revolution had stopped the creation of further debts of this nature and the legislature did its best to prevent the collection of those debts which were still outstanding. But the Revolution had also, to a great extent, destroyed the market for Virginian products and nearly everyone in the state was rich in land and poor to a proverb in cash, or, at least, in cash that circulated outside the state. Nearly every session of the legislature saw the introduction of bills tampering with the currency; bills to make debts easier to pay, and bills to make debts harder to collect.

The government of the state was conducted with an almost complete absence of settled policy. This was partly due to the doctrinaire constitution which prevented the development of executive leadership and partly to the lack of parties and organs of public opinion. Nearly all the important decisions were made by the legislature and the action of the legislature was most unpredictable. During the different stages in the passage of a bill the majority would frequently shift from one side to the other and then back again. Nor did the bills which passed indicate any consistent program unless an obvious dislike of paying debts can be regarded as a program. The needs and obligations of the central government, which would be humbly presented to the legislature, were contemptuously disregarded. The whole performance indicated the adolescence of democracy but what marked it chiefly in the eyes of a critical observer was the lack of a sense of responsibility.

That lack troubled Marshall deeply for his outward carelessness concealed some very strongly held convictions. One of these was a Calvinistic belief in the inviolability of contractual obligations. What a man promised he should perform. Marshall's whole belief in popular government depended on the validity of that principle in public as well as in private conduct. The political theory of the great state papers of the first Continental Congress as well as the political theory which underlay the numerous constitutions which had been drawn after the Declaration of Independence was that government was a compact, a contract. Organized society came into being as a result of the mutual promises of its members set forth, in the case of each of the American states, in a written agreement called a constitution. Marshall accepted this theory wholeheartedly and wished to see not only it, but all its logical implications, carried out in practice. If it was once admitted that men were entitled to judge for themselves whether or not they would carry out the promises which they had made it seemed to him that the props were knocked out from under organized society.

He was not alone in his premises. The contract theory of society was to continue for many years to be the generally accepted political theory in the United States. It was even accepted by those whose specific political actions were directly opposed to Marshall's. The road to political success lay in harmonizing the desires of the people, or of that vociferous portion of the people which determines the outcome of elections, with this theory of government. Even the scholarly but unpopular Madison finally followed this road. He was politically ambitious and his political ambition, working behind the veil of his subconsciousness, enabled him finally to rationalize to his own satisfaction what appeared to the world to be his change of principles. To say that this change alone saved Madison from political extinction is not to say that elections in eighteenth-century Virginia were determined by logical debates on the theory of government. Few of the members of the House of Delegates could have explained their actions in terms of any political theory. The theorists are always a minority but a necessary minority. A popular movement must always have a creed, however few of its followers understand it. Jack Cade might have succeeded if he had had a Marx to furnish him with a theory. So throughout the period of Marshall's career cultivated minds were busy harmonizing with subtle logic the populist desires of the Virginians with the contract theory of society.

If Marshall had been politically ambitious he too might have done so. Few men find it difficult to adjust their theories to their desires and the greatest source of political corruption is the desire to be re-elected. Marshall's freedom from the ambition for political success meant that his interferences in public affairs were always dictated by conviction but it also meant his gradual estrangement politically from almost all the other rising young men of Virginia. It is remarkable that it was not until after he had become Chief Justice that this estrangement lost him any of his personal popularity. It is more remarkable that a man with his apparent carelessness and love of popularity should be the one to withstand the pressure of the group to which he belonged. It cannot all be ascribed to his revolutionary experiences. His winter at Valley Forge undoubtedly influenced him in favor of a stronger government but he was not the only ex-Continental officer in Virginia. The example of Washington had a great effect in the development of Marshall's views but there was never a time when he was the only man in Virginia who respected the opinions of the master of Mount Vernon.

Marshall was not at first identified with an unpopular political group. The demarcation into political parties did not take place until after the adoption of the constitution. During his two terms in the legislature Marshall watched democracy in action and did what he could to defeat debtors' legislation and legislation which ignored the treaty obligations of the United States with Great Britain and Spain. His actions did not diminish his personal popularity. In

1786, when he had been admitted to the bar scarcely five years, he received a "handsome vote"[23] in the legislature for the office of Attorney-General. The vote was complimentary for Marshall was not especially anxious to obtain the office. The action of the legislature indicates, however, the position he had already attained at the bar. The speed with which he had attained that position was due in part to the fact that he had been unusually old when he commenced to practice. He was now thirty-one but the average life span was then much shorter than it is now and thirty-one probably represented the same grade of seniority that forty does in the twentieth century.

His popularity also helped him in the only branch of the state government to which he did not begrudge his time. This was the militia in which he rose so rapidly that, by the time he emerged on the national scene, he was universally known as General Marshall.

He was drawn from his practice and the militia by his desire to see the constitution ratified. He was not yet of sufficient importance to be a delegate to the constitutional convention but he accepted the work of the convention wholeheartedly. To him, as to most of the thoughtful men of the country, it was the last chance to preserve the fruits of the Revolution; the last chance to prove that it was possible for the American people to govern themselves. Virginia was, at that time, the largest and most populous of the states and its ratification of the proposed constitution was essential if the new government was ever to go into effect. But Virginia was also one of the states whose ratification was most doubtful. The opposition was led by statesmen like Patrick Henry and George Mason who feared that the proposed national government would be an engine of tyranny but its rank and file consisted of individuals who feared that ratification would mean that

---

[23] Letter dated December 4, 1786 from James Madison to Thomas Jefferson, HUNT, II at 294.

debts would have to be paid. The latter group was so strong
in the legislature that it was doubtful whether a convention
would even be called to consider ratification.

The chief asset of the ratificationists was brains. The
majority of the leaders were on their side; they had the
immense prestige of Washington behind them; they were
well organized, and they knew what they wanted. They
planned their campaign carefully. Their first step was to
get as many of their members elected to the legislature as
possible. For this purpose Marshall was asked to run for
the House of Delegates from Henrico County, the county in
which Richmond is located. Party lines were not yet drawn,
so the question of his views on ratification did not enter
into the election. He was easily elected. The anticipated
struggle over the calling of a convention turned into a
struggle over the wording of the call. It gave Marshall his
first opportunity to display his statesmanship for he succeeded in suggesting a form of words which satisfied both
sides.

The ratificationist managers appreciated his value. The
majority of the inhabitants of Henrico County were known
to be opposed to ratification but his personal popularity
was so great that, despite this fact, he was elected to the
convention. His was not the only vote which was cast in
the convention in favor of ratification which had been won
through the personal popularity of the member casting it.

The lack of an effective press and of sharply drawn party
lines meant that there were many members of the convention whose views were still undecided when that body went
into session. Great care was used in debate, for votes might
actually be won by a telling speech. Marshall was one
of the minor ratificationist leaders and was used by his
party both on the floor and outside the convention hall.
He was undoubtedly of more use in the latter capacity.
The unpopular Madison, the ratificationist manager, could

lebate but he was unlikely to win many votes over a tavern
able.

Marshall at the time had a reputation as an orator but
he speeches he now delivered were, in quality, far below
his later judicial utterances. There were gaps in the logic
and he inclined to declamation. But in one respect he was
superior to many of the ratificationists. He accepted democracy, and his definition of the proposed government as a
"well-regulated democracy" [24] helped to repair the damage
which had been done by one of the ratificationist speakers
who had contemptuously referred to the people as a "herd."

The constitution was debated clause by clause and the
defense of the judiciary article was assigned to him. The
chief interest of the debate on this clause lies in the fact
that Henry, the leader of the anti-ratificationists, based part
of his attack on the ground that the federal judiciary would
not be sufficiently independent to declare acts of Congress
unconstitutional. Judicial review was not a new and un-
heard-of thing, for the Virginian state judges had already
taken the position that they had power to interpret the
state constitution. "Yes, sir," said Patrick Henry, "our
judges opposed the acts of the legislature . . . They had the
fortitude to declare that they were the judiciary and would
oppose unconstitutional acts. Are you sure your federal
judiciary will act thus? Is that judiciary as well constructed,
and as independent of the other branches, as our state judiciary? . . . I take it as the highest encomium on" Virginia
"that the acts of the legislature, if unconstitutional, are liable
to be opposed by the judiciary."[25] Marshall did his best
to set Henry's fears at rest.

Marshall's services in the convention were appreciated so
highly by Washington that, on the organization of the new
government, he offered the former the position of United
States Attorney for Virginia. A district attorney was not

---

[24] BEVERIDGE, I at 410.
[25] BEVERIDGE, I at 430.

then required to devote his full time to the service of the government but merely to treat the government as a client from whom he had a permanent retainer. Nevertheless Marshall declined the appointment on the ground that its acceptance would interfere too much with his private practice. He could not escape so easily from public life. For a short time he devoted himself to his practice which, in the decade of the nineties, yielded him an average of between four and five thousand dollars a year.

His return to public life was due, not to ambition for political success, but to his desire to serve what he considered to be the best interests of the public. Those who had been opposed to ratification were now in complete control of the state government. At the urgent solicitation of the Federalist leaders Marshall was again induced to give them the benefit of his vote-getting abilities. He ran for the legislature from Henrico and was again elected. He now rapidly rose to the position of Federalist leader of the state. His name began to be known to the northern Federalists and Washington attempted to bring him into the service of the central government by offering him the position of Secretary of War. The offer was refused. Marshall was willing to lend a helping hand now and then when it was badly needed but he had no intention of abandoning his practice, his farming and his pleasant afternoons at the Richmond quoit club for the uncertain sea of national politics.

Only once did he take a different attitude and then his decision was governed by the fact that the position offered him carried a remuneration in excess of what he could expect to earn from his practice. The position was that of special envoy to France. In those days, when the United States had not yet developed a class who sought diplomatic appointments for the sake of the prestige, the government paid its diplomats on a different scale from that of its other employees. Diplomatic salaries, excessively generous when measured by the American scale, were graduated to those of the minor European courts but never approached those paid by Great Britain and France. Marshall received altogether for his diplomatic services, which took up about a year of his time, nearly twenty thousand dollars. His expenses, which are included in this sum, probably did not exceed five thousand dollars for, as his official position was never recognized in France, he incurred few of the ordinary social expenses of diplomacy.

He was not the sole American envoy but a member of a commission of three of whom the other two members were Charles Cotesworth Pinckney of South Carolina and Elbridge Gerry of Massachusetts. This mission preceded by several years the one headed by Ellsworth. It was occasioned by the callous disregard which France had shown for the neutral rights of America. Whatever restraint had been evidenced in Paris before Jay's treaty was signed was abandoned after that document became known. The French regarded this treaty as a violation of the treaty of alliance concluded with the government of Louis XVI during the Revolution. The Directory now treated the United States as in the list of its enemies and seized any American ships or property that happened to come within its clutches. This conduct was encouraged by the belief in Paris that there was a numerous party in America waiting for an opportunity to refashion the government along French lines; to change the federal republic into a government modeled on that numerous group of states, such as the Batavian Republic, the Helvetian Republic and the Ligurian Republic, which the French were organizing all over Europe.

The pro-British New England Federalists had been carefully ignored by Adams in making up the membership of the mission. Pinckney was a South Carolina Federalist. Gerry, by far the least able of the three, was that rare thing, a Jeffersonian from Massachusetts. Marshall and Pinckney met in Holland and went on to Paris where Gerry shortly afterwards joined them. From the first the envoys received the most contemptuous treatment from a government which had been advised by Talleyrand that "the United States merit no more consideration than Genoa or Geneva."[26] The object of Talleyrand and the members of the Directory was to extract money from America; money for themselves in the form of bribes and for their government in the form of a loan. Were not the second and third rate powers all over Europe paying tribute to the French Republic and graft to its officials? And in what respect did the United States differ from the sovereign duchy of Parma?

The Americans were made acquainted with what was expected of them through a nondescript man of business named Hottenguer who called on the envoys and explained that a gift of a quarter of a million dollars to Talleyrand to distribute among the various members of the Directory would be necessary before the diplomatic status of the mission could even be acknowledged. The flat refusal of the Americans to give the bribe which Hottenguer demanded or even to treat with Hottenguer did not end the matter. Other shady characters, who were to go down in history as X, Y and Z, followed. Even a woman was employed before the end to see whether she could not seduce the envoys. The proposals were all to the same effect. Gerry, anxious to show that he was a man experienced in the ways of the world, insisted on the envoys listening to all these proposals and, after nearly every one of these visits, there were sharp words between him and Marshall. The latter always insisted that they should refuse to have any part in such underhand negotiations but Gerry was sure that this merely showed how unacquainted the Virginian was with the mysteries of diplomacy. Pinckney always backed Marshall, who soon became the real head of the commission, against Gerry. In order, however, to keep the commission from breaking up completely, Marshall and Pinckney continued to listen to X, Y and Z.

[26] BEVERIDGE, II at 251.

Ultimately Marshall induced his colleagues to join with him in a series of memorials to the French government which he drafted in that clear and closely woven logic which he was soon to use from the bench. They had to be translated before presentation as he knew only such French as he had learned from his study of a French grammar on the voyage over and as he had picked up since his arrival. But it made little difference, for the memorials only brought forth further insults and further demands for money. Finally Marshall and Pinckney gave up in despair and left Paris.

The reports of the envoys had at first been received in America with incredulity but when Marshall's reports, the X Y Z papers, were published there was a burst of popular resentment against the French government which for the first time made the Adams administration really popular. Steps were taken to build up an army and navy. "Hail, Columbia," the first real national song, was written by a Philadelphia lawyer, Joseph Hopkinson. It was not long before the country had embarked on its informal war with France.

Marshall was given the chief credit for upholding American rights and for refusing to allow the negotiations to be drawn into any unsavory by-paths. The memorials which Talleyrand had treated so contemptuously seemed to Marshall's fellow countrymen to set forth their position with almost ideal dignity and perspicacity. The author of the memorials was a national hero. On his arrival at Philadelphia, which was the seat of government, "the Secretary of State and many carriages," to quote Vice-President Jefferson, "with all the city cavalry, went to Frankfort to meet him . . . the bells rang till late in the night, and immense crowds were collected to see and make part of the show, which was circuitously paraded through the streets before he was set down at the city tavern."[27] Banquets were ten-

---

[27] Letter dated June 21, 1798 to James Madison, P. L. FORD, VII at 272.

dered him on every side at one of which the new national motto, "millions for defense but not one cent for tribute," was coined as a toast. Adams expressed the goodwill of the nation by tendering Marshall the vacancy on the Supreme Court arising from the death of James Wilson. It did not tempt Marshall who still preferred private life in Richmond to the service of the government.

He was not to escape so easily. The Federalists rapidly destroyed their unusual popularity by the passage of the Alien and Sedition Laws. The first of these provided for the deportation of any alien whom the President might deem dangerous and was aimed at the large number of foreigners in the ranks of the Jeffersonians. The second had as its chief objective the prevention of publications in opposition to governmental measures. The informal war against France continued for some time but the passage of these acts gave the anti-Federalists an issue. They were soon as strong in Virginia as they had ever been.

This growth of anti-administration feeling alarmed the Federalist leaders. They had no wish to be a sectional party and the size and importance of Virginia made them particularly anxious to have at least one member of Congress from that state. Marshall was the only possibility but he stoutly refused to run. Finally Bushrod Washington enlisted his uncle's help. Marshall was invited to Mount Vernon. He went, and for four days Washington argued with him that it was his duty to run. Marshall could not withstand entreaties from such a source and he finally agreed. The decision marked the turning point in his career.

He did not win this election as easily as his previous one. His personal popularity was as great as ever but politics was passing out of the heroic age. The opposition was now a well-organized party and it charged Marshall with the sins of all the Federalists. He was an aristocrat, a monarchist and a Tory. He was a tool of the group which hoped to shackle the press by means of the Sedition Act. This last charge Marshall answered by refusing to support that act and by stating that if he had been in Congress at the time of its passage he would have voted against it. Even this might not have saved him if his opponents had not made a tactical blunder. There was only one man whose personal popularity in the district exceeded Marshall's. This man was Patrick Henry and the Jeffersonians now circulated a report that Henry had denounced Marshall as an aristocrat. They made the mistake common to many who confound those who opposed ratification with those who opposed the subsequent Federalist administrations.

The anti-ratificationists and the anti-Federalists were by no means the same. Jefferson himself had been out of the country at the time of the adoption of the constitution so he was never called upon to express himself definitely on the subject but it is probable that if he had been in America he would have been in favor of ratification. His ablest lieutenant, Madison, had been an important factor in the drafting of that instrument and the leader of the ratificationists in Virginia. McKean, the leading anti-Federalist in Pennsylvania, was also the man who had forced ratification by that state in a manner which bordered on the scandalous. And the leading Federalist lawyer of Marshall's early years on the bench, Luther Martin, whom Jefferson described as "that old Federalist bulldog," had been a member of the constitutional convention but had gone home before it completed its work because he was so scandalized at the turn which affairs were taking. So Henry, who had expected nothing but evil to follow ratification, was now well satisfied with the government under which he lived. He had long been out of active politics but he had early taken a friendly interest in Marshall. Even when Marshall had opposed him in the Virginian ratifying convention Henry had indicated his personal liking for the younger lawyer. So now, when the old orator learned of the manner in which his name was being used, he was furious. He wrote a letter to Marshall emphatically denying that he had made any such remarks and speaking of Marshall's conduct in the most laudatory terms. This letter, when made public, was sufficient to turn the election and Marshall was elected to Congress by a narrow margin.

His repudiation of the Alien and Sedition Laws chilled his welcome when he came to Congress. Because of the fierce opposition which those laws had aroused the Federalists regarded their support as the cardinal test of Federalism. A few thought that Marshall's heresy in this respect was a concession to the political realities of his own district but the majority feared that it was a step in the direction of Jeffersonianism. The majority were satisfied that their analysis was correct when Marshall joined with the Jeffersonians in passing a bill which repealed the Alien and Sedition Laws. The parties were so evenly balanced in the House that if it had not been for his vote the repeal bill would not have been passed.

But what exasperated the Federalists most was that attitude in Marshall which the Speaker of the House, Sedgwick, described as his disposition "to express great respect for the sovereign people and to quote their expressions as evidence of truth."[28] Marshall had not, like so many of the leaders of his party, lost his faith in a "well-regulated democracy." He had been exasperated by the incompetence of much of the popular government which had come before his eyes; by the virtual breakdown of the government of the Articles of Confederation; by the debtor legislation in Virginia and other states, and by the childishness, irresponsibility and general incompetence which the House of Delegates had displayed while he was a member. But it was clear to him that no other basis of governmental authority than the will of the people was possible in America. There is no evidence that he ever despaired of democracy

[28] BEVERIDGE, II at 432.

but if he did his experiences with the Directory brought him back to his early faith. And at least from the time of his first term in the House of Delegates the attitude which he expressed by the adjective "well-regulated," was an essential part of his political faith.

His refusal to see eye to eye with the extreme Federalist leaders soon brought him into close touch with President Adams. Marshall had early demonstrated his ability on the national scene by defending the conduct of the administration in surrendering a fugitive from justice, who claimed he was an American citizen named Jonathan Robbins, to the British government. His speech on that occasion was so magnificent that Gallatin, the Jeffersonian leader in the House, refused to reply and answered the pleas of his followers with a curt, "Answer it yourselves, for my part I think it unanswerable."[29] Marshall's refusal to support an election bill which was designed chiefly to ensure Adams' own re-election did not alter the regard which the New Englander was rapidly acquiring for the Virginian congressman. The cabinet which Adams had inherited from his predecessor had little respect for the President. As the latter put it, "I had all the officers and half the crew always ready to throw me overboard."[30] The Hamiltonian wing of the party acknowledged Adams as their nominal leader only because they had nobody with whom to replace him. And the President kept his Hamiltonian advisers in the cabinet for the same reason; because he did not know where to find substitutes.

Marshall's emergence on the national scene removed the President's difficulty in this respect. Both men detested the extreme anti-democratic and pro-British tendencies of the Hamiltonians. Both men believed in a truly national foreign policy which did not play favorites among the warring

[29] BEVERIDGE, II at 475.
[30] Letter dated March 4, 1809 from John Adams to Dr. Rush, BIDDLE (Series A), at 219.

nations of Europe. And Marshall had the supreme advantage that he was not from New England, for Adams was sensitive of the fact that his party was becoming a sectional party. Before the Virginian's first term in Congress was completed he had become Secretary of State. It was too late to save the Federalist party but for the few remaining months of the administration Marshall was the virtual head of the government. Adams, completely satisfied with his new subordinate, had, immediately after the appointment, rushed off to his home in Massachusetts and thereafter paid little attention to public affairs.

Marshall was in this strategic position when Ellsworth's resignation left the Chief Justiceship vacant. The election of 1800 had already taken place and, while it was still uncertain whether the next President would be named Jefferson or Burr, it was certain that he would not be a Federalist. That fact had caused the judiciary to take on a new importance in the eyes of that party. Even so, the choice of Marshall was almost an accident. He himself had recommended Associate Justice Paterson but Adams refused to listen to the suggestion. Jay was his choice and, Marshall relates, "when I waited on the President with Mr. Jay's letter declining the appointment he said thoughtfully 'who [sic] shall I nominate now?' I replied that I could not tell, as I supposed that his objection to Judge Paterson remained. He said in a decided tone, 'I shall not nominate him.' After a moment's hesitation he said, 'I believe I must nominate you.' I had never before heard myself named for the office and had not even thought of it. I was pleased as well as surprised and bowed in silence."[31]

This time there was no hesitation on Marshall's part in accepting the appointment; no complaints about the inadequate remuneration of public office and the necessity for providing for a growing family. It was not that the Chief Justiceship paid better than the Justiceship which Marshall

---

[31] DICTIONARY, Article: John Marshall.

had previously refused, for the custom which is still followed by which the head of the Court receives only five
hundred dollars a year more than the associates had already
been established. Nor was it because he had made sufficient
money to satisfy him, for it was to be a good many years
before the Fairfax estate was entirely paid for. Marshall
undoubtedly felt that the country was approaching a crisis
from which he could not shrink, for with all his level-headed-
ness and calmness of judgment he shared somewhat in the
Federalist fears of Jefferson. But he was also acquiring a taste for public life; after acting the diplomat in
Paris and the Secretary of State in Washington, Richmond
seemed somewhat dull. And he could not be oblivious of
the fact that, next to the Presidency, the Chief Justiceship
was the most important office in the government. That
these latter considerations entered into his decision is obvious from the fact that, once at the head of the Court, he
retained the position until his death in extreme old age.

*   *   *   *   *   *

So when the new administration took office Marshall was
left in Washington, that "wilderness city set in a mudhole,"
to hold the pass for what he considered sound government;
for that "well-regulated democracy" which he feared was
about to be overthrown by the French theories of the visionary Jefferson. Party government was a new thing and
men still believed what they said about their political opponents. Jefferson was actually surprised that the government was turned over to him without a struggle; that the
Federalists, many of whom he sincerely believed plotted for
a monarchy, had not attempted to execute a *coup d'état.*
That, in truth, was the chief plank in his platform. He
had talked largely about the monarchical and pro-British
tendencies of the government and about the dangers to
democracy. What he had to offer was rather a change of
atmosphere than a change of policy. This was undoubtedly
what was expected. The balance of voting power in the

country lay in the hands of people who had little complaint about the actual administration of affairs by Washington and Adams but who were tired of hearing Hamilton thunder, "the people—your people, sir, is a great beast." Jefferson's "revolution" was largely spiritual and it is doubtful whether one who had the statute books as his only guide would discover that there had been even a change of party.

The change was also to a great extent a change from a government of New Englanders to a government of Virginians. Jefferson had small respect for the former; they were, he said, "marked, like the Jews, with such a perversity of character, as to constitute, from that circumstance, the natural division of our parties."[32] He was not alone in his view that, during the Adams administration, the country had been "completely under the saddle of Massachusetts and Connecticut," and the change in government can in a sense be described as a decision by the Middle Atlantic states, by the Low Dutch of New York and the High Dutch of Pennsylvania, that a government by Virginians was preferable to a government by Yankees. The people of these central states had little sympathy with the more theoretical aspects of the Virginian group. Jefferson's ideal of an agricultural United States patterned after Virginia had little appeal for them; they already sensed, although they had no leader to express it, that the social organization of Pennsylvania rather than that of Virginia or Massachusetts, was destined to become the dominant one in the new nation.

This divergence between the theories of the leaders and the desires of the most substantial group of their followers is vital to an understanding of the relations between Chief Justice Marshall and the political party which was dominant in the other two branches of the government throughout the period that he sat on the Court. In many respects the northern section of Jefferson's party was Federalist in practice.

[32] Letter dated June 1, 1798 from Jefferson to John Taylor, P. L. FORD, VII at 265.

His northern followers were interested in building roads and developing manufactures, not in spreading the Virginian social system. Jefferson had hardly taken office when, under the leadership of Gallatin, the chief of the Pennsylvania Jeffersonians, they tacked a provision on to the bill admitting Ohio as a state requiring that a portion of the proceeds from the sale of public lands in that state be used to build roads to the seaboard. This was directly contrary to all the states' rights theories of the Virginian school but so was much of the legislation of the Jeffersonian period. When Marshall upheld the power of the federal government to organize banks he was not passing upon the existence of the bank which Hamilton had organized but on the bank which had been chartered in the administration of James Madison. Jefferson himself stretched the powers of the federal government almost to the breaking point by his purchase of Louisiana. Both incidents were typical of the era. The Jeffersonian statesmen were constantly being driven, partly by the force of circumstances and partly by the sectional interests of the western and northern wings of their party, into doing things which were directly contrary to their principles. It was left to the Federalist at the head of the Supreme Court to furnish the logical justification for their acts.

In many respects both Marshall and Jefferson were in false positions. Jefferson, the theorist, was in the executive position—a position in which he never felt particularly happy. Marshall, whom one would suppose from his background to be much better suited to executive work than to the writing of essays on government, wielded the essentially intellectual, but negative, power of the Court. It was not the most important respect in which the two men were in false positions. Jefferson had come into power as the great democrat, elected to save the country from the monarchical and aristocratic proclivities of the Federalists. But he himself was essentially an aristocrat, both intellectually and socially.

His efforts to disregard convention and to appear to be just one of the common people always carried the atmosphere of the library with them; they were the actions of the conscious, intellectual democrat rather than of the unconscious, born democrat. The President never was, as the Chief Justice was even after he had sat on the bench for many years, hail-fellow-well-met at the Richmond quoit club. No one ever saw Jefferson come to that institution, as Chester Harding, the artist, saw Marshall come to it, "with his coat on his arm and his hat in his hand, which he was using as a fan. He walked directly up to a large bowl of mint julep, which had been prepared, and drank off a tumblerful of the liquid, smacked his lips, and then turned to the company with a cheerful 'How are you, gentlemen?' . . . before long I saw the great Chief Justice . . . down on his knees, measuring the contested distance with a straw, with as much earnestness as if it had been a point of law; and if he proved to be in the right, the woods would ring with his triumphant shout."[33] Nor did they see Jefferson, as Bishop Meade saw Marshall, also long after he had become Chief Justice, riding through the streets of Richmond with a bag of clover seed on his saddle which he was taking to a farm which he owned nearby.[34]

That the two men detested each other goes without question. It is not apparent when they first met but in view of the fact that they were related and that Richmond was a small place it must have been early. Nor does it appear when their enmity first arose but as Jefferson was in Europe during most of the period between Marshall's admission to the bar and the adoption of the constitution it was probably subsequent to that date. The enmity did not arise out of any specific incident. Its basis was rather temperamental. Jefferson was very outspoken in his letters and the shortcomings of his cousin Marshall was a subject on which he

---

[33] Quoted by J. B. Thayer, DICKINSON at 35.
[34] MEADE, II at 222.

wrote much, yet for a long time the most specific thing he could find to denounce about Marshall's conduct was the latter's "lax, lounging manners."[35]

The phrase gives the key to the cause of their enmity. Jefferson, the sensitive intellectual, envied the ease with which the backwoodsman mingled with the bulk of the population and was accepted by all as one of themselves. And the frontiersman, with his quiet skepticism as to the value of an unregulated and extreme democracy had small faith in the practicality of his thin-skinned cousin who shrank from too intimate contact with the common people, yet who was forever preaching of the rights of man and of the value of democracy. It is not impossible, indeed it is quite easy, to reconcile their views on government but it was impossible to get two men of such divergent characters to respect and trust one another.

Their religious activities bring out the difference as clearly as anything else. Jefferson was a deist but he expressed his aversion for state churches and narrow creeds so freely and so often that a great many of his fellow countrymen became convinced that he was an atheist. Marshall, on the contrary, never openly departed from the creed in which he was raised. The Church of England was the established church in Virginia and the one to which his family belonged. That church became very unpopular because of its connection with the imperial government and its disestablishment almost completed its ruin in Virginia. It took years before any considerable number of the pre-Revolutionary Anglicans could be induced to become Episcopalians. Marshall was one of the first to join in the move to reorganize the Episcopal Church and helped, not only with his purse, but with his attendance. Nor was he at all backward in reproving those of his friends who failed to attend services but for his entire mature life his devout friends, and particularly his

---

[35] Letter dated November 26, 1795 from Jefferson to Madison, P. L. FORD, VII at 36.

numerous friends among the clergy, wondered why he himself had never been known to take communion. In other respects his participation in religious ceremonies showed the utmost fervor; it was even known among his intimate friends that he made it a practice to repeat the Lord's Prayer and "Now I Lay Me Down To Sleep" every night before retiring. He kept this latter custom up until his death but it was not until long after his death that the reason for his failure to take communion was known. A daughter who had been much with him in his old age had obtained the explanation from him and had kept it secret for years. The explanation was, in the language of the clergyman to whom she ultimately repeated it, that "he was a Unitarian in opinion . . . he believed in the truth of the Christian revelation, but not in the divinity of Christ; therefore he could not commune in the Episcopal Church."[36] Marshall's action in staying in, and actively supporting, the Episcopal Church when he held these views can only be explained on the supposition that he believed it was his duty to suppress his individual opinion and to lend his support to the maintenance of an established institution. It is hard to conceive that Jefferson would have taken such an attitude.

The essentially false position in which Jefferson found himself appears in Marshall's first great constitutional opinion. When Madison, Jefferson's appointee, became Secretary of State he found in his office a commission as Justice of the Peace for the District of Columbia made out to a William Marbury and fully signed. It was one of a number of similar commissions which had been filled out and signed by the outgoing Federalists in their desire to leave members of their party in as many positions as possible. The fact that some of these documents had never been delivered was largely Marshall's fault for he had been, despite his assumption of the Chief Justiceship, acting Secretary of State to the end of the Adams administration. Marbury was not content

[36] Quoted at MEADE, II at 223n.

to lose his appointment quietly but brought suit in the Supreme Court asking for a writ of mandamus directing Madison to deliver the commission.

The decision was not rendered for some time for one of the first acts of the Jeffersonians on coming into office had been to pass a statute adjourning the Court for more than a year. Since the legal procedure under which the Court acts —in this case the times at which it held its sessions—are fixed by statute it is always possible, by changing the statutes, to delay or prevent a particular case from reaching the Court. This action, naturally, had not been taken because of the Marbury case. It was to prevent a far more serious matter from reaching the Court, a matter which, in fact, never was passed on judicially.

One of the last acts of the outgoing Federalists had been to repair the defects in Ellsworth's Judiciary Act. That act, it will be recalled, provided for three grades of courts but only two grades of judges. The circuit courts, the intermediate grade, had no judges of their own but were held by the traveling members of the Supreme Court acting with local district judges. The system had been unpopular with the members of the Supreme Court from the beginning but their complaints went unheeded until the Federalist leaders saw a party reason for remedying the situation. In the last session of Congress which they controlled an act was passed providing for a separate group of circuit court judges. President Adams did what he was expected to do and promptly appointed Federalists to all the newly created judgeships. The appointments had been made at such a late date that an indubitably false story soon became current that on the night of March 3 Marshall, as acting Secretary of State, had sat at a desk signing and sealing the commissions while Lincoln, the incoming Attorney-General, stood, with a watch in his hand, waiting for the hour of midnight and the end of the Adams administration to arrive. Yet the popular effect of an anecdote does not depend on its truth and from this story, which Jefferson himself never used, the new judges were commonly known as the "Midnight Judges."

The Jeffersonians were determined to get rid of the Midnight Judges but it was difficult to work out a constitutional way of doing so. They had no intention of flagrantly disregarding the organic law for they had taken office largely as the defenders of the constitution against the monarchical and aristocratic machinations of the Federalists. Yet that instrument provides clearly that judges are to hold office for life unless convicted on an impeachment. The Jeffersonians attempted to solve the difficulty by drawing a distinction between removing a man from an office and abolishing the office. An act was passed abolishing the separate circuit court judgeships. But the Jeffersonian leaders were plainly frightened by their action. A considerable number of their northern congressmen had refused to vote for the repeal bill, partly because of constitutional scruples and partly because the additional judgeships were popular in commercial circles.

The repeal of the Federalist Judiciary Act of 1801 created no practical difficulties for that act existed only on paper. The new judges had their commissions but none of them had taken his seat or rendered any decisions. Yet the Jeffersonians were fearful of what they had done; fearful particularly that one of the ousted judges would bring an action of some sort which would give the Supreme Court an opportunity to declare the repeal act unconstitutional in so far as it deprived the Midnight Judges of the positions to which they had been constitutionally appointed. If such a decision were to be rendered it would hurt the Jeffersonians enormously not to acquiesce for they would then be guilty of doing the very thing which they had charged the Federalists with doing—ignoring the constitution. It was not yet appreciated that the constitution is always the issue of the outs; that the object of constitutional guarantees is to protect political minorities. The art of party government was new

and politicians were still inclined to take their platforms
seriously. The position that the Court had no authority to
render such a decision was hardly tenable as a historical
fact and the history involved was not then at all ancient.
Both Jefferson and Madison were men of too much conscience blatantly to ignore that history. Both must have
recalled that one of Jefferson's chief criticisms of the constitution, like Patrick Henry's, was that the judiciary did not
have sufficient power over legislation.[37] It was for these
reasons that the Supreme Court was prevented from sitting
for more than a year.

None of the ousted judges ever brought suit to test the
legality of the repeal act but when the Court reconvened
even Marshall gave indications of being worried about a
possible political assault on the courts. He was the heir to
a Federalist precedent which constantly troubled the Court
during the earlier years of his term. The harmony between
the previous Chief Justices and the Presidents had been too
perfect. There had been some truth in the Jeffersonian
charge that the judiciary was not in reality an independent
branch of the government. Jay and Ellsworth had consulted
with Washington almost as if they had been members of his
cabinet. This precedent made Jefferson feel that he was not
receiving the cooperation to which he was entitled; it gave
rise to a subconscious belief on his part that the decent thing
for his cousin Marshall to do was to resign, as ambassadors
are today expected to resign upon a change of administration.

Marshall did not become more than a minor irritation in
Jefferson's life until the decision in the *Marbury Case* was
announced. The decision was the first important one rendered in a new court room for, as if to symbolize the coming
of age of the American political system, the seat of government had been moved to Washington almost simultaneously
with the change of administration. The new "Federal City"

[37] See BEARD, at 126-127.

had been planned with a grandeur which excited more ridi-
cule than admiration but no provision had been made for
the Court. Finally one of the Senate committee rooms,
thirty feet long by twenty-four feet wide, was set aside for
this purpose. Here Marshall presided for the first eight
years of his administration and here he rendered his decision in the *Marbury Case*.[88] The opinion set the style which
he subsequently followed in all his great decisions. The
practice disappeared by which each of the judges wrote an
opinion. Marshall spoke not as a member of the Court but
for the Court. There is no record of how he induced the
associates to agree to this procedure but it is easy to imagine
that the change came about through their general fear of the
Jeffersonians.

In writing the opinion the Chief Justice analyzed the case
point by point. He came to the conclusion that Marbury was
entitled to his commission and that if the Court, by issuing
a writ of mandamus to the Secretary of State, ordered the
delivery of the commission it would only be doing what common law courts had always done. The issue of such a writ
would not interfere with the proper discretion of the executive branch of the government since it would order the doing
of a purely ministerial act, of the handing over of a piece of
paper which was already signed and sealed. But the permanent importance of the case lies in the fact that the Court
did not issue the writ. Marshall's opinion apparently con-
ceded Marbury's case and the government had not presented
any argument. Marshall himself had found the fatal defect.
Ellsworth's Judiciary Act, which had provided the procedure
for the federal courts, contained a section providing for the
issue of writs of mandamus by the Supreme Court under
these circumstances. This section of the Judiciary Act
Marshall now declared to be unconstitutional.

He devoted only a few paragraphs of his rather lengthy
opinion to this point. His reasoning, as in most of his great

---

[88] *Marbury* v. *Madison*, 1 Cranch 137, 2 L. Ed. 60 (1803).

cases, was based on a literal construction of the exact wording of the constitution. That document stated that the Court was to have only appellate jurisdiction except in a few enumerated cases. The granting of writs of mandamus was not one of the enumerated cases. Therefore, said Marshall, the section of the Judiciary Act which purports to confer original jurisdiction upon the Supreme Court in such cases is unconstitutional.

The decision was so abstract in its nature that it did not arouse any great popular interest. What reaction there was was largely favorable for the doctrine that government was a necessary evil was then generally accepted. The public was pleased to discover that the judiciary had some of that independence which Jefferson and his followers had claimed that it ought to have. The decision itself did not hurt Marshall but the process of establishing the proper spheres of the various branches of the federal government was one in which all sides had lessons to learn. If Jefferson expected the Chief Justice to act as a subordinate of the President, Marshall had yet to learn that if the judiciary was to be independent it would have carefully to confine itself within the limits which clearly belonged to it. If he had confined his opinion to the constitutional point, there would have been no criticism. But he had said that if the case had arisen in a constitutional manner, the Court would have had authority to order the delivery of the commission. This statement, elaborated over many pages, gave Jefferson an opening and the administration press followed the cue from the White House. The judicial branch of the government, it was charged, was attempting to dictate to the executive branch.

This reaction had its roots in Jefferson's subtle personality. He himself had complained many times about the constantly increasing power of the executive, about the weakness of the judiciary and about the ineffectiveness of the constitution. He could readily have accepted the deci-

sion as a reform due to his own activities. There was no
political advantage to be gained by taking the course he
took. The decision was not distasteful to any portion of the
electorate and certainly in the end Jefferson's various attempts to interfere with the judiciary were not helpful politically. It arose in part from his feminine habit of looking
on those who opposed him not as misguided but as wicked.
It arose in part from his personal dislike of Marshall. But
its chief basis was Jefferson's curious conservatism, a conservatism which led him to oppose all reforms but his own.
Outside of his disagreements with Marshall the most startling
example of this innate conservatism had been Jefferson's
attempt to induce the Virginian legislature to provide by
statute that the common law of the state was the common
law of England as it stood at the accession of George II. His
avowed object was to "get rid of Mansfield's innovations."[39]
If the law of contracts had been in the medieval condition
in which Mansfield found it, Jefferson would have had a
scheme for reforming it. Since the reforms had already
been made, Jefferson was for ignoring the reforms. So he
was in favor of an independent judiciary, boldly upholding
the constitutional limitations on the other two branches of
government, until he saw such a judiciary coming into existence without his assistance. If the judges who asserted the
independence of the judiciary had been of his own choosing
he might have felt differently.

It was here that the weak point in Marshall's position lay.
Jay and Ellsworth and their colleagues had indubitably not
acted as though the Court was an isolated institution having
nothing in common with the President. Ellsworth, especially, had always acted as though he were a subordinate of
the President. The Court was now to answer for his sins.
The Virginian group in Congress, with the more or less
covert assistance of Jefferson, impeached Justice Chase. He
was a signer of the Declaration of Independence and an

[39] Pound, *The Growth of Administrative Justice.*

opponent of the adoption of the constitution who had been appointed to the Supreme Court by President Washington. He was a fairly able judge and had been suggested several times for the Chief Justiceship but his roughness, irascibility and general lack of temper and tact had made him many enemies. He had particularly infuriated the extreme democrats by a charge to a Baltimore grand jury in which he stated that "universal suffrage . . . will . . . take away all security for property and personal liberty. . . . Our republican Constitution will sink into a mobocracy—the worst of all possible governments."[40]

Probably many even of the Jeffersonians agreed with Chase in this and in any event his conduct, however lacking in propriety it may have been, did not constitute a crime. It was a heritage from the custom which Jay had begun of making the charge to the grand jury a sort of review of the state of the nation. Even the most rabid of the Virginian group recognized that it, alone, was not sufficient to justify impeachment. Chase's record was combed for other instances of misconduct. A number of instances were uncovered where Chase had been insolent and overbearing in the conduct of trials but nothing which could be regarded as criminal within the ordinary meaning of the word. The case resolved itself into this: Did the constitution, when it stated that judges could be impeached only for "high Crimes and Misdemeanors," use those words in their ordinary meaning or did those words mean "any conduct which two-thirds of the Senate deem sufficiently improper to justify removal?"

Marshall was frankly worried about the matter; so worried that his habitual calm left him even in public. He was called as a witness on some minor matters and the occasion was one of the few times when he made an unfavorable impression in public. "The Chief Justice," one of the senators entered in his diary, "really discovered too much cau-

---

[40] ADMINISTRATION OF JEFFERSON, II at 149.

tion—too much fear—too much cunning. . . . That dignified
frankness which his high office required did not appear. A
cunning man ought never to discover the arts of the *trimmer*
in his testimony."[41] But none of the senators knew how
thoroughly upset the Chief Justice really was. He had convinced himself that the removal of Chase was to be a prelude
to his own impeachment and had actually suggested in a
private letter that the storm be averted by a constitutional
amendment giving Congress appellate jurisdiction over the
Supreme Court. The fact that he had made the suggestion
did not come to light until long after his death for the Senate
disappointed the Virginian group and acquitted Chase.

Marshall could go back to the boarding-house, where the
judges lived together during sessions of the Court, with his
mind at rest. There were to be no more attacks by legal
means on the independence of the judiciary. There were
still ample ways of restricting the power of the Court if that
had been Jefferson's object. The Judiciary Act could have
been amended to restrict, or even almost destroy, the Court's
jurisdiction. To do so would not have satisfied the President. He was not aroused over any specific decision the
Court had rendered. What irritated him was that the judges
owed him no sort of allegiance. His hostility was not a
political hostility against the Court as such but a personal
hostility against his cousin the Chief Justice. That had been
the weakness of all the action he had taken so far for his
followers did not share his personal hostility. It was difficult to convince them that the tall, spare, good-natured
Marshall, with his plain yet dignified manners, was at bottom
an imp of Satan.

Jefferson had been very anxious to have a bill of rights
in the constitution because of "the legal check which it puts
into the hands of the judiciary"[42] for at one time he had
feared that the President would develop into a tyrant who

[41] BEVERIDGE, III at 196.
[42] Letter dated March 15, 1789 from Jefferson to Madison. P. L.
FORD, V at 80.

would imprison and punish citizens without a fair trial. His fear was justified for he himself, one of the most enlightened and civilized men who ever lived in the White House, was also the only President who attempted to override the bill of rights in order to punish a personal enemy.

Jefferson hated his Vice-President as thoroughly as he hated the Chief Justice but for more tangible reasons. And when Burr, on his failure to be re-elected at the end of their first term, began traveling up and down the Mississippi Valley, the President readily convinced himself that Burr's object was treasonable, that he plotted to separate the Western states from the Union. To this day no one knows exactly what Burr had in mind. He himself claimed that he intended to found a settlement in Arkansas; it is probable that he intended to conduct a filibustering expedition into Spanish territory on the order of those later expeditions by which Texas was detached from Mexico. In any event Jefferson, with the help of the incredible Wilkinson, who, in addition to being the highest ranking officer in the United States army, received a secret salary from Spain, announced the discovery of a plot to break up the Union by force. Burr was arrested in the western territory and brought east on horseback. During the long time that this slow journey took the President committed himself thoroughly and publicly to the position that Burr had planned to break up the Union; that there was no doubt that Burr was guilty of treason, and that the administration had the evidence in its possession with which to convict him beyond question. By the time Burr was arraigned Jefferson had given the case a political complexion; the obtaining of a conviction had become a party necessity. When one of Wilkinson's subordinates called on Caesar A. Rodney, the Attorney-General, to report that he had reason to believe the General was himself a traitor Rodney told him bluntly, "What would be the result, if all your charges against General Wilkinson should be proven? Why, just what the Federalists and the enemies of the present Administration wish—it would turn the indignation of the people from Burr on Wilkinson. Burr would escape, and Wilkinson take his place."[43]   It was, in short, precisely the type of case that had led the members of the Constitutional Convention to provide, even though they inserted no bill of rights, as one of the three sections of the judiciary article, that "Treason against the United States, shall consist only in levying War against them, or in adhering to their Enemies, giving them Aid and Comfort. No Person shall be convicted of Treason unless on the Testimony of two Witnesses to the same overt Act, or on Confession in open Court."

The action of the framers was not due entirely to the fact that they themselves had all at one time been traitors. The definition of treason had been stretched by the crown lawyers of the seventeenth and eighteenth centuries to such preposterous lengths that even Dr. Johnson "was glad Lord George Gordon had escaped, rather than that a precedent should be established for hanging a man for *constructive treason.*"[44]   But the punishment was usually much more severe than hanging and was, indeed, the main reason why the crown preferred to prosecute for treason rather than for lesser crimes. By the end of the eighteenth century the public taste was becoming a little too squeamish for tearing a man's bowels out while he was still alive; for hanging him until he was not quite dead and then tying his limbs to wild horses and tearing him to death, or for burning women alive, but those punishments still remained on the books. In any case a conviction for treason carried with it punishments against the traitor's family which were not inflicted on other criminals. In England as late as 1794 the members of a society which advocated universal suffrage were prosecuted for treason but the jury refused to bring in a conviction.[45] Nearly two centuries earlier Bacon had given his opinion

---

[43] ADMINISTRATION OF JEFFERSON, III at 455.
[44] Boswell's Johnson (Hill's ed.), IV at 101.
[45] HOLDSWORTH, VIII at 318.

that the mere saying in private conversation that the king was incapable constituted treason.[46] Two generations later Algernon Sidney was convicted and executed for writing in a book which was never published, that the supreme power was lodged in Parliament rather than in the king. "This book," said Chief Justice Jeffreys in summing up, "contains all the malice and revenge and treason that mankind can be guilty of; it fixes the sole power in the parliament and the people...."[47] Nor did the English revolution put a stop to the growth of the doctrine of constructive treason although it changed its direction for in 1710 some individuals were convicted of treason "for raising a riot to destroy all dissenting meeting-houses."[48] And now Jefferson, the liberal, the reformer, the believer in the rights of man, found himself the heir to the Tudors and the Stuarts, to the Star Chamber and the Bloody Assizes, to the obsequious chancellor of James I and the inhuman chief justice of James II.

The chief difficulty about the prosecution of Burr consisted in that portion of the constitutional definition which limits treason to "levying War." Where was the war? A war is not usually looked upon as something that is carried on secretly, without anybody knowing of its existence. If there had actually been a war there should have been plenty of witnesses to that fact. The nearest approach to a war had been a gathering of about twenty men on Blennerhassett's Island in the Ohio. Burr had not even been with them. They claimed that the object of their gathering was to travel down the Ohio-Mississippi with Burr and settle in Arkansas. It is true they were armed but there was nothing unusual about guns on the frontier. Very likely they intended to attack the Spaniards but even under the broadest English rule that did not constitute treason against the United States. Jefferson was too intelligent not to realize the ridiculous position into which his hatred of Burr had led him but he vented his

---

[46] HOLDSWORTH, VIII at 314.
[47] HOLDSWORTH, VIII at 315n.
[48] HOLDSWORTH, VIII at 320.

irritation with himself by blaming the whole fiasco on the judge before whom the case came.

That judge was Marshall, sitting in Richmond on circuit, for Blennerhassett's Island was then within the state of Virginia. Burr had, up to then, been in the custody of the military so Marshall was the committing magistrate before whom he was originally brought, the judge who impaneled the grand jury which found the indictment and the trial judge before whom he was tried. The prisoner was represented by an unequaled array of counsel headed by Luther Martin, who had been Chase's counsel on his impeachment trial, and including Edmund Randolph and Marshall's intimate friend, John Wickham. That Martin, a man who had refused to sign the constitution, should now, voluntarily and without pay, represent the administration's enemy marks the difference between Jefferson the philosopher and Jefferson, the head of the government. The District Attorney, Hay, was a man of inferior ability but one to whom Jefferson's wish was law. The government had, in addition, retained several special counsel including William Wirt whose brilliant career was just beginning.

Richmond took on the aspect of a fair, for men, both famous and unknown, flocked from far and wide to see the proceedings. The capacities of the town of five thousand people were taxed to overflowing and, at Hay's request, in order to accommodate as many as possible of the sightseers, the court met in the barnlike structure used for meetings of the House of Delegates. The request had been made in the hope that the court would be overawed by the temper of the crowd but Burr, who had as great a gift for popularity and was as shrewd a politician as any man in America, soon began to win the sympathy of the onlookers. On both sides counsel addressed themselves to this audience as much as to the court. Nor was Marshall who, despite his general easy-goingness, always managed to create an impression on the bench of great dignity, oblivious to the political aspects

of what he did. So it was, amid streams of tobacco juice
and clouds of smoke, for neither were forbidden in the court
room, that the most famous criminal trial in American history took place.

In many respects the case revealed what we have since
come to regard as the worst features of our administration
of justice. It took up an excessive amount of time, the better
part of a summer; the behavior of the audience gave it some
of the circus atmosphere so frequently found in notorious
criminal cases today; the court allowed endless argument on
every trivial point that arose, and counsel obviously addressed themselves as much to the newspapers and the
public as to the court and the jury. The proceedings were
lifted above the sordidness of the ordinary sensational mur-
der trial by the dignity of the judge, the brilliance of counsel,
the nature of the accusation and the importance of the
prisoner, but above all by the issues involved. The question
was not whether a particular individual was guilty, not even
whether a former Vice-President was guilty of a plot to
destroy the government, but whether those legal safeguards
of the rights of individuals which had been so carefully
written into all the constitutions in America would hold
when put to the test.

Again Marshall was the heir of the Federalist mistakes.
The judges and lawyers of that party had shown no great
respect for the constitutional definition of treason in the
prosecutions which followed the Whisky Rebellion, and the
Jeffersonian newspapers now delighted in showing how the
law of treason varied with the political faith of the defendant. Yet even they could not charge Marshall with sympathy
with the supposed conspiracy for it was universally known
that the Chief Justice was a strong nationalist, a fixed believer in the inviolability of the Union. He himself made
one bad mistake in the course of the proceedings. One is
constantly surprised in the lives of the earlier Chief Justices
by their apparently defective sense of judicial propriety.

Judges frequently discussed their decisions with outsiders before rendering them and sat in cases where we would now consider them disqualified because of their relationship to counsel or the parties. Marshall was not in advance of custom in this respect. He saw no impropriety in sitting in the *Marbury Case* even though it was his negligence as Secretary of State which was responsible for Marbury's failure to receive his commission. So now, in spite of his political acumen and his awareness of the real issues involved, Marshall committed what was even then considered an impropriety.

He and Wickham were old friends and both were famous for their lawyer dinners; dinners at which the best obtainable food and liquor were combined with the best conversation of a bar which dominated the intellectual life of the community. In the interval between Burr's arraignment and the impaneling of the grand jury, while the prisoner was out on bail, Wickham gave one of these dinners. Marshall was invited and, despite his wife's forebodings, he allowed the carefree frontiersman in him to overcome the astuteness which was hidden behind his apparent frankness. When he arrived he learned that the situation was even worse than his wife had feared. Burr was one of the guests. But Marshall stayed and thus gave the Jeffersonian press a theme on which it could endlessly harp. What outcome could be expected for a trial in which the judge went out to dinner with the prisoner and his counsel? The incident radically altered Marshall's ideas of judicial propriety; so much so that when, some years later, he and Bishop Meade in traveling together came to a particularly bad piece of road and the Bishop suggested that they cut across a field at a place where the fence was down and it was obvious that others had done so before, Marshall refused. "It was his duty," he told the Bishop, "as one in office, to be very particular in regard to such things."[49]

---

[49] MEADE. II at 222.

Jefferson had taken a bear by the tail when he announced to the country that Burr's guilt was beyond question. At first the crowd that had flocked to Richmond all wanted a conviction. But as the case began to unfold the crowd began to divide in sentiment. The grand jury gave the first indication of the change of weather.

Wilkinson was the government's chief witness and "Wilkinson," wrote Washington Irving who was covering the case for a New York newspaper, "is now before the grand jury, and has such a mighty mass of *words* to deliver himself of, that he claims at least two days more to discharge the wondrous cargo."[50] When discharged it made such an impression that it was only by a narrow vote that the General himself escaped indictment. The foreman of the jury, Randolph of Roanoke, who had been the manager for the House in the Chase impeachment, gave it as his opinion that "Wilkinson is the only man that I ever saw who was from the bark to the very core a villain . . . yet this man stands on the very summit and pinnacle of executive favor."[51] Soon Hay reported to Jefferson that Burr's partisans were becoming bold and numerous. The way the anti-administration sentiment was forming appears from the statement of an eye-witness that, as he was "crossing the court-house green, I heard a great noise of haranguing some distance off. Inquiring what it was, I was told it was a great blackguard from Tennessee, one Andrew Jackson, making a speech for Burr and damning Jefferson as a persecutor."[52]

Jefferson was soon called upon to make good his public pronouncement of Burr's guilt. The defense moved for a subpœna directing the President to appear as a witness and to bring with him the papers on which his conclusion was based. The motion raised a delicate legal point. No one

---

[50] BEVERIDGE, III at 464n.
[51] Letter dated June 25, 1807 from Randolph to Nicholson, ADAMS' RANDOLPH, at 219.
[52] ADMINISTRATION OF JEFFERSON, III at 460.

had ever dreamed of subpœnaing a king but was a President the same as a king? After exhaustive argument Marshall decided that he was not; that the Court would issue the subpœna but that Jefferson would be under no compulsion to obey it.[53] The opinion intensified the President's false position and his decision to disregard the subpœna did not help the administration in the court of public opinion to which he had referred his quarrel with the Chief Justice.

When, at the conclusion of the long trial, the jury brought in a verdict of acquittal Jefferson's resentment against the Chief Justice became greater than ever. Marshall himself galloped off to his estate at Oak Hill but the President was again talking of impeachment. The threat had been thrown in the face of the court by Hay in the course of the trial but Marshall had appeared unmoved. Jefferson went so far as to insert a suggestion that the Chief Justice be impeached in his next annual message but was persuaded by his cabinet to leave it out.

Their action indicates the nature of what has been called the Jeffersonian attack on the Supreme Court. That attack from the beginning had had a personal aspect which constantly increased. The country as a whole was well satisfied with the administration of justice. Jefferson subconsciously felt the need to vindicate his character from the imputation of tyranny which it seemed to him that the Burr case had left on it but his cabinet knew the politically vulnerable position in which such a proceeding would place them. An impeachment would have to depend largely on the testimony of General Wilkinson and they had no desire to entrust their political fortunes to the veracity of that doughty warrior. The outcome of the trial had stirred up sufficient resentment among the more rabid Jeffersonians so that a mob hanged Marshall, along with Burr and his counsel, in effigy in Baltimore. It was the gust that indicated the

---

[53] *United States* v. *Burr*, 25 Fed. Cas. (Case No. 14,692d) 30 (1807).

storm was over and never again, during Marshall's long tenure of office, was there any talk in responsible quarters of removing him from office. But the Jefferson-Marshall quarrel left its mark on American political history. Throughout the remainder of his life Jefferson never tired of discussing whether the founders had been wise in attempting to set up an independent judiciary and whether, if they were, they had ever intended that it should be as independent as Marshall's decisions showed it to be. Those questions were not coeval with the federal government.

Marshall was to be subjected to many bitter attacks in the course of the next quarter-century, but hereafter those attacks were not to be personal; they were not even, in many instances, attacks on the judiciary. Instead, they were attacks on the federal government as such and, as such, however much lip service Jefferson's successors paid him, they could not be countenanced by Presidents and cabinets. In the administration succeeding Jefferson the executive branch of the government still talked the language of anti-Federalism but in practice its actions were Federalistic. The logical justification for the actions of Jefferson's heirs was left to Marshall, Adams' appointee.

*   *   *   *   *   *

During the thirty-four years that Marshall presided over the Supreme Court his personal views can, except in a few relatively unimportant instances, be treated as equivalent to the views of the Court. No Chief Justice before or since has dominated his colleagues the way Marshall did. When he came to the Court the associate justices were Cushing, Paterson, Chase, Washington and Moore. Cushing could be relied on to follow the majority. Washington, a competent but not a brilliant judge, had originally been appointed to fill the vacancy on the Court which Marshall refused. He and his chief were old friends and seldom disagreed about anything. Moore, a man of the same age as Marshall, was almost a nonentity. The strong men among the associates were Paterson and Chase. The latter had violated even the judicial etiquette of 1800 by electioneering for Adams and, when Jefferson was elected, Chase was glad to make himself as inconspicuous as possible. Paterson had been the candidate for Chief Justice of the Federalist senators and it was only when they were satisfied that Adams would never appoint him that they had voted for Marshall's confirmation. But Paterson did not dispute the gentle leadership which Marshall, with his knack of handling men, imposed on the Court.

His leadership was different from that of either his predecessors or his successors. Prior to his time the opinions of the Court had been delivered *seriatim*, that is, each judge, beginning with the junior in time of appointment, had delivered a long or short opinion on every case. The Chief Justice had closed with his own opinion but there was no one opinion which could be said to be the opinion of the Court. This practice Marshall immediately changed. His opinion in *Marbury v. Madison* was the opinion of the Court and his action gave notice that hereafter in great cases the Chief Justice would speak for the judicial branch of the government. So far as is known the associates all cheerfully acquiesced in the change. Marshall was such a pleasant companion that it was always difficult for anyone to withstand his wishes and, during Jefferson's administration, none of the judges was anxious to stand out as the mouthpiece of the Court.

The appointment of Jeffersonian judges did not affect Marshall's dominance. Great constitutional cases do not arise every day and most of Marshall's great decisions were rendered after the majority of the Court were Jeffersonians, appointees of Jefferson and Madison. Marshall himself remained a Federalist but long before his death he was the only member of that party on the Supreme Court. His great opinions cannot be looked upon as party decisions for, while spoken by a Federalist, they represented the con-

clusions of a predominantly Jeffersonian Court. Jefferson
himself never recognized this but until his death he clung
to the opinion that Marshall was one of the old "monocrats"
who by some mysterious, but undoubtedly nefarious, means
corrupted one after another of the good democrats who
were appointed to control him.

Marshall's career can almost be interpreted in terms of
feud and friendship for the appointment which made the
majority of the Court Jeffersonian resulted in a friendship
which was as close as the feud was bitter. Cushing's death,
shortly after Jefferson's retirement, created the opportunity
for which that President had been waiting. The death had
reduced the Federalists in the Court to a minority. Jefferson
was profuse in his written advice to Madison regarding the
vacancy. It was necessary that Cushing's successor be appointed from New England and nearly all the eminent lawyers of that region were Federalists. The appointment, at
Jefferson's suggestion, was offered first to Levi Lincoln who
refused it. Alexander Wolcott of Connecticut, one of the first
of American party bosses, was nominated but the nomination was promptly rejected by the Senate. J. Q. Adams,
who had drifted away from his father's party, was then
nominated and confirmed but declined the appointment.
Finally, with some misgiving, Joseph Story was nominated.
He was only thirty-two but the misgiving was not on account
of his age. Story, a poet in his youth and a man of sprightly
and mercurial temperament, had started life as a Jeffersonian. The lack of leaders of that party in Massachusetts had
given him a free field and he had already been a congressman and speaker of the lower house in the legislature. He
had already, too, begun to gain that reputation for profound
legal learning on which his fame rests and the old Federalist
leaders in Boston had been carefully courting him. Jefferson was afraid their efforts were bearing fruit.

Story had first met Marshall in 1808 and had immediately
taken to the older man. The Chief Justice had not lived up

to the impression which Story had gained from the Jeffersonian papers. "I love his laugh," wrote the future associate,
"it is too hearty for an intriguer,—and his good temper and
unwearied patience are equally agreeable on the bench and
in the study."[54] It was the beginning of a life-long friendship. When Story joined the Court in 1811 the judges still
all lived together in a boarding-house during the terms of
Court. It was in this family circle that Marshall gained his
influence over his associates. None of them ever brought his
wife to Washington, which was a dismal village in which
most of the inhabitants lived in boarding-houses and in
which practically the only amusement was bachelor dinners.
Calhoun established a great social reputation by having
women at his parties. Both Marshall and Story loved female
company although both were devoted to their wives. The
bar of the Court consisted of a small body of distinguished
lawyers, many of whom were also from time to time senators
and cabinet officers, who came to Washington every year for
the sessions of the Court. The judges and the lawyers constituted the most stable element in a city whose population consisted largely of a shifting body of congressmen. The place
was so dull that the few ladies in town would attend court
to hear their friends argue. A stranger was scandalized to
see the marshal, after the opening of court, hand their
"cards of invitation" to the judges who thereupon answered
them from the bench.

Marshall did not enjoy Washington dinners quite so
much as Story did. The etiquette of the town was scarcely
stiff but it was a little too formal for the old frontiersman.
He still came to court with his hair tousled, dressed in a
coat that did not look as though it belonged to him, with a
shirt that needed washing and with shoes which revealed
plainly the town's lack of pavement. He would sit and tell
stories in his rather hesitating drawl with anybody that

---

[54] Letter dated February 25, 1808 to Samuel P. P. Fay. Story,
I at 167.

happened to be present until court opened; he was even known to go out into the yard and play marbles with a boy, but all agree that when he put on his judicial robe his manner changed completely. There is no hint that Marshall on the bench was ever anything but dignity personified. The physical surroundings gave him little help in preserving that dignity. After the British burned the Capitol during the War of 1812 the Court sat for several terms in such quarters as could be rented in Washington. Finally a basement room under the Senate chamber was fixed up for its use. A mahogany desk and a comfortable chair were provided for each judge but the Court did not even have a robing room. The marshal would help the judges into their gowns in the court room proper and they would thereupon go behind the railing which separated their seats from the rest of the room and take their places. It was here that Marshall listened to the interminable arguments that preceded nearly all his famous decisions. He not only did not demand brevity but insisted that every point be argued to the fullest possible extent. It was Marshall's way of learning law but it was only the lightness of the docket which enabled him to allow one case to be argued for nine days. While Marshall was famous for his courtesy from the bench even he did not always listen with rapt attention when a lawyer took three days to present a point. He is never known to have cut counsel short but he once defined "the acme of judicial distinction" as "the ability to look a lawyer straight in the eyes for two hours and not hear a damned word he says."[55]

Marshall and Story were poles apart in their attitude toward "learning" but together they made an admirable team. If Marshall was the father of American constitutional law Story was the father of American common law. The stream of legal treatises which Story turned out was one of the most important influences in the development of Ameri-

---

[55] BEVERIDGE, IV at 83.

can law and they established their author as one of the first
American scholars, in any field, with an international reputation. Story's learning was the perfect complement to
Marshall's power of logic. Story's reading was voracious
and included everything from the Year-books to the latest
novel. The latter class of literature appealed to both men
equally. Marshall would wait impatiently for Sir Walter
Scott to produce his next novel and the Chief Justice chided
Story for not sufficiently appreciating Jane Austen. Their
mutual taste for light literature indicated the sentimentality
and the love of fun which the two men had in common. It
is probably due to Story that all but the eldest of Marshall's
five sons attended Harvard.

The judges in their Washington boarding-house, like
other men, occasionally had spasms of reform in one of
which they determined to get along without wine at dinner
"except on rainy days." Marshall loved his Madeira after
dinner and it was not long before he broke into a conversation at the end of a meal with "Brother Story, step to the
window and see if it does not look like rain." The latter's
doleful report that the sun was shining brightly did not stop
the Madeira for the Chief Justice ruled that "our jurisdiction
extends over so large a territory that the doctrine of chances
makes it certain that it must be raining somewhere."[56]
The judges obtained their Madeira by a special importation
every year from the islands where it was produced. This
habit was soon so well known that one of the most popular
brands of that wine was called "Supreme Court."

*   *   *   *   *   *

The peculiar relationship which the Federalist Chief
Justice was to bear to the party in power never came out
more clearly than in the second of his historical decisions.
The case was decided the year before Story's appointment
but he, too, was involved as he was of counsel on the win-
ning side.

---

[56] BEVERIDGE, IV at 88.

Georgia was the poorest and most underpopulated of the original thirteen states but its lack of population did not prevent it from claiming title to the future states of Alabama and Mississippi. The boundaries of its claims were vague and conflicted with those of the British in West Florida and of the Spanish in Louisiana but the vagueness of the boundaries made little difference. The western territory of Georgia was actually in the possession of the Creeks and Choctaws, the most civilized Indians in eastern North America. So far were the Georgians from being able to subdue these Indians that it was at least equally probable that the Indians, who could always obtain arms and ammunition from New Orleans or Pensacola, would end by subduing the Georgians. This did not prevent the Georgian title to the Creek and Choctaw lands from having a value.

Land speculation was the business of every American. Those that had money bought paper titles to western land; those that had no money earned their land by living on it. So during Washington's administration the Georgian legislature disposed of its western lands to companies organized for the purpose who paid the state somewhat over a cent an acre for its doubtful title. It is at least questionable whether the state could have made a better bargain but it is certain that a great many members of the legislature made a good thing for themselves out of the transaction. The purchasers promptly sold the land to investors in the north and east so, as usual, by the time the cry of fraud was raised the land, or at least the paper title derived from Georgia, was in the hands of people who were unquestionably innocent of any wrongdoing. But the invention of the cotton gin had increased the value of southwestern land and a wave of indignation swept through Georgia at the venality of the legislatures which had sold the Yazoo lands, as they were called. The last legislature to make such a sale was succeded by one pledged to undo the work of its predecessor. It revoked the acts making the grants and thus took the legal position that a land grant was like any other act of a legislature and could be revoked by a succeeding legislature. Later Georgia ceded its claims to Alabama and Mississippi to the federal government.

The matter was at this stage when Jefferson became President. The Yazoo claimants, as the innocent purchasers were called, were clamoring for the recognition of their titles by the federal government. A substantial party in Congress deemed it outrageous that any claims should be recognized which had originated in the corruption of the representatives of the people. Three members of the cabinet, Madison, Gallatin and Lincoln, were appointed a commission to work out a settlement. Their eminently fair report recommended the setting aside of five million acres to settle the claims which was considerably less than the face amount of the claims. The compromise had Jefferson's whole-hearted support but it aroused so much antagonism in the southern wing of his party that the matter was still unsettled when he left office.

In the meantime it occurred to the claimants that they might get some help from the Supreme Court. The function of the judiciary in the government was still so little appreciated that it took years before it occurred to the claimants that their case, a matter fundamentally of the validity of a land title, was one which properly belonged in the courts. Their attitude was correct. When they finally did obtain a decision it was not treated as law but rather as an authoritative exposition of what the constitution intended that the law should be. In many of Marshall's most famous cases the conclusions of the Court did not represent the will of the state; they were rather in the nature of pronouncements on morality by a distinguished ecclesiastical body.

The Yazoo question reached the Court in the form of a case known as *Fletcher* v. *Peck*.[57] Peck had transferred one of the claims to Fletcher who sued to get his money back

---

[57] 6 Cranch 87, 3 L. Ed. 162 (1810).

on the ground that the claim was worthless.   There was plenty of evidence that it was not a real controversy but, as Justice Johnson called it, "a mere feigned case."   All the parts of the constitution did not grow up together.   Today the Court would unquestionably throw out such a case as not within the constitutional grant of power to the judiciary but Marshall always seems to have been singularly blind to the need for a "case or controversy."

On the merits the decision was unanimous and was expressed, with the exception of a brief opinion by Johnson, in the opinion written by Marshall for the Court.   The action of the Georgia legislature in rescinding its grant was the type of careless disregard for private rights which the framers of the constitution had had in mind when they had inserted the clause forbidding the passage of laws by any state impairing the obligations of contracts.   The real question was whether the fact that the original grant had been brought about by fraud and corruption made a difference. The Court answered this by an application of the established doctrine of English law that fraud in the original transaction does not affect a subsequent innocent purchaser for value. It was on this point that the decision was attacked.   There was as yet by no means universal agreement that the law of England prior to the Revolution was now the law of America. The law of nature and of revelation still had its advocates and the prevailing anti-British sentiment had led to attempts to introduce the civil law.   These last attempts failed largely through the inability of the bench and bar to use authorities written in any language but their own but now a Georgia congressman denounced the decision as an attempt to destroy the "rights and liberties of the people" by a "maxim of English law."[58]

The decision had no effect as a legal proceeding but was of great help to the administration in getting its bill to compromise the Yazoo claims through Congress.   It was the first

---

[58] BEVERIDGE, III at 598.

of a line of decisions in which the great Federalist Chief
Justice wrote opinions for a predominantly Jeffersonian
court upholding acts passed by a Jeffersonian Congress
under the guidance of a Jeffersonian President.

The most striking instances of the fusion of Federalist
theory and Jeffersonian practice were the bank cases. The
original break into parties in Washington's administration
had turned on the power of Congress to organize a national
bank. The charter of that bank had expired by limitation
but it had proved such a useful institution that, a few years
later, the Jeffersonians, in Madison's administration, organized another one. It was this second, or Jeffersonian, bank
which was haled before Marshall. The organization of the
bank was not due to any change in the principles on which
the Jeffersonian party was founded but was brought about
purely by the force of factors extrinsic to the administration.
The professions of the party in power remained the same
but the necessities of the situation compelled it to act in
accordance with the professions of its opponents. Perhaps
it is the fact that party platforms have made so little difference in America that has enabled democratic government to
survive here but in any event it was left to the Federalist
Chief Justice to give the logical defense for the inconsistent
act of the Madison administration in organizing the second
central bank.

However satisfactory the organization of that institution
was to the Jeffersonian leaders in Washington it was not
equally popular throughout the country. The state governments felt a natural sympathy for the home boys, the local
bankers, whose business was likely to be injured by this new
monster chartered in Washington and controlled in Philadelphia. It was a struggle between different groups of bankers
rather than a struggle between economic or social classes.

The bank was itself a sort of federated institution in
which each branch was semi-independent. The first clash
arose over the branch in Baltimore, a city which was then

of much greater relative importance in the financial life of the country than it is today. It is impossible to judge to what extent the rivalry between Philadelphia and Baltimore entered into the dislike of the bank in Maryland but, in any event, the local bankers succeeded in having a statute passed which was designed to drive the national bank out of the state. They were too subtle merely to forbid the bank to do business in the state. Instead, they planned to accomplish their purpose through the use of the taxing power. A statute was passed by the legislature of Maryland imposing a heavy tax on the issue of notes by the Baltimore branch of the Bank of the United States; a tax so heavy that it amounted to a prohibition. It was the same device which was later successfully used by the national government to drive state banks of issue out of existence.

The validity of the statute was tested in a case,[59] decided in 1819, in which the state sued McCulloch, the cashier of the Baltimore branch of the bank, for failing to pay the tax. The questions involved were whether the federal government had power to organize a bank and, if it did, whether the bank was subject to state taxation. A unanimous Court, speaking through what is probably the most famous opinion that Marshall ever wrote, decided both questions in favor of the bank. There was considerable popular disapproval of the decision but the disapproval cannot be described as Jeffersonian. The names of the counsel alone are sufficient to indicate how little the decision followed the old political alignments. The man who had been the ablest of government counsel in the trial of Aaron Burr, William Wirt, appeared for the bank while Luther Martin, who had been the leader among Burr's lawyers, represented the state.

Maryland acquiesced in the decision but the power of the Court was still largely moral. If a state refused to accept

---

[59] *McCulloch* v. *Maryland*, 4 Wheat. 316, 4 L. Ed. 579 (1819).

a decision the Court had no real physical power with which to compel it to do so. A committee of the Ohio legislature discovered this interesting fact and determined to act on it.

Instead of bringing suit to enforce an Ohio statute taxing the bank, similar to the Maryland statute, they simply had the state auditor, Osborn, seize the money, consisting of about a hundred and twenty thousand dollars, which was in the bank's branch at Chillicothe, in payment of the tax. The injunction which the bank obtained from the circuit court was disregarded. The bank then sued Osborn, personally, for the return of the money and the state legislature thereupon adopted a resolution stating that Marshall's opinion in the Maryland case was invalid. The bank won in its suit against Osborn but he refused to obey the decree ordering him to return the money. He was thereupon jailed for contempt, the key of the state treasury was taken from him and the money found in the state treasury was seized, all by order of the circuit court. The legislature adopted various resolutions denouncing the circuit court but was unable to stir up much public sympathy in other states. Ohio was not willing to break with the Union over the matter and its law-abiding habits finally forced its champions of liberty to carry the controversy to the Supreme Court. When, five years after the *McCulloch Case,* that Court handed down a decision[60] in favor of the bank, the state quietly submitted. It was the first case in which Ellsworth's "coercion by law— that coercion which acts only upon delinquent individuals" had been put into practice.

The Yazoo land case and the bank cases stood out in Marshall's life as pre-eminent examples of the fact that the position which the Court, under his guidance, was obtaining in our governmental system was not a party position. Those cases by their support of acts of nominally anti-Federalist administrations showed that the Court was not a Federalist

---

[60] *Osborn* v. *The Bank of the United States,* 9 Wheat. 738, 6 L. Ed. 204 (1824).

institution but one which was inextricably bound up with the whole governmental system. There were other cases during the same period which were not tied up with any political policy yet which were of far-reaching effect in the gradual unfolding of a system "partly national; partly federal."

The first of these,[61] which was decided in 1819, the same year as the *McCulloch Case,* belongs legally in the same category as the Yazoo land case. Like it, it turned on that section of the constitution which forbids the passage of laws by any state impairing the obligation of contracts. This time the contract in question was not a fraudulent land grant but the charter of a college. Dartmouth in New Hampshire had been founded in colonial times under a royal charter. It had continued to exist under this charter into the nineteenth century, when a long and obscure quarrel which was supposed to have originated in scandal-mongering among the members of the college church, ended in an attempt by the state government to take over control of the college. The college administration took the position that the original charter constituted a contract between the crown and those who donated the endowment. The opposite position is at least arguable but the opinion which Marshall wrote for the Court adopted that analysis of the nature of a charter. The case was to be cited often in the future. If a college charter was irrevocable by a legislature so were the charters of business corporations. But a remedy was speedily discovered and today many state constitutions and practically all state incorporation laws reserve a power of revocation to the state.

Cases such as the *Dartmouth College Case* always left a feeling of resentment against the Court in some group. In course of time that resentment found a theory around which to crystallize. That theory did not originate purely as a reaction against the Court. It expressed rather the

---

[61] *Dartmouth College Case,* 4 Wheat. 518, 4 L. Ed. 629 (1819).

feelings of those who felt that they were in a hopeless minority. Originally it had no geographical habitat. It had appeared among the New England Federalists during the War of 1812. Later its headquarters was South Carolina. After Marshall's death it was at one time popular in Wisconsin. But as the South gradually became the principal minority section that theory became a peculiarly Southern possession.

The theory of state sovereignty, the theory that the federal government and the states are sovereignties equal in rank and that, therefore, the Supreme Court, a branch of the federal government, is not entitled to decide conflicts of jurisdiction between them, gained nourishment from a number of minor decisions which cannot be described in detail here. Resentment was aroused in Virginia by a decision,[62] in a case in which Marshall did not sit, affirming the validity of the old British land grants. At a later date the Court gave satisfaction to many Virginians equal to the resentment aroused by the first case by upholding[63] the validity of the grants of Kentucky land which they had obtained from Virginia while Kentucky was still part of that state. This decision aroused as much antagonism in Kentucky as the decision on the British land grants had aroused in Virginia, but, Henry Clay sadly wrote, "when the thunders of that Court were directed against poor Kentucky, in vain did she invoke Virginian aid ... not a Virginia voice is heard against this decision."[64]

The theory of state sovereignty had so far had its greatest development among the little oligarchy which ruled Virginia and a miserable police court case from that state, which was decided two years before the Kentucky land case, involved the most thorough threshing out in Marshall's time of the theory of the federal judicial power. This first important

[62] *Martin* v. *Hunter's Lessee*, 1 Wheat. 304, 4 L. Ed. 97 (1816).
[63] *Green* v. *Biddle*, 8 Wheat. 1, 5 L. Ed. 547 (1823).
[64] WARREN, I at 642.

appearance of the developing doctrine of state sovereignty on the national scene was unconnected with the peculiar local interests of any section. The federal government had set up a lottery and two men of the name of Cohen were convicted in a Virginian court of selling tickets in this lottery in violation of a state statute. The defendants appealed to the Supreme Court of the United States from the highest state court to which they could carry their case. On appeal the case became known, by a curious pluralizing of the defendants' names, as *Cohens* v. *Virginia.*[65]

In time the most famous section of Ellsworth's judiciary act came to be that known as section twenty-five. It had been used a few times before but it was the lottery case which first dragged it into the political spotlight. That section is still law and is as much imbedded in our system of government as if it were part of the constitution itself. As it stood in Marshall's day it provided for appeals from any state court of last resort when the validity of any treaty or law of the United States was called into question and the decision of that court was against its validity. This last condition was abolished in the twentieth century but the members of the first senate were unable to conceive of a condition of affairs in which a state court would hold a federal statute valid and the Supreme Court would hold it invalid.

In the *Cohens Case,* which was decided in 1821, the Supreme Court, again speaking through Marshall, held that it had jurisdiction to hear the appeal. So far as the Cohens personally were concerned the decision gave them little comfort for the Court went on to hold that Congress had not intended to permit the sale of the lottery tickets in Virginia and that they had therefore been properly convicted. Like so many of Marshall's decisions the case was academic but it called forth the most furious denunciation from the rulers of Virginian state politics. The dominant figure in that state's affairs was Spencer Roane, the Chief Justice of the

[65] 6 Wheat. 264, 5 L. Ed. 257 (1821).

state and an able and acute lawyer. He and Thomas Jefferson seem to have been the only personal enemies that
Marshall created in the course of his long life. It was well
known that Jefferson had intended to appoint Roane Chief
Justice whenever he got Marshall out of that office. Disappointed in this ambition, Roane, like most of the purely
Virginian group among the Jeffersonians, retired to state
politics. That group had found itself less and less important
on the national scene as the strength of the northern and
western wings of their party grew. Determined to be first
in their village rather than second in Rome, they were now
busily engaged in the development of the more extreme
forms of the doctrine of state sovereignty.

Roane started a war of pamphlets against the Court, and
Marshall in particular, which culminated in the next session
of Congress in a number of proposals to curb the power of
the Court. While the proposals were various the particular
power which had been exercised in the *Cohens Case* could
easily be disposed of. No constitutional amendment was
necessary. All that was required to repeal section twenty-
five of the judiciary act was a bare majority of Congress.
The proposal was made that that section be repealed but that
bare majority could not be obtained. When it came to the
point, responsible statesmen realized that there had to be
some method of settling conflicts between the states and the
federal government. Roane complained that "Jefferson and
Madison hang back too much in this great crisis"[66] for,
however they might permit their followers to talk, neither of
them had any desire to convert the United States into a mere
league of sovereignties. In one respect the attacks had
changed since those of Jefferson's administration. This time
there was, outside of Roane's outpourings, nothing personal.
Most of those speaking against the Court in Congress started
with a tribute of respect to the Chief Justice. Marshall's
background was a peculiar advantage to him. The center of

[66] WARREN, I at 558.

dissatisfaction was Virginia and Kentucky. In the former state he had innumerable personal friends and was universally popular. He still maintained his home in Richmond and as his five sons grew up and married he had deeded them portions of his holdings in Fauquier County. There they lived the lives of country gentlemen for the Marshalls were by now very thoroughly established in the Virginian squirearchy. Marshall was not personally as well acquainted in Kentucky as in Virginia but Thomas Marshall and many of his fifteen children had gone across the mountains at the close of the Revolution. There the clan had prospered both economically and politically. The congressmen from Kentucky and Virginia were not likely to have any virulent hatred of Marshall.

The doctrine of state sovereignty had not yet become connected with the South's "peculiar institution." But in this respect, too, Marshall was in a particularly strong position. He had acquired a dislike of slavery in his youth when the leaders of Virginian politics were almost all opposed to that institution. His tenacity, his conservatism and his isolation from elections kept him from changing his views with the change of sentiment in his community. To the day of his death he believed slavery an evil but he did not believe that the solution lay in the creation of a large population of free negroes. The only way out that he could see was to return the negroes to Africa. He gave freely of his time and money to the African Colonization Society which was engaged in the work of settling freed negroes in Liberia.

The congressional discussions in regard to the functions of the Supreme Court continued for some years after the *Cohens Case* but produced nothing. Meanwhile a case arose in which the Court's use of its power to review state legislation gained it far more popularity than it had lost by any of its previous decisions. It brought home to the public as no previous decision of the Court had done that a system which worked according to logic, rather than passion, could not be the agent of any political group.

A few years before, Robert Fulton and Chancellor Livingston had developed the steamboat to a state where its commercial operation was possible. Shortly after the *Clermont* made its first successful run against the current of the Hudson River, the New York legislature granted the two promoters an exclusive monopoly of steam navigation in the waters of the state. This grant was immediately attacked in the state courts but the act of the legislature was upheld. The monopoly also obtained a similar grant from the legislature of Louisiana. This gave Fulton and Livingston control of the mouth of the Mississippi which, together with the control of New York harbor, practically gave them control of the commerce of the country for in the early years of the nineteenth century the internal communication of the country was almost entirely by water. There was plenty of popular resentment over the growth of this "trust." New Jersey, Connecticut and Ohio passed retaliatory statutes forbidding any boats licensed by the monopoly from coming within the waters which those states controlled. The feeling between the first two of these states and New York was so bitter that, as Wirt said in the Supreme Court, they were "almost on the eve of war" for "the war of legislation, which has already commenced, will, according to its usual course, become a war of blows."[67]

The question of the validity of the steamboat monopoly was brought to an issue over a ferryboat line from Elizabethport, New Jersey to New York City which had been established by ex-governor Ogden of New Jersey in defiance of the monopoly. Livingston and Fulton made so much trouble for Ogden that he was compelled to buy a license from them. He had hardly done so when a former partner of his, Thomas Gibbons, started a competing ferryboat line without a license. Ogden immediately brought suit in the New York state courts to enjoin Gibbons. That staunch old Federalist, Chancellor Kent, upheld the validity of the

---

[67] *Gibbons* v. *Ogden*, 9 Wheat. 1, at 185, 6 L. Ed. 23, at 67 (1824).

monopoly and enjoined Gibbons from running his line. The Chancellor's decision was upheld in the New York Court for the Trial of Impeachments and Correction of Errors and after a number of years the case reached the Supreme Court. There has seldom been a case in which more money was involved and most of the leading lawyers of the country appeared on one side or the other.

The attack on the steamboat monopoly was based on two clauses of the constitution, that which gives Congress power to regulate interstate and foreign commerce and that which authorizes Congress to pass patent laws. The defense was that this did not mean that the states might not also pass laws on those subjects any more than the power of Congress to levy taxes meant that the states could not also levy taxes. The monopoly was greatly helped by an opinion Marshall had written a few years before[68] in which he had indicated that the power of Congress to pass bankruptcy laws did not deprive the states of all power to pass statutes regarding insolvents.

His opinion in the bankruptcy case evidently now troubled Marshall greatly. While he had been too much of a statesman in that case to lay down a hard and fast rule that all state insolvency laws were necessarily invalid, he realized that the type of interference with navigation which had been occasioned by the New York steamboat laws was not only the very type the framers of the constitution had had in mind when they had vested the power to regulate interstate and foreign commerce in the central government but was also the very type of interference which had brought about the calling of the federal constitutional convention in the first place. In fact, it had been the navigation laws of New York which had been chiefly responsible for arousing nationalistic sentiment in Connecticut and New Jersey. Marshall also recognized the enormous practical difficulties which would arise if the validity of the monopoly was con-

---

[68] *Sturges* v. *Crowninshield*, 4 Wheat. 122, 4 L. Ed. 529 (1819).

ceded. If it was once admitted that the monopoly was valid,
the most important means of communication in the country
would be thrown open to regulation by the various states
with the probable result that it would be regulated to death.
While that result might have given a great impetus to the
nationalism that was Marshall's one great passion, he was
not willing to leave the evil of excessive state regulation to
be legislated out of existence by Congress. But he did not
desire to incur the practical and doctrinal difficulties which
a decision holding the monopoly invalid purely because it
was an attempt by a state to regulate interstate commerce
would involve.

There was a subsidiary point in the case which gave him
a way out. Gibbons, the owner of the independent ferry
line, had a federal coasting license and Marshall based his
decision on this fact. That license, said the Chief Justice,
entitled Gibbons to run his boats in all American waters.
The New York statute creating the monopoly therefore
directly contravened the federal licensing act. Congress
had exercised its regulatory power and it was therefore
unnecessary to determine whether, if there had been no
federal statute on the subject, the monopoly would have
been valid.

The decision in the steamboat case met with almost
universal popular satisfaction but it was only the beginning
of an immense mass of cases construing the commerce
clause—a mass which is still growing. Marshall, himself,
three years later, wrote one of his most famous decisions in
a case[69] holding a Maryland tax on importers invalid but
the difficulties of the subject are best illustrated by one of
his minor decisions made in 1829, five years after the steamboat case.

The state of Delaware had authorized the organization
of a company to drain a marsh. For that purpose the

---

[69] *Brown* v. *Maryland*, 12 Wheat. 419, 6 L. E. 678 (1827).

company was also empowered to build a dam across what was known as Blackbird Creek, a body of water which Marshall described as one of "those small navigable creeks into which the tide flows, and which abound throughout the lower country of the Middle and Southern states." One Willson, in reliance upon Marshall's decision in the steam-boat case, sailed up the creek in his sloop *Sally,* which had a federal coasting license, and, when he came to the dam, broke through. The owners of the dam promptly sued him for damages and, to Willson's surprise, Marshall agreed with them.[70] His opinion cannot be ranked along with the great legal essays which he wrote in his famous cases. It is in that that its interest lies. Marshall obviously was puzzled. He was well acquainted with "those small naviga-ble creeks . . . which abound throughout the lower country of the Middle and Southern states" and he had no mind to apply the same rule to them that he had applied to the Hudson and the Mississippi. Yet he had difficulty in finding a satisfactory legal distinction, a distinction which would enable a lawyer to advise a client whether the particular river over which the client proposed to sail fell within the class of the Hudson or of the Blackbird. It was typical of the problems which Marshall left for his successors.

His work was not in the development of flexible and delicately balanced legal principles. Constitutional law as he left it had that rigidity which is characteristic of all legal systems in their youth. He might be said to have developed the common law of the constitution; his successors were left the task of developing its equity. Marshall laid down the broad principle in the *McCulloch Case* that the power to tax was the power to destroy. It was left to succeeding judges to work out the types and degrees of taxation which were unlawful, to add, in Holmes' words, the proviso to Marshall's statement, "not while this court lives."

---

[70] *Willson* v. *Blackbird Creek Marsh Co.,* 2 Pet. 245, 7 L. Ed. 412 (1829).

Even in Marshall's lifetime there were signs of revolt against his rigid construction of the constitution. In the early days his colleagues had left constitutional matters largely to him but now that all had learned from him the technique of this new branch of the law the other judges developed ideas of their own. Finally, in 1827, a case arose in which Marshall found himself in a minority. The case[71] involved the constitutionality of a New York insolvency law which provided for the discharge of the debtor under certain circumstances. The division was not along party lines for the only Federalist besides Marshall still on the bench, Bushrod Washington, went with the majority while not only Story but Duval, who had likewise been appointed by Madison, sided with Marshall.

Outside of the field of constitutional law Marshall's fame rests chiefly on his opinions in international law. During much of the time that he sat on the bench a great portion of the cases which came up for decision had to do with the law of the ocean. Some of the cases were due to the Napoleonic wars and the War of 1812 but there was an even more fertile source.

In the early years of the nineteenth century the revolt of the Spanish colonies in the Americas had filled American waters with all sorts of nondescript privateers and pirates. There was much sympathy in the United States for the Spanish colonists and plenty of American adventurers were willing to take letters of marque from the innumerable governments that were being set up in South America and go out looking for Spanish loot. Ships were constantly being fitted out in New Orleans, Charleston and Baltimore which, as soon as they had cleared, would hoist the flag of some struggling and unrecognized South American republic and proceed to plunder any Spanish property they could find. Innumerable and loud complaints were lodged by the Spanish diplomatic representatives in Washington. The

---

[71] *Ogden* v. *Saunders*, 12 Wheat. 213, 6 L. Ed. 606 (1827).

government did what it could to prevent breaches of neutrality but was hampered by public sympathy with the adventurers in the United States and by the vagueness of the international law on the subject.

Marshall had almost as free a hand here as he had in the formulation of the fundamental principles of constitutional law. He recognized clearly the nature of his task. "If a great system of public law is ever to prevail on the ocean," wrote Marshall, "it must, in analogy to the municipal system, result from decisions and reasonings, appealing through the press to the common judgment of the civilized world. Heretofore, admiralty proceedings . . . have been substituting for principles the capricious mandates of power and of belligerent policy. . . . Neutral tribunals should be heard on subjects in which neutral nations are equally concerned."[72] The last remark was occasioned by the American familiarity with the British admiralty courts in which their vessels had constantly been condemned as prizes on one flimsy pretext or another during the years before the War of 1812, frequently with little or no opportunity for a hearing and seldom on any definite principle which could be used as a guide in the future.

In developing the law of the ocean Marshall attempted to introduce much higher standards of international morality than had theretofore prevailed. Due to the fact that most of the cases which came before the Court arose out of acts done by Americans, Marshall had many more opportunities to develop the obligations of neutrals than their rights. This latter field is still largely open. Perhaps this was the reason the English courts were so ready to take over his doctrines in the flood of the same type of problems which reached them during and after the World War. The English courts cited Marshall frequently in solving those problems and their judges, as one of them, Lord Craigmyle, has remarked, "ranked Marshall with the highest

[72] WARREN, I at 568-569.

not only when he gave a leading judgment, but even, and this is a superlative test—even when he dissented."[73]

The same thing cannot be said of his activities in the field of private law. Here he was a strong, rather than a pre-eminent, judge but his great reputation in constitutional and international law gave an additional weight to any decision by him. That reputation has resulted in firmly entrenching several questionable decisions which he rendered on points of private law.

He was indolent but he did not dislike pen work as his predecessor Ellsworth had done. Yet the spectacle of Story at his side turning out a constant stream of legal treatises never moved Marshall to try his hand at it. Only once did he turn author and that was before he met Story. On Washington's death his nephew, Justice Bushrod Washington, came into possession of his papers and asked Marshall to write with their help a definitive life of his uncle. Marshall was still in debt for the Fairfax estate and agreed in the sanguine expectation that the book would have an immense sale. He was greatly disappointed. He had adopted the same principle as in the writing of his opinions which always was to start with his analysis as far back as possible. He started in his *Life* with the discovery of America and the book grew to interminable length before he even reached his real subject. While he seems to have enjoyed writing legal opinions, which he frequently did sitting under a tree in the yard, he found that he thoroughly hated the writing of this book. Its value today lies in the fact that in writing of the Revolutionary and post-Revolutionary period Marshall was frequently writing from his own knowledge; it was not history but autobiography.

Marshall's work was done when Andrew Jackson became President. The Chief Justice was then nearly seventy-four. He had placed the Court on a secure foundation; he had proved that the American experiment, the experiment of

[73] CRAIGMYLE, at 82.

protecting political minorities by written limitations on power, enforced by judicial means, was workable.

Marshall, the backwoodsman who had gone east to civilization, had no sympathy for Jackson, the backwoodsman who had followed the frontier over the mountains. Jeffersonianism had by now become Toryism. In the Virginia state constitutional convention of 1829 Marshall, Madison and Monroe fought side by side to retain the oligarchic features of the state constitution which the convention had been called to abolish. The Chief Justice feared that Jackson's election spelled the ruin of his life's work and a case soon arose which confirmed his worst fears. Georgia flagrantly disregarded a writ of the Court in order to hang an Indian named Corn Tassel.[74] It was on this occasion that the President is supposed to have remarked, "John Marshall has given his decision, now let him enforce it." Jackson's disregard for Marshall in this instance was not based on any system but on his frontiersman's belief that Indians were a kind of vermin that should be exterminated by any means, fair or foul.

Jackson's attitude toward nullification in South Carolina cheered Marshall somewhat but he still feared to leave the selection of his successor to the Tennesseean. So Marshall, as his successor was afterwards to do, set to work to outlive the President then in office. It was a difficult task for his health was rapidly failing. At first he had a stone in his kidneys which made work almost impossible for him. Dr. Physick, the leading physician of the country, was consulted and, while he undertook to perform an operation, he warned Marshall that the chances were that it would prove unsuccessful. But the Chief Justice was insistent and, in that day before anæsthetics, managed with a calm which astonished the physicians to hold himself steady while more than a

[74] Referred to in the statement of the case in *Cherokee Nation* v. *Georgia*, 5 Pet. 1 at 12-13, 8 L. Ed. 25 at 29 (1831). Another case which arose out of the same general situation is *Worcester* v. *Georgia*, 6 Pet. 515, 8 L. Ed. 483 (1832).

thousand calculi were removed. Marshall had scarcely recovered from the operation when the death of the wife he had married nearly forty-eight years before threw him into a mental despondency as severe as the physical illness from which he had just recovered. He never overcame the shock of her loss and soon he developed a liver complaint from which he likewise never recovered. From the time of his operation in 1831 both friends and enemies expected his death at any time. Those with whom his political sympathies lay dreaded that event not only because of their love for him but because of their fear of the appointment that Jackson might make in his place. They realized that not only the Chief Justice but the whole Court was about to change. The Court as a whole was old and before Jackson left office he had appointed not only a Chief Justice but five Associate Justices.

In the summer of 1835 Marshall returned to Dr. Physick in Philadelphia in the hope that something could still be done for his liver. The chances of his recovery were desperate and on July 6, 1835, when he was almost eighty years old, he died in that city.

There were very few of his old enemies left to rejoice over his death. Throughout the land meetings were held to do honor to his memory for by now he occupied much the same position in popularity that George Washington had had. Even *Niles' Register*, a newspaper which had attacked nearly every one of his famous decisions, announced that "a great man has fallen in Israel. Next to Washington only, did he possess the reverence and homage of the American people."[75]

*   *   *   *   *   *

When Marshall left the Supreme Court that institution had attained the position in our system of government which it has retained ever since. Marshall's success in establishing

---

[75] BEVERIDGE, IV at 591.

the independence of his branch of the government had destroyed any possibility that the Chief Justice would develop into a Lord Chancellor, a judicial officer who came and went with changes in party. This result was largely a personal triumph. If Adams had left a different man at the head of the Court it is possible that a custom might have arisen by which, while all the judges in theory held their offices by the same tenure, the head of the judiciary would be expected to offer his resignation upon a change of Presidents. There are many other means besides impeachment by which such a custom, if it had once arisen, could have been enforced. That it did not arise is Marshall's greatest contribution to the development of constitutionalism.

His success in retaining his position against Jefferson's open hostility must be ascribed to character and personality rather than to cleverness. The complete control which Jefferson and his group had over the other two branches of the government, and over the greater part of the press of the country, during the early years of Marshall's Chief Justiceship, made cleverness an impossible weapon. It was easy for statesmen to deliver speeches, and for newspapers to print editorials, fulminating against Marshall as an aristocrat holding a position in the government which had been created in flagrant violation of the fundamental tenets of democracy. On paper it was easy to identify Marshall with the sins of his party, with the pompousness of Adams and the snobbishness of Hamilton. The difficulty was that he did not live up to the description. "I love his laugh," as Story had said after first meeting him, "it is too hearty for an intriguer." That laugh, in the case of this one New England Jeffersonian, undid the effects of all the attacks. The Jeffersonian charges simply were not believed by people who had seen the Chief Justice, in a garb which made one of his own relatives-in-law, who had never seen him, mistake him for the butcher, riding circuit in his gig, without a servant, stopping at the common taverns and spending the evenings swapping anecdotes with his fellow travelers or pitching horseshoes in the street.

The establishment of the independence of the judiciary was of far more importance than any doctrine of constitutional construction enunciated by Marshall. The country would not have fallen apart if Marshall had decided that the federal government had no authority to organize a bank. That very conclusion was later arrived at by the political branches of the government and the failure to recharter the Bank of the United States did not break up the Union. If he had held the steamboat monopoly valid Congress could always have remedied the situation by legislation. The states learned in time how to protect themselves against the doctrine of the *Dartmouth College Case.*

His great opinions accomplished their chief work in persuading public opinion that the great experiment of the constitution, the attempt to enforce written limitations on power by judicial means, was feasible. To view Marshall, as both friends and enemies have done, as a man who, through his position on the Court, imposed a strong central government on the country in defiance of popular sentiment is absurd. His decisions at times irritated various noisy minorities, but if any of those minorities had been at any time a majority it could easily have overturned both him and the Court. Marshall's survival and steadily increasing prestige under such attacks indicate that in the long run his work satisfied his countrymen. That work was far higher than the mere construction of the constitution; far higher than the creation of guiding principles in a new branch of jurisprudence. His work was to prove to the world that limitations on power can be made effective; that disputes over those limitations can be settled better in other places than on the battlefield; that force is not the only means of adjusting social conflicts.

Chapter V.

ROGER BROOKE TANEY

Important Dates

Born, March 17, 1777 in Calvert County, Maryland.

Graduated, Dickinson College, 1795.

Admitted to bar, 1799.

Elected to the House of Delegates of Maryland, 1799.

Settled in Frederick, Maryland, 1801.

Married Anne Phebe Charlton Key, January 7, 1806.

State Senator, 1816-1821.

Moved to Baltimore, 1823.

Appointed Attorney-General of Maryland, 1827.

Appointed Attorney-General of the United States, 1831.

Appointed Secretary of the Treasury, September 23, 1833.

Nomination as Secretary of the Treasury rejected by the Senate, June 24, 1834.

Appointed Associate Justice, Supreme Court of the United States, January 15, 1835; action on nomination postponed, March 3, 1835.

Appointed Chief Justice of the United States, December 28, 1835; confirmed March 15, 1836.

Mrs. Taney died, September 29, 1855.

Died, October 12, 1864.

[NOTE: Taney is pronounced "Tawney."]

ROGER BROOKE TANEY

From the portrait by Emanuel Leutze,
painted when Taney was over eighty

Any system of government worthy of the name must rise above individuals; it must be such that it can survive the death of any person connected with it. If it cannot so survive it is a mere tyranny, a dictatorship, bearing more resemblance to the power of an underworld overlord than to a civilized organization of society. The death of the individual under whose direction any social institution has been founded or developed always raises the question whether he has succeeded in giving his work the civilized quality of perpetuity; whether his work has resulted in the creation or development of a true social institution or whether it was merely a reflection of his own ego, destined to die with that ego.

Viewed dispassionately, Marshall's death scarcely seems to raise this question. He was not the founder of the Supreme Court; his was not the mind which had conceived a system "partly national, partly federal," in which the powers of each part would be limited not only as to each other but as to the individuals by whom and over whom those powers were exercised. Nor had he originated the means of making such a complicated system workable. The conception of the judiciary as an independent and coordinate branch of government drawing the limits of power on the other branches of the central government and between the local governments and the central government so as to protect the citizen from his government and the different units of government from each other had existed long before Marshall became Chief Justice. He was not even the first Chief Justice; not even the first to breathe life into this conception of the judiciary.

Yet the question of whether that conception could survive his death arose in the minds of many people, both people who favored that conception and people who opposed it.

199

This was partly due to the birth of a contrary theory during the long years that Marshall had presided over the Court; a theory that it was not the function of the Court to draw the limits on power between the local governments and the central government, between the states and the nation. The advocates of this contrary theory hoped that at last their conception of the nature of state sovereignty would be adopted by the Court; a hope which was increased when Taney's nomination as Chief Justice was accompanied by the nomination as Associate Justice of Philip P. Barbour who, as counsel for the state of Virginia, had, in the *Cohens Case,* presented the extreme states' rights theory to the Supreme Court. Taney himself had never given even lip service to that theory. The level-headed Marshall had, a few months before his death, attempted to bring about the confirmation of Taney's nomination as Associate Justice.[1] But the more excitable Story, shortly after the appointment of the new Chief Justice, wrote that the Supreme Court was "gone."

The difference of opinion was due to the political habit of lumping all sorts of incongruous, and even contradictory, hopes and aspirations together into one party. Many of the extreme states' rights men were followers of Jackson but Taney was not among them. His reasons for joining that party had been very different. To him that party was not one which would introduce a new theory of government or a new social system but one which would restore the old. To restore the old it was necessary to destroy certain things, specifically the Bank of the United States, which Taney regarded not as the embodiment of conservatism but as the symbol of a new and dangerous social tendency. It was for this reason that he appeared to the public of 1835 as a radical. The truth was exactly the opposite. He was a conservative of the deepest dye in the true meaning of the word for he longed ardently to maintain the social system

---

[1] Letter from Marshall to Benjamin Watkins Leigh, TYLER, at 240.

in which he was born, a system which had served its time and was now rapidly disintegrating.

*   *   *   *   *   *

Superficially his background resembled that of Marshall. Social conditions in Maryland and Virginia were much the same and the Taneys were a substantial family in the former, as the Marshalls were in the latter, state. Here the resemblance ends. The Marshalls were a new and vigorous family, aggressively on the way up. They had been of small account before Thomas Marshall went to seek his fortune in the wilderness. But the plantation where the Taneys resided was one, to quote the words of the Chief Justice, which his family "had owned and lived upon . . . for many generations before I was born."[2] It was located in one of the oldest portions of the state, in what was very distinctly a tidewater region. The plantation faced on the estuary of the Patuxent River, in Calvert County, in the southern part of the Western Shore.

The founder of the family had been an indentured servant who came to the colony in the middle of the seventeenth century and, at his death, left the estate on which Roger was born. The Chief Justice was the sixth in descent from the original Taney but the family circumstances had remained at the same level. The estate descended by primogeniture and the younger children were turned out into the world. The Taneys had originally been Anglicans but at some unknown time had turned Roman Catholic. Michael Taney, the Chief Justice's father, had been educated at St. Omer's in northern France where, since the time of Queen Elizabeth, a school had been maintained for the education of English Catholics. Michael was the eldest son and inherited the family estate. On his return to America he was content to live his life as his father had done and was only distinguished from his fellow planters by his habits of

---

[2] Autobiography, TYLER, at 20.

reading for, according to his son, he "read every work he could obtain in the then scant libraries of the country."[8]

It was only in their reading habits that there was much similarity between the two men. His mother, rather than his father, was the parent to whom Taney's affections were drawn. She was of the Brooke family whose plantation was separated from that of the Taneys by Battle Creek, a tributary of the Patuxent. The Brookes had been established in the state as long, if not longer, than the Taneys and were distinguished from the latter family only by the somewhat higher social position of their founder. One member of the family had been a Cromwellian governor of the province but, like the Taneys, the Brookes had later adopted the faith of the proprietary family. Neither followed the proprietors when the latter joined the Church of England.

Roger was the second son and, as such, was given to understand from the time he was a boy that he would never own the big clapboard family mansion but would have to earn a living. It was perhaps fortunate for Taney that this was so. He was not adapted physically or mentally to the life of a tobacco planter on an almost inaccessible plantation, located in a county which did not boast a single town or even a good-sized village. He had none of the physical attributes which are supposed to come from a country up-bringing. He was as tall and had as big a skeleton as Marshall but, unlike Marshall, his skeleton was not the basis of a robust body. His chest was remarkably flat and from his boyhood to the time of his death he was always in poor health. As a boy he learned from his father to shoot ducks and to follow the hounds but he cared for neither amusement. He relates that during the winter he spent at home after leaving college his father would "invite some other gentleman, who also kept fox-hounds, to come with his pack on a particular day, and [hunt] with the two packs united. Other gentlemen, who were known to be fond of the sport,

---

[8] Autobiography, TYLER, at 27.

were also invited, so as to make a party of eight or ten persons, and sometimes more. The hunting usually lasted a week. The party always rose before day, breakfasted by candle-light,—most commonly on spare-ribs (or bacon) and hominy,—drank freely of eggnog, and then mounted and were in the cover, where they expected to find a fox, before sunrise."[4] The ground was rough, the chase was usually a long one and the party seldom returned home until late in the day. They spent the evening drinking and playing cards. While Mrs. Taney remained at home a certain amount of decorum prevailed at these parties but, sometime after Roger had established his own home, she went to live with him. She never returned for, in her absence, her husband stabbed a man named Magruder to death at one of these parties and was compelled to flee the country.

When Taney came to write his autobiography in his old age he claimed to have been very fond of life on his father's plantation although he still remembered that "eggnog was very apt to give me a headache." But he never set up a country place of his own. Fox hunting and duck shooting did not appeal to him. As a boy he loved to roam in the woods alone or to lie under a tree on the banks of the river. His love of the country was more that of the poet than that of the squire and his love of the poetry of the country never left him. His courtship was passed largely in searching the woods for flowers and after his marriage his chief amusement was long horseback rides through the hills with his wife. Even in his seventies he wrote her, "I find the hyacinths in bloom in the Capitol grounds, and walked about them alone after the Court adjourned, to enjoy the marks of the opening spring. In a week they will be beautiful."[5] It seems to have been well known that the easiest way to approach the Chief Justice was through his love of

---

[4] Autobiography, TYLER, at 55.

[5] Letter dated April 1, 1850. TYLER, at 471.

flowers for one of his sons-in-law states that Taney "always thought well of one who liked them."[6]

His strong sensitivity to nature was not his only peculiarity in the workaday world. Even as a boy there was some trace of that almost ethereal appearance which was later his most prominent characteristic. His eyes were dark and deep sunk, his face was long and bony with an extremely high forehead topped by a mass of rather unkempt dark hair which does not seem to have become appreciably gray until he was in his sixties. It was a figure for an El Greco portrait. As he grew older his dignity and his unworldly look increased to an extent which is most clearly revealed in a petulant remark by one of the leaders of the bar: "I can answer his arguments, I am not afraid of his logic, but that infernal apostolic manner of his, there is no replying to."[7] The apostolic appearance reflected an innate unworldliness. Taney always gives the impression of a man who was never quite at home in everyday affairs.

In one respect his appearance and his tastes belied him. His unworldliness was not the unworldliness of the cloister. It was rather the unworldliness of one of those medieval saints who drew from their asceticism a faith and a strength of will which moved mountains. His colleagues on the bench refer frequently to his "iron will" and "ardent temperament." Neither are very apparent in what we know of his early life. They were probably secondary characteristics which were developed by his need for making his own way. If he had been the eldest son and had inherited the estate he might have developed into a charming but ineffectual recluse.

As a young man he deferred entirely to the wishes of his superiors. From the day he was born it had been settled that, as the younger son of a landed family, he should be a lawyer. His preliminary education was the same as that of

---

[6] Letter dated November 4, 1864 from J. Mason Campbell. TYLER, at ix.

[7] William Pinkney, quoted in STEINER, at 87.

his elder brother. Both started by attending a school "kept in a log-cabin by a well-disposed but ignorant old man, who professed to teach reading, writing and arithmetic as far as the rule of three. . . . Our only school-books were Dillworth's spelling book and the Bible; and these, I believe, were the only books our teacher had ever read."[8] Later various private tutors were employed who stayed with the family. But when Roger left for college at the age of fifteen he left alone for there was no need for his elder brother, the prospective squire, to acquire any further education.

The college selected was Dickinson, which had recently been founded by the Presbyterians at Carlisle, Pennsylvania. It had been selected chiefly because two other boys from the vicinity were attending it and Roger made the journey with them. It was a real journey. They started by water, "on board one of the schooners employed in transporting produce and goods between the Patuxent River and Baltimore, and, owing to unfavorable winds, it was a week before we reached our port of destination." From here to Carlisle there was no regular means of conveyance at all. The students stayed at an inn in Baltimore until they could find a wagon returning to Carlisle which had room for them. Finding such a wagon, together with the ride to Carlisle, took them another week. Due to the lack of banking facilities, they were obliged to carry all their money, for the period until their return home, along with them. This money was entirely in specie and therefore too bulky to be carried about in their pockets. It was "necessarily placed in our trunks, and much exposed in an open wagon in a public wagonyard, while the wagoner and ourselves were somewhere else." So great were the difficulties of travel that Taney went home only twice during his three years in college. On both of those journeys, he "walked from Carlisle to Baltimore with one of" his "school-companions, performing the journey in a little over two days."

---

[8] Autobiography, TYLER, at 27-28.

In college he was a hard student but showed no independence. He studied docilely what he was supposed to study and took voluminous notes in all his courses. The college was little better than a preparatory school but he later had these notes carefully bound and kept them all his life. After he had started to practice he decided that his general education was not sufficient and these notes were then used by him as a basis for further study. He was always studious but his intellectual curiosity was never very wide. He never indulged in any extensive general reading although, at least as an old man, he was a regular reader of *Blackwood's* and some other of the English magazines. Even when he became aroused over the bank question he does not seem either to have realized his deficiencies as an economist or to have attempted to remedy them.

The same tendency to be a model pupil, to accept what his teachers taught him, and to stay within the bounds of orthodoxy appears when he studied law. He was probably the better lawyer for it for there is much less place for irregular methods in study for a profession than there is in general education. His professional preparation was superior to that of any of his predecessors except Rutledge. Taney, unlike any of his predecessors, was always primarily a lawyer. He had a taste for technical and abstruse learning which they had all lacked. He was always the learned lawyer and his interest in other directions was less than that of any of them. Taney's apparent inability to manage his personal business affairs successfully brings out the distinction forcibly.

He studied law for three years under Judge Jeremiah Chase, one of the three judges of the General Court. This was both a court of last resort and a court of first instance. It sat alternately at Annapolis and Easton for the two Shores, respectively. The sessions at the former town were far more important and it was there that Taney did his studying. His family connections procured him a ready welcome into what was, during the sessions of the legislature, the social center of the state but he refused all invitations. He made it his business to read law twelve hours a day. While he did associate with the twenty or thirty other law students in the town it was only for the purpose of discussing legal problems. These discussions were informal for Judge Chase did not approve of moot courts and debating societies. Instead, he directed Taney to attend all the sessions of the General Court and to take notes on what occurred. When the court was not in session he read and, as through Chase he had access to a considerable stock of books, he had, when he came to the bar, a thorough knowledge of all the classic texts of the common law.

Taney afterwards complained that he would have been better off if he had studied in the office of a practitioner rather than a judge as in that case he would have been required to write out pleadings, instead of acquiring merely a theoretical knowledge of what they should contain. As a young lawyer his lack of knowledge of the ordinary rules of thumb to be used in the preparation of pleadings may have seemed a drawback but in order to learn those rules of thumb he would have been required to spend his time, as many law students then did, as a mere copy clerk. In the long run his thorough acquaintance with all the English books on special pleading was a great advantage. Common law pleading then flourished in Maryland in all its intricacies and nothing raised a lawyer higher in the eyes of his brethren than a reputation as a special pleader. The intimacy which Taney established in Annapolis with the theory of traverses, rejoinders and surrebutters was the basis of the reputation which he established in the Supreme Court as an expert in procedure.

He undoubtedly received a much more thorough grounding in the law in Chase's office than he would have received in the office of a lawyer in active practice. The chief drawback was that it accentuated his tendency to keep to him-

self. The ability to mingle with people is much more easily
acquired than the solid and scholarly knowledge of the law
which Taney now had but when he was first admitted to the
bar he felt his shyness as an extreme handicap. There is
nothing very unusual in the fact that in his first case—an
assault case which was tried in the Mayor's Court—he had
difficulty in speaking and had to press his knees against the
table in order to keep steady on his feet. What is unusual
is that he never entirely got over his timidity and even when
he was a well-known public figure he had occasional attacks
of stage-fright.

Taney soon had another experience which made him
decide to devote himself systematically to acquiring ease
in social intercourse. His father was convinced that the
best way for his son to get established in practice was for
him to become a member of the House of Delegates, the
lower house of the state legislature. It was no great honor,
for Calvert County with scarcely eight thousand inhabitants,
only half of whom were white, had four delegates. Usually
there was not even a contest but when Roger ran for election
there were, to the surprise of the Taneys, five candidates
for the four seats. As there was a property qualification
there were only a few hundred voters. National party lines
were not yet followed in local elections which were conducted on a purely personal basis. Roger must have known
many of the voters personally but even so he found cam-
paigning extremely distasteful. He was elected but he always ascribed his election purely to the exertions of his
father and his father's fox-hunting friends.

So the following winter he returned to Annapolis as a
member of the legislature. This time he did not confine
himself to his room but took every opportunity to mix "freely
in the society of the place, which, at that period, was always
gay during the session of the General Assembly, and highly
cultivated and refined." He did not particularly enjoy his
new mode of life and blamed his lack of enjoyment on his

inability to take part in "that light and playful conversation which usually prevails at such assemblies."[9]

His venture into politics was short-lived. The next election was fought along national party lines and Taney went down to defeat with John Adams. The planter aristocracy of Maryland, unlike the planter aristocracy of Virginia, seems to have been on the whole Federalist, for the national parties split along different social lines in different sections. In Maryland, the border state, the Jeffersonian party took on more of the complexion of its northern than of its southern wing. There it was inclined to be the urban party, the industrial party. New England Federalism was not an industrial party but a commercial party. Pickering and his associates did not want to develop industries but to protect and expand the carrying trade, the import and export trade, which New England had originally developed under the protection of the British navigation laws. The Taneys had always been Federalists and Roger adopted the family political faith without question. In his early days he never showed any inclination to rebel, to develop ideas of his own and to follow them in the face of social disapproval. The frequent charges that the Jeffersonians were a French party may also have had some effect in confirming his, and his family's, Federalism. The Taneys were not likely to feel much sympathy for either the anti-clericism of the Jacobins or the deism of Jefferson.

Taney continued to call himself a Federalist long after that party had disappeared from national politics. His failure to be re-elected to the House of Delegates necessitated a complete change in his plans. The political advantages were the only temptation that Calvert County had and now that they were gone both he and his father agreed that it was advisable for him to set up in practice in a city. Baltimore naturally occurred to them but Taney "feared I should be lost in a large city" if he mingled with the thirty thousand

[9] Autobiography, TYLER, at 86.

inhabitants of that town. So he selected Frederick instead which was located in the extreme northern portion of the state and some ways inland. It had been founded in 1745 and its population was derived largely from Pennsylvania. While Carrollton Manor was located nearby, the hilly country, interspersed with fertile valleys, fostered a social system patterned after that of the North rather than after that of the South.

Taney lived and practiced law here, with an occasional interlude of politics, for twenty-two years. There was nothing spectacular about his career. Nor did he expect anything spectacular. He did not develop a protective armor of arrogance under which to conceal his shyness and modesty. That shyness and modesty appeared rather in a habitual humility and deference to the views of others. The outward humility and deference never left him but under it he gradually developed that iron will which afterwards distinguished him on the national scene. It was the humility of a medieval churchman, a type which Taney curiously resembled. Even the most distinct anecdote of his humility has a very ecclesiastical flavor. When he attended church he would, his priest reports, "stand at the outer door leading to the confessional, in a crowd of penitents, majority colored, waiting his turn for admission. I proposed to introduce him by another door to my confessional, but he would not accept of any deviation from the established custom."[10]

He had not come to Frederick as a total stranger. Several of his fellow students from Annapolis were practicing there and he was well supplied with introductions. The town was small but its bar was not excessively crowded and the older lawyers helped him to get started in practice. One of the fellow students was Francis Scott Key whose family had a plantation near the town. Taney soon became a frequent visitor there and found in Frank Key's sister, Ann Phebe, a girl who shared his love of flowers and of the contempla-

---

[10] Letter dated March 2, 1871 from (Father) John McElroy. TYLER, at 476.

tion of nature. His courtship did not proceed hurriedly. He did not regard the economic aspects of marriage lightly and it was not until five years after he settled in Frederick that he felt himself in a position to support a wife.

She was as devout an Episcopalian as he was a Roman Catholic but their religious differences did not stand in the way. Prior to their marriage they made what seems to have been the customary agreement at the time. This provided that the sons were to be raised as Catholics and the daughters as Episcopalians. As Taney had no sons who grew to manhood all his children were Episcopalians except a daughter who, in middle age, became a Catholic. Devout as he was, Taney never tried to break either the spirit or the letter of the agreement. He certainly looked forward to a future life with his wife and, if that involved any heterodoxy on his part, he was to that extent heterodox. Religion was not a subject which he cared to discuss and his extreme courtesy did not prevent him from cutting short a priest who, at a dinner at the Taneys, had begun to expatiate on the advantages of Catholicism, with the sharp remark that he never allowed religion to be discussed at his table.

Taney's study of common law procedure gradually made him, during his years at the Frederick bar, an expert special pleader. A decision acquired through the use of the intricacies of pleading was much more highly valued by the bar than one acquired on the merits but he seems never to have taken an undue advantage of his superior skill. Maryland lawyers boasted that the action of ejectment had been developed in their state to an extent unknown elsewhere but a young lawyer from Pennsylvania who settled in Frederick never forgot one of his first ejectment cases, a case in which Taney appeared for the other side. While the two lawyers sat in the courtroom waiting for the case to be called the latter leaned over and whispered to the Pennsylvanian that his "locations" were "all wrong" and suggested that he ask for an adjournment.

Taney had more difficulty in learning the art of persuading a jury than he had in acquiring a knowledge of pleading
but he gradually acquired this art also. It was never his
strong suit but he in time developed a style of address which,
coupled with his apostolic appearance, made him very effective in obtaining verdicts. A younger member of the Frederick bar described his method of obtaining verdicts as
consisting in the summing up of "the whole pith of his
argument in a single terse sentence, that would fix itself,
like an arrow of truth, in the hearts of the jury. In defending a person charged with an assault, who, though first
assailed, had so used his privilege of self-defense as to make
himself the aggressor by the heavy blows he had dealt,"
Taney "said, 'Gentlemen of the jury, if a man have [sic] a
head like a post, you must hammer him like a post.' "[11]

He mixed in politics to the extent that has always been
usual among small-town lawyers but he never allowed
politics to become his primary interest. He continued to be a
Federalist which in Maryland was largely the country party,
while the Jeffersonians, with their center of strength in
Baltimore, were the city party. A few years after his arrival
in Frederick, no doubt for the purpose of getting himself
established in his new home, he ran for the House of Delegates and was defeated. As his professional reputation increased his political importance increased for in his case it
was distinctly his professional reputation which carried him
forward politically rather than his political reputation which
carried him forward professionally. The War of 1812 split
the Maryland Federalists into two factions, one of which
opposed the war and the other of which believed it to be the
duty of everyone, now that war was declared, to support the
administration. The latter faction were called Coodies from
a newspaper character named Abimelech Coody. Taney was
the most prominent man in his county to join the Coodies
and was consequently for a time known locally as "King
Coody." His Coodyism did not lead him to desert his party

---

[11] TYLER, at 136.

and when, at the end of the war, the two factions were reunited, he was elected a Federalist state senator.

His Federalism, in truth, had little to do with national politics for that party had ceased to be a national party. What had once been its national program had been taken over almost bodily by the Jeffersonians as soon as they acquired control of the central government. Whatever it professed, the latter party was now the party of strong government. It had taken over the major portion of its opponents' platform. Jefferson had denounced his opponents as a pro-British faction but he himself had hardly become President before he meditated an alliance with England. Even during his administration the federal government had taken steps to provide roads and waterways, those internal improvements which were so badly needed and which, out of office, he had claimed were no business of the central government. And his successor went so far as to recharter the Bank of the United States. The party which still bore the name of Federalist survived in a few states only as a local party, divided from its opponents on local issues and united with the Federalists of other states only through the use of a common name.

Prior to the War of 1812 Taney showed little interest in national politics. He called himself a Federalist originally because his father had done so. He continued to do so because to him that party represented the rural type of civilization which he preferred. He did not recognize the Jeffersonians as the rural party, the party of the countryside. To him they were rather the industrial and commercial party whose strength lay in the bustling metropolis of Baltimore where he himself had refused to live for fear he "would be lost in a great city." As he saw the Jeffersonians purchase Louisiana, commit the central government to the building of roads and canals and finally recharter the central bank of issue that party became more and more identified in his mind with that tendency in American society which he abhorred—the tendency toward industrialization, expansion and exploitation of natural resources.

As he grew older and the slavery question became more and more important he analyzed the situation as a struggle between two types of civilization, that of New England and that of the South. On this analysis he did not hesitate to align himself with the South. It is significant that he seems to have disregarded the middle states and to have treated the opposing type of civilization as the peculiar product of New England. The South to which he gave his allegiance was not the South of Jefferson Davis, not the South of cotton, sugar and rice but the South he had known in Calvert County and perhaps even more the South he had known in Frederick. It was a South in which the factors which brought on the war between the sections were largely absent. He had been glad to leave Calvert County for even the long established and relatively undeveloped plantation system of the tidewater regions had not appealed to him. Frederick, a few miles south of the Mason and Dixon Line, where both the crops and the small farms on which most of them were raised were much the same as in Pennsylvania, and where only the presence of slaves as house servants and a certain social veneer partook of the South, expressed his social ideal. It was much the same as that of the great Virginians of the previous generation, of Washington, of Jefferson and of Mason.

Taney was no advocate of slavery. He regarded the slave trade with the deepest disgust but he did not favor Marshall's desire to solve the problem by transporting the negroes to Africa. There can be no question that Taney regarded negroes as a definitely inferior species of humanity. But he did not think that for that reason they should be exposed to all the rigors permitted by the institution of slavery. As an inferior people, as weak members of society, they were entitled to special help and consideration from the stronger members of society. He did not favor forced emancipation; he looked forward rather to a gradual and voluntary eman-

cipation. He favored particularly a practice which the
Maryland law made possible by which a slave could, with
the consent of his master, buy his freedom. This procedure
took the form of a conveyance of the title to the slave, by
the master, to a third party to be held in trust. If the slave
made the payments provided for in the deed of trust the
trustee would emancipate him. If the payments were not
made, title to the slave would revert to the master. The
trustee under such an arrangement occupied a rather thank-
less position and the number of times that Taney occupied
it indicates clearly that he took pleasure in doing so. To him
there was not only a general moral obligation to aid slaves
who desired to improve their status but a professional obligation to give them the aid of his legal skill by acting as
trustee. It was typical of his conception of his professional
duties. He always thought of himself as primarily a peace-
maker and only secondarily as an advocate. He always did
his best to work out a reconciliation between the parties
before proceeding to litigation.

Although he was not the eldest son he seems to have inherited some slaves. It is not clear whether this was at the
death of his father or when his elder brother later either died
or disappeared. Taney followed a higher moral course with
these slaves than he advocated for other people. He was not
a rich man, he never was a rich man, and slaves were valuable property. Taney never indulged in business speculation
and it was a number of years after he was married before he
was able to buy a house. When he did, it was a very modest
dwelling which, while detached, was built with the flat sides
which indicated that the builder had in mind the possibility
of attaching houses on either side in accordance with the
thrifty habit that is still followed in eastern Pennsylvania.
Despite the substantial addition which the slaves must have
made to his fortune Taney emancipated them. It was an act
of charity even for those who were too old to work, for he
paid pensions to the latter until they died.

In this last procedure he reveals his solution of the negro

question. He was convinced that the negroes were an inferior race, incapable of managing their own concerns, but
at the same time he abhorred "those reptiles who live by
trading in human flesh, and enrich themselves by tearing the
husband from the wife, the infant from the bosom of the
mother."[12] His solution was gradual freedom for the slaves
without governmental intervention. The negroes thus freed
were to live in a state of dependence on their former masters
who, in turn, were to have the obligation of helping and defending their former slaves. It was to be a relation like that
of client and patron in ancient Rome. The similarity is more
striking when it is recalled that many of those clients were
freedmen.

His solution of the slavery question appeared practicable
in Frederick where free negroes were not uncommon but it
overlooked the great commercial plantations of the far South
and, above all, it overlooked the pecuniary, rather than
patriarchal, nature of the civilization in which he lived.
Taney was not blind to this last objection. He realized the
constantly increasing pecuniary character of American civilization and he hated it. He ascribed the origin of the pecuniary element in the life around him to New England and its
political fostering to Jefferson's successors.

His analysis of the social forces at work in the country
brings out that element in his character which was responsible for his great judicial mistake—his provincialism. It was
a refined and cultivated type of provincialism which was
concealed in ordinary intercourse by the urbanity of his
manners but it was none the less deep for all that. There is
no record that he ever made a journey of any consequence
on his own initiative. There is not even any indication that
he ever made any business trips out of his own state before
his appointment to Jackson's cabinet. He does not seem to
have kept up any acquaintances he may have made in college and he seems never to have visited Carlisle after his
graduation. Even as a judge he did not travel extensively

---

[12] Taney, quoted by TYLER, at 130.

for the circuit court system had been considerably modified
since Jay's time and Taney's circuit was always the one
closest to Washington. Nor did he make up for his lack of
travel in other ways. He read, but his reading was never
very catholic. The society of Frederick was limited but he
did not particularly cultivate the limited society which the
town afforded. He never evidenced any desire to enlarge
his acquaintance or to meet new people. Even when, late in
life, he emerged onto the national scene, he was inclined to
keep to himself and to limit his company to old friends and
to the friends and relatives of old friends. So during his two
decades in Frederick he was content to remain by himself,
or in the company of his family, and to satisfy his intellectual
desires with professional study.

Almost as soon as Taney was established at the Frederick
bar he had become counsel to the local bank. He was retained purely for professional reasons for he never showed
any liking for, or interest in, banking or any other form of
business. All these local banks which were scattered
throughout the country issued their own notes which usually
circulated only in a limited area. No attempt was made in
connection with the establishment of the Bank of the United
States to drive these local currencies out of circulation. The
states continued to charter as many banks as they wished
and to grant the privilege of issuing notes to all of them.
The charters of these banks were nearly always granted as
a matter of political favor. They were the source of endless corruption in the state legislatures and, together with
similar charters for other purposes which were granted during the same period, the origin of the phrase "special privi-
leges"—a phrase which did not lose its political usefulness
long after these special acts of incorporation had been superseded nearly everywhere by general incorporation and banking laws. These local banks were subject to practically no
supervision; their management was frequently incredibly
scandalous, and they had a habit of suspending payment of
their own notes without closing. These practices resulted in

endless losses not only to the commercial but even more to the wage-earning classes. The local bankers made it their business to see to it that the people understood that these evils were not due to the mismanagement of the local banks but to the wicked moneyed monster, the Bank of the United States, in which even Englishmen were stockholders and which President Madison, with a flagrant disregard of the principles of his party, had rechartered. The local bankers were in much more intimate contact with the people than the national bankers; they were influential in state politics or they would not have received their charters in the first place, and their hatred of the Bank of the United States helped build up a great popular antipathy for that institution. This antipathy first manifested itself in Maryland in the passage of the taxing act which was declared unconstitutional in the *McCulloch Case* but it was also the force which pushed Taney into the Chief Justiceship.

The first step in bringing him upon the national scene was his removal to Baltimore in 1823. This action was governed by professional motives. So long as he remained in Frederick a good part of his time was necessarily taken up in jury work but he had argued enough appeals to get himself known to the bar of the whole state and to satisfy him that it was the form of activity most suited to his talents. In the early part of the nineteenth century the Baltimore bar was the most brilliant in the country. There was as yet no Washington bar of any importance and, as Baltimore was the large city nearest to the capital, its lawyers were frequently retained on appeals to the Supreme Court.

For a long time the Maryland bar had been dominated by Luther Martin but his continual drunkenness finally ended in paralysis. He was succeeded by William Pinkney whose habit of shocking the judges by wearing purple doeskin gloves, "fit for a ballroom," when arguing a case, did not seem to interfere with his ability to obtain decisions. When Pinkney's death was announced to the House of Representatives by Randolph of Roanoke in that speech in which, himself a layman, he so magnificently eulogized the profession of the law, Taney knew that it was now or never. He was forty-six, he was at the head of the bar in his own community, he had mingled in politics sufficiently to be generally known throughout the state and he had had enough cases in the Court of Appeals and had handled them well enough so that he could reasonably expect that his brethren of the bar would turn to him when they wanted the help of an experienced appellate lawyer. So he sold his house in Frederick—at a loss—and moved to the city. He apparently never visited Frederick again.

His expectations were partly realized. The practice which Pinkney had left was too rich a prize to be allowed to drop into the hands of a relatively unknown man from the interior of the state. William Wirt who had been for years Attorney-General of the United States likewise aspired to succeed Pinkney and it was to him that the major share of Pinkney's business fell. There was enough left to satisfy Taney but the most important client he acquired in Baltimore was the Union Bank. A separate class of corporation lawyers had not yet arisen and Taney advised the bank on all its affairs. That institution was controlled by Thomas Ellicott, an aggressive and, as events showed, unscrupulous Quaker. Ellicott looked on the Bank of the United States as a competitor whose superior currency kept the notes of his own bank from circulating as freely as they might otherwise have done and whose superior solvency attracted deposits which his bank might otherwise have obtained.

The great advocate was as clay in the hands of the Quaker. The banker, as is usual in such cases, found moral reasons for his business desires. He was soon a frequent visitor at Taney's house and the two engaged in long discussions of the banking situation. The lawyer did not profess to know anything about banking; he had accepted the national bank on the word of the many eminent statesmen of all parties who had said that some such institution was necessary to act as a depositary of government funds, to provide a stable currency and to transfer capital from those sections of the country where it was plentiful to those sections where it was scarce. He knew that central banks were usual and that the Bank of the United States was modeled after the Bank of England and the Bank of France. He had previously thought that the public interest was amply protected by the government ownership of part of the stock and by the government nomination of five of the directors. He respected property rights and the bank had paid a substantial cash bonus for its charter at a time when United States bonds were in default and the government was in desperate need of money. He knew, too, that the bank was so far from being a private institution that Nicholas Biddle, its president and the dominant figure in its affairs, was not even a financier by trade but a Greek scholar, literateur and amateur architect who sat on the bank's board not as the representative of the private stockholders but as one of the government directors. Biddle had taken the position rather against his will and only at the insistence of President Monroe but once on the board of the bank he had taken his new duties with a zeal and success which can be measured by our national habit of depositing our money in imitation Greek temples—a monument to Biddle's curious assortment of talents.

Taney had never professed to know anything about banking and had never given the subject serious thought. He had always given his clients legal advice without troubling himself about the way they conducted their business. But, as he smoked his ever-present cigar and listened to Ellicott talk, a great light dawned. The bank, that great financial institution run from Philadelphia, Taney discovered, was the citadel of those tendencies which were undermining American culture—his culture, the rural, semi-patriarchal culture which he had known in Calvert County and in Frederick. He had long appreciated that that culture was in danger but he had never before had any clear notion what could be done to save it. But it took Peggy O'Neale's reputation to put him into a position where he could apply his new knowledge.

Party lines had disappeared. The Federalists were only a local party and in state politics Taney remained one of their members. He was rewarded with the appointment of Attorney-General of Maryland in 1827—a position which did not require him to give up his private practice. He was appointed as a Federalist by a Federalist governor but his allegiance to this party in local affairs had not prevented him from supporting Jackson for the Presidency in 1824. Taney saw in the Tennessee frontiersman the best prospect of maintaining the rural culture which he loved. Jackson again received his support in 1828 but Taney did not enter into politics so actively that he could reasonably expect to be offered an appointment. He was content with his practice and with the leadership of the state bar which the possession of the Attorney-Generalship implied.

Jackson had never even heard of him until the refusal of Mrs. Berrien, the wife of his Attorney-General, to call on Peggy O'Neale, now Mrs. Eaton, required him to find a new head for the Department of Justice. The President's rule was adamant. Either his cabinet officers made their wives call on Mrs. Eaton or they themselves left the cabinet. Jackson had no definite idea how to fill the resulting vacancy.

His choice was limited by the fact that the Attorney-General was not a full-fledged member of the cabinet. The government was still conducted on such a primitive scale that it did not require a full-time legal staff. The Attorney-General was merely a distinguished lawyer in private practice who was retained by the government to represent it in the rare cases before the Supreme Court in which it was involved and to give occasional opinions to the other cabinet officers. Yet the Attorney-General had to be located reasonably close to Washington. The part-time nature of the job and the difficulties of communication combined to limit the occupants of the position largely to lawyers from Virginia or Maryland. As the ablest lawyers from that region tended to gravitate to Baltimore, the President naturally looked in that direction.

He asked his physician, a Marylander named William
Jones, for suggestions. "I know a man," replied the doctor,
"who will suit for Attorney-General." "Who is he?" was the
answer. "Roger B. Taney, of the Baltimore bar. He is now
the leading lawyer of Maryland, and a zealous friend of
your administration. I learned his character while I studied
medicine with your friend Dr. William Tyler, of Frederick,
where Mr. Taney then resided. He was a Federalist, but
after war was declared in 1812, gave it his hearty support."[13]
The rumor soon went around that Taney was being considered and, after some wire-pulling by his brother-in-law,
Francis Scott Key, the position was offered and accepted.
There is no record of Mrs. Taney's views on Peggy O'Neale
but as Taney kept his home in Baltimore perhaps the problem never arose.

With Taney's appointment the nature of the Attorney-
Generalship changed. The new occupant of that office was
content to be the government's law officer with one exception but that exception involved the most controversial policy
of the administration. His long conferences with Ellicott
were to bear fruit. Taney felt that he understood the banking situation and that now that he was in a position of influence it was his duty to do something about it. He had seen
in Jackson the champion of a rural, unmonetized culture;
he intended to test the validity of that conception.

The President was known not to have any great love for
the bank but he had certainly not taken office as its enemy.
A few members of his kitchen cabinet were its enemies,
largely because they thought of it as a branch of the government and were disgusted to find that they were unable to
apply the spoils system to it. None of the cabinet officers
was particularly opposed to the bank and it might have
survived and obtained a new charter if it had not been for
Taney. Urged on by his Attorney-General, Jackson first
vetoed the act to recharter the bank and then determined
not to wait for the expiration of the existing charter but to

[13] TYLER, at 167.

remove the government funds from the bank immediately. By statute, the control of those funds was in the hands of the Secretary of the Treasury who was required to render his report, not to the President, but directly to Congress. This position was held by McLane who was known to be friendly to the bank. He was disposed of by promoting him to the state department. William J. Duane, a Philadelphia lawyer, was appointed to the vacancy chiefly because he was a notorious enemy of the bank. Unfortunately for him he was also an honest man and a clear thinker. He had never come under the spell of Thomas Ellicott. He hated the bank as much, if not more, than Taney but he was unable to appreciate Taney's distinction between the morality of a banker who did business under a state charter and the morality of a banker who did business under a federal charter. Duane could not understand how the average man was necessarily benefited by the substitution for the stable currency of the "moneyed aristocracy" of the numerous, fluctuating and unsound currencies of the "people's" banks. He hated the bank but he did not want to destroy it until a satisfactory substitute had been devised.

Neither Jackson nor Taney agreed with the Secretary of the Treasury. Taney, with the help of his banking mentor, Ellicott, prepared a statement of why it was necessary that the government funds be removed from the bank immediately. This document Jackson read to the cabinet as his own but, while even Duane admitted that it was a strong paper[14], it did not meet the supreme test of strength for none of the cabinet officers was convinced by it. The President had stronger weapons in his arsenal than argument. Since Duane could not be convinced he was removed.

So when Taney put his feet on his desk and a cigar in his mouth and leaned back to see how the paper on the deposits which he had written for the President read in print he did so not as Attorney-General but as Secretary of the Treasury. He had not wanted his new position. He was not a financier

---

[14] SWISHER, at 232.

and had no desire to become one. He had never practiced law as a stepping stone to something else. There was to him no intellectual pleasure equal to the study of a knotty problem in special pleading and no triumph equal to obtaining the decision of an appellate court in a hard case. He accepted the Treasury purely from a sense of duty. He had been the chief factor in causing the President to decide to remove the deposits and since no other member of the cabinet would carry out that policy Taney had to become Secretary of the Treasury.

He immediately stopped making further deposits of government funds in the bank. He was fearful of the power of the "moneyed aristocracy" and knew not how the bank would take revenge. As a protection against any possible retaliation he made out large drafts against the government's existing balance in the bank. He sent these drafts to individuals whom he believed he could trust, located in various leading cities, with instructions to present them only in certain specified contingencies. He entrusted one of these drafts, for half a million dollars, to Thomas Ellicott. Taney's faith that Ellicott's financial advice was governed by a disinterested zeal for the public good had a rude awakening. The bank made no move to retaliate against Taney's order forbidding further government deposits with it but Ellicott, in total disregard of his instructions, immediately presented his draft. It was honored and, as soon as Ellicott had received the money, he used it in a personal stock speculation.[15] The Quaker could not even find a good excuse to give Taney for this conduct.

All this occurred during a recess of Congress but when that body met it was in no mood to approve the government's course. Its first result had been a stringency of credit and there were foreshadowings of the long depression that was soon to come. A congressional committee was appointed to investigate the action of the Secretary of the Treasury and promptly dug up the Ellicott scandal. Probably no man

[15] CHANNING, V at 449.

could have been found who felt an imputation of graft as
deeply as Taney and there does not seem to have been any
serious accusation that he had profited personally but the
incident did not add to the already feeble financial prestige
of the new Secretary of the Treasury. The situation was so
bad that Jackson did not send Taney's nomination to the
Senate until he was forced to do so by the approaching end
of the session. Upon receiving the nomination the Senate
promptly rejected it.

So Taney returned to private life with the feeling that he
had been unjustly treated. He saw the bank everywhere.
He was sure that Nicholas Biddle, its president, was schem-
ing to break up his practice. Even the numerous public
banquets tendered him did not weaken this feeling. His
close relations with Jackson continued and their correspondence on public affairs was intimate and frequent. The
Senate's rejection of Taney as Secretary of the Treasury had
only increased the President's high regard for him. Jackson
was determined to get Taney back into public life as speedily
as possible and, very likely, if Taney had been ambitious to
do so, he, rather than Van Buren, might have been Jackson's
heir. Taney was not ambitious in that direction and he and
Van Buren were the best of friends.

The newspapers and politicians of the country were unable to conceive how Taney could be both an able, learned
and conservative lawyer and the radical enemy of the bank.
Many people never were able to grasp the conception of such
a character and the shifts in Taney's reputation are among
the most curious in the history of reputations. When Taney
was first appointed to the Supreme Court, a large proportion
of the population regarded him as a radical of some sort or
other—they did not all agree as to exactly what kind. He
was later to be denounced—in a fervor of denunciation
such as no other American judge has ever aroused—as the
wicked Chief Justice who conspired with President Buchanan to force slavery on a free people. Long after his death
there was a reversion to the original conception. Taney the

lawyer was forgotten. The Dred Scott decision was over-looked or explained away. He was remembered simply as the enemy of the bank and with that one fact as a basis he now seems well on the way to gaining a reputation as an enemy of property.

These shifts in his reputation do more than overlook specific aspects of his career. They overlook the very nature of the judicial process. Courts undoubtedly legislate but so does every non-legislative branch of the government. The decision of a court establishes a rule of law which influences conduct but so do the decisions of traffic policemen, tax col-lectors and customs inspectors. The difference between these different types of decisions lies partly in their scope but more in the manner in which they are made. To take an illustration from Taney's own conduct in regard to the bank: It is possible that if the question of the constitutionality of the act incorporating the Bank of the United States had come before him judicially his opinion of the political unwisdom of that act, working through that portion of his mentality which psychologists call the unconscious, might have led him to favor the arguments against its constitutionality. But the specific conduct for which the Senate refused to confirm his appointment as Secretary of the Treasury was his action in refusing to deposit further government funds in the bank. It is impossible to conceive of Taney, as a judge, restraining any Secretary of the Treasury from depositing further funds in the Bank of the United States. As a politician he was ardently in favor of preventing such deposits. As a judge it would have been necessary to justify his decision by fitting it logically into the general body of law which he was adminis-tering. The logic would not necessarily have to be infallible but it would have to be at least such that the general body of law after the decision—of which general body that deci-sion would now be a part—would retain the essentials of predictability and stability. Those factors do not carry great weight in the determination of rules of conduct by the legis-lature.

It is difficult even for men who are themselves able lawyers to bear these differences in mind in the thick of a
political fight. The news gradually got around Washington
that Jackson intended to appoint Taney to the Supreme
Court on the first vacancy. Mr. Justice Duval of Maryland
was very old and very ill but he clung to his seat in the hope
of outliving Jackson's administration. When he learned that
Taney was to be his successor his fears vanished and he
resigned immediately. Marshall shared Duval's view that
Taney's financial heresies would not prevent him from being
an able judge. The Chief Justice did a little discreet lobby-
ing in the nominee's behalf but the Senate was not to be
moved. Probably more as a punishment for Taney's political
actions than through fear of his decisions, the Senate adjourned, on the night of March 3, after voting to postpone
action on the nomination. When the passage of this motion
was announced to Jackson he "replied that it was past twelve
o'clock and he would receive no message from the damned
scoundrels."[16] By the next session the Chief Justiceship
itself was vacant, an event which had not occurred in the
political life of any of the men then in power.

The more difficulty Jackson had in inducing the Senate to
ratify one of his nominations, the better he liked the nominee.
The Senate had twice refused to ratify his nomination of
Taney and had also refused to ratify his nomination of Van
Buren as minister to England. These rejections by the
Senate automatically made Taney and Van Buren the special
favorites of the President. Now that Marshall was dead and
his own term was drawing to a close, Jackson easily divided
the honors. Van Buren was to be his successor in the White
House and Taney was to succeed Marshall on the bench. So
when the Senate met for its next session one of the first items
of business to come before it was the nomination of Roger
Brooke Taney as Chief Justice. The Senate struggled with
the nomination for nearly three months. But it was no
longer possible to withstand the President's overwhelming

---

[16] WARREN, I at 802.

popularity. Taney's nomination was confirmed and, two months after he took his seat, he had the pleasure of swearing in his friend Van Buren as President.

In a sense the appointment put the Court to a test similar to that which had been imposed on it when Marshall had been left to face Jefferson. Then the question had been whether the Court was really an independent and coordinate branch of the government; whether it could survive when it was headed by a man who was out of sympathy with the party in control of the other two branches of the government. The question now was whether there really was such a thing as constitutional law; whether the decisions of the Court would continue to have that stability and logical continuity which are essential to a body of law or whether they would show that sudden about-face which is characteristic of the decisions of a political body.

If Taney had been the radical that Clay and Webster pictured him to be it is possible that there would have been such an about-face, but a careful analysis of his early life makes such a conception of his character seem almost incredible. He was born in a family of country gentry—the class which in every country and every age has always been regarded as the most conservative. As a young man he had never shown any traits of rebellion in his character. He had followed his father's wishes in the choice of a profession and in the selection of a mode of establishing himself in that profession. He had been very happy in that profession. So far was he from a reformer that he had made himself a master of that branch of his profession—special pleading— which reformers were even then attacking on every side. Those reformers never gained his sympathy and he remained until his death a champion of common law procedure in all its nicety. He had even clung to the political party of his father despite the fact that during most of Taney's mature life it must have been as evident to him as it was to everyone else in the country that that party was dead beyond recall. It was not a background which frightened Duval—who had

been the judge before whom Taney had pleaded his first case
—or Marshall with his keen and dispassionate judgment of
character.

The Whig leaders, in their eagerness to find an issue on
which to focus their dislike of Jackson, had selected the
bank. It was an issue which had proved disastrous in the
election but it had resulted in identifying Taney in the public mind with all the various brands of the radicalism of
the 1830s which had assembled around Jackson. In only one
case during Taney's long tenure of the Chief Justiceship did
the identification prove correct and then he voted against the
majority of the Court. His dissenting opinion in that case
more nearly expressed the extreme theory of state sovereignty than any other opinion ever delivered in the Supreme
Court. Rhode Island brought suit against Massachusetts to
settle a dispute over the boundary between the two states.[17]
Massachusetts argued that the Court had no jurisdiction in
view of the sovereign nature of the parties and Taney agreed
with this argument.

This dissent represented the limit of his deviation from
Marshall. When that case was decided the extreme Whig
fear of Taney had already passed. The case [18] which in the
popular mind of the time—and which still in the minds of
many historians—measured the difference between Taney
and his predecessor was decided in 1837, before Taney's reputation as a politician had had an opportunity to be forgotten.

In the latter part of the eighteenth century the Massachusetts legislature had granted a franchise to a group incorporated as the Proprietors of the Charles River Bridge to build
a toll bridge from Boston to Charlestown over the Charles
near its mouth. At the time there was no comparable piece
of engineering in the country and to many the idea of building a bridge over the tidewater portion of a fair-sized river

[17] *Rhode Island* v. *Massachusetts*, 12 Pet. 657, 9 L. Ed. 1233
(1838).
[18] *Charles River Bridge* v. *Warren Bridge*, 11 Pet. 420, 9 L. Ed.
773 (1837).

seemed fantastic. Investing in the project was regarded as highly speculative. But all the roads from the territory north of Boston converged in Charlestown Square near the Charlestown end of the proposed bridge and, if such a bridge could be built, the profits would undoubtedly be great. The lure was sufficient so that the promoters or "adventurers," as they were called, finally succeeded in raising the necessary capital. They succeeded also, after many difficulties, in building the bridge. When completed, it was regarded as an engineering marvel and was widely copied. The profits of the promoters were great and the stock of their corporation became gilt-edged. By the next generation the difficulties had been forgotten, for it was no longer such a feat to build a bridge, and the profits alone were remembered. It seemed an outrage to the people of the Commonwealth of Massachusetts that they should have to pay for the privilege of driving a wagon from Charlestown to Boston. A scheme was devised to destroy the lucrative monopoly held by the Charles River Bridge Company. A new bridge company was chartered, under the name of the Proprietors of the Warren Bridge, with power to build a competing bridge on which they were to charge lower tolls and which was to belong to the Commonwealth in a comparatively short time.

The stockholders in the old bridge company brought suit to prevent the building of the new bridge. Their case was built on the doctrine of the *Dartmouth College Case* decided by Marshall nearly twenty years before. That case had decided that an act of a state legislature interfering with a college charter constituted a violation of the constitutional provision that "No State shall . . . pass any . . . Law impairing the Obligation of Contracts." If a college charter was a contract so was the charter of a bridge company. And, said they, while their charter did not expressly say so it clearly implied that no competing charters would be granted.

Taney refused to admit this minor premise. The case had been in the Court for years and it was well known that it was only the inability of the Court to agree which had pre-

vented it from being decided during Marshall's Chief Justiceship. Taney now wrote the majority opinion and the approach to the problem which he adopted seems to have been
his own. It was a most lawyerlike approach and revealed
the man who had drunk deep of the tradition of the common law. The ancient English precedents had established
the doctrine that grants by the Crown were to be strictly
construed. This principle was the basis of Taney's opinion.
A state charter, like a Crown grant, gave the grantee only
what was expressly set forth. Since this charter did not
expressly state that no charters to build competing bridges
would be granted no such prohibition could be implied.

Reduced to the actual points involved the *Charles River
Bridge Case* does not sound revolutionary. The basis for the
horror with which erudite lawyers such as Story and Kent
viewed the decision is not to be found either in the facts of
the case or in Taney's opinion. That horror was based
entirely on the perfervid politics of the period. It was not
Taney's law, but his character, which Story and Kent feared.
They knew that legalistically his opinion was perfectly de-
fensible; that the most that could be said against it was that
they took a different view of a technical question than he
did. Nor could the conclusion which Taney had reached by
the use of technical arguments reasonably frighten any conservative. That conclusion may have destroyed a great part
of the value of the investments of many of the stockholders
in the old bridge company but it certainly did not destroy
property values to anything like the same extent as Marshall's decision in the steamboat case. A monopoly of toll
bridges over the Charles River was a peanut business compared with a monopoly of steam navigation at the mouths of
the Mississippi and the Hudson.

In the glow of the fire which Taney's fight against the
bank had lighted few stopped to make a dollar and cents
comparison of the effect of the bridge case and of the steamboat case. Most of Taney's enemies deemed it unnecessary.
They did not view Taney's opinion as merely adding shading

to the rough sketch of the law of the contracts clause which Marshall had made. The immediate view of the new Chief Justice's enemies was that he was merely preparing the ground for a total abandonment of the doctrine that a state could not pass a law impairing the obligation of contracts.

In the bridge case Taney had followed one Marshall precedent which he never adopted as his own. This was the habit which had so irritated Jefferson; the habit of having the Chief Justice act as the spokesman of the Court in great constitutional cases. That custom died with Marshall. Almost simultaneously with the bridge case, Taney assigned the writing of the majority opinions in two important cases[19] to two of his associates. The change may have been in part due to the extreme courtesy with which he was accustomed to treat his fellow judges. But the same judges who testify to his unfailing ease and courtesy in the conference room also state that he could be very stubborn in his own opinion. The stubbornness was a trait which he developed with age for there is little evidence of it in his early life. It would not have been surprising if that trait, combined with his position as Chief Justice, had now made him endeavor to rule the Court as Marshall had done. Neither his courtesy nor his apparent humility can explain his failure to make the attempt. Neither had prevented him as Attorney-General from forcing his way into a question of financial policy —a question which was clearly outside his province. It may be that the position of the Court had changed so much between 1801 and 1835 that if Marshall had been appointed in the latter year instead of in the former he would never have gained his dominant position. The curious thing about Taney is that he never attempted to gain such a position. The explanation must be sought not in Taney's character but in the nature of the cases which came before him.

The clause of the constitution which most often came up

---

[19] *Briscoe* v. *Bank of Kentucky,* 11 Pet. 257, 9 L. Ed. 709 (1837); *City of New York* v. *Miln,* 11 Pet. 102, 9 L. Ed. 648 (1837).

for construction during Taney's tenure of office was the clause giving Congress power over interstate and foreign commerce. The *Blackbird Creek Case* during Marshall's time foreshadowed the difficulties which now faced the Court. The first of these cases to arise involved the validity of a state statute requiring a report on every passenger who was landed in the ports of that state. [20] Taney himself did not write the opinion but the statute was upheld by a statement that it was within the police power of the state. The invention of a name for the reserved powers of the state over interstate and foreign commerce was of little help. This case was followed a decade later by the *Passenger Cases* [21] which involved somewhat more stringent state regulations of the same general type. The question split the Court wide open and Taney, who thought the regulations valid, was among the minority. Even that case did not fully indicate the difficulty which the Court had in working out a predictable line of demarcation between the power of the states and of the central government over interstate and foreign commerce. Two years before the *Passenger Cases*, in 1847, a case [22] was decided which involved the validity of a New Hampshire statute which forbade the sale of intoxicating liquor without a license from the selectmen of the town in which the sale was made. In defiance of these laws a Boston merchant took a keg of gin into New Hampshire and sold it. All the members of the Court agreed that his conduct was not justified by the constitution but they could not agree why. It took six separate opinions to set forth the unanimous conclusion of the nine judges.

Taney evidenced throughout his tenure of office a disinclination to hold state acts void as violations of the commerce clause. This disinclination did not extend to other clauses of the constitution. His peculiar attitude toward the commerce clause may have been in part a reflection of his dis-

---

[20] *City of New York* v. *Miln,* supra, note 19.
[21] 7 How. 283, 12 L. Ed. 702 (1948).
[22] *License Cases,* 5 How. 504, 12 L. Ed. 256 (1847).

like for the pecuniary civilization which he saw rising about
him for after his experiences with the central bank he may
have seen some connection between the power of the central
government over commerce and the growth of the commercial classes. Such a disinclination to interfere with the independence of the state governments can scarcely be traced in
his decisions on other constitutional points.

The first case in which he showed what might be called
the Federalist aspect of his judicial character was *Earle* v.
Bank of Augusta. [23] This case arose out of the purchase in
Alabama by a Georgia bank of a bill of exchange. The bill
had been drawn by an Alabama firm on a New York firm to
the order of Earle, a resident of Alabama who indorsed it, in
Alabama, to the Georgia bank. After a protest for non-pay-
ment that bank sued Earle in the federal court. He defended
on the ground that a Georgia bank could have no existence
outside the State of Georgia and that therefore there had
been no transaction between him and the bank. There was
little in the way of precedent to restrain Taney from taking
any view of the case which he desired. If he had wished to
live up to his political reputation as a states' rights man he
could easily have taken the judicial position that a corporation could have no existence whatever outside the state of its
incorporation. He did not do so. He took the position, instead, that a corporation could, through its agents, do business in a state other than the state of its incorporation, at
least until the second state forbade it to do so. The case became the basis of that tangled mass of law concerning the
doing of business by corporations outside the states in which
they are incorporated which was to grow up as the business
of the country became organized along national lines but
remained in the hands of corporations with state charters.

The popular representation of Taney as a judge whose
constitutional views were diametrically opposed to those of

---

[23] 13 Pet. 519, 10 L. Ed. 274 (1839). For a full discussion of this
case and its effects see HENDERSON.

Marshall is based, so far as it is based on his judicial conduct and not on his Jacksonianism, on a few cases which happened to come up in the first few years after his appointment. Thereafter, with the exception of cases involving the commerce clause, the landmarks in the stream of constitutional decisions in which Taney took part were strongly Federalistic. In the first of these [24] it was decided that the governor of Vermont had no power to seize, at the request of the Canadian authorities, a fugitive from justice and extradite him to Canada. The ground of the decision was that the action of the governor was an interference with the exclusive authority of the central government in foreign affairs. It was followed by a case [25] in which a state moratorium law which had been passed in the depression of the late 1830s was held invalid. The statute in question was very mild. It merely provided that the mortgaged property could not be sold on foreclosure for less than two-thirds of the appraised value and that the mortgagor was to have a year after the sale in which to redeem the property sold.

Taney's enemies had charged him with destroying the value of the contracts clause in the constitution by his opinion in the *Charles River Bridge Case.* If they really believed the charge his opinion in the mortgage case must have seemed incredible. This moratorium law would probably have passed the Court of the 1930s without great difficulty but Taney, in the opinion which he wrote for the Court of 1843, found that, so far as it applied to mortgages which had already been made, it impaired the obligation of contracts. A few years later he wrote an opinion in a case [26] greatly extending the federal admiralty jurisdiction over inland waterways, a jurisdiction which, in the heyday of the river steamboats, was by no means popular. The tendency of Taney's mind which had appeared in his refusal to pass on a disputed state boundary cropped up only once thereafter. This time it appeared not in a dissent but in a majority

---

[24] *Holmes* v. *Jennison,* 14 Pet. 540, 10 L. Ed. 579 (1840).
[25] *Bronson* v. *Kenzie,* 1 How. 311, 11 L. Ed. 143 (1843).
[26] *The Genesee Chief,* 12 How. 443, 13 L. Ed. 1058 (1851).

decision; an opinion which has, in addition, since stood the test of time.

Rhode Island, which had been practically independent as a British colony, had not, on becoming a state, adopted a new constitution. The old colonial charter had simply been continued as the constitution of the new state but in course of time the method of representation which it provided had become intensely unpopular. The charter government, as the "ins" were called, refused to entertain any suggestion of reform. Finally the "outs" fell back on the contract theory of government. They purported to organize a new state government through the action of the people themselves. A man named Dorr was elected governor under the constitution which they thus adopted. The charter government declared martial law and succeeded in suppressing the Dorr government. The rebels contrived to arrange a piece of private litigation so as to raise the question of the legality of the Dorr government. Taney wrote the majority opinion in which the Court refused to hear the controversy on the ground that the dispute was purely political in character and its decision was outside the scope of the judicial power. [27]

*   *   *   *   *   *

Taney had now reached the height of his career. He had come into office as a demagogue but no one could find a trace of the demagogue in his judicial actions. It was impossible that everyone should be completely satisfied by his decision in every case but they were now all well satisfied that in every case his decision was judicial, not political. The suspicion of his integrity as a judge which was to cloud the latter years of his life had yet to arise. For the present, in the calm twilight of the era which preceded the storm of civil war, as his apostolic figure was seen administering the oath of office to one undistinguished President after another, there was universal agreement that he was the ideal Chief Justice. Even Clay felt moved to apologize for the virulence with which he had opposed Taney's confirmation and before

[27] *Luther* v. *Borden*, 7 How. 1, 12 L. Ed. 581 (1849).

returning home from one of his last sessions the Kentuckian was seen to seek out the Chief Justice and express his second judgment. "Mr. Chief Justice," said Clay, "there was no man in the land who regretted your appointment to the place you now hold more than I did; there was no member of the Senate who opposed it more than I did; but I have come to say to you, and I say it now in parting, perhaps for the last time,—I have witnessed your judicial career, and it is due to myself and due to you that I should say what has been the result; that I am satisfied now that no man in the United States could have been selected, more abundantly able to wear the ermine which Chief Justice Marshall honored." [28]

Yet with the benefit of hindsight we can see the personal factors which, when they came into contact with the mighty political problem of slavery, were to produce the later catastrophe. Taney was still in essentials the Maryland Federalist—the product of, and believer in, the Jeffersonian social system. His provincialism had, if anything, increased with age. He even went so far as to object to his daughter and son-in-law spending a summer in Newport on the ground that it showed a preference for the North over the South. "I have not the slightest confidence," he wrote them, in the "superior health of Newport over Old Point, and look upon it as nothing more than that unfortunate feeling of inferiority in the South, which believes everything in the North to be superior to what we have." [29] There is no definite evidence that Taney himself was ever so far north as New York in his life. Nor did he travel any further in any other direction.

The circuit system was still in force but the judges were now assigned to permanent circuits. The increasing sectionalism also demanded that each judge live in the circuit over which he presided. As Taney was from Maryland his circuit duty did not require any extensive traveling.

---

[28] WARREN, II at 16.
[29] Letter, dated June 26, 1855, from Taney to Campbell. SWISHER at 466.

As Chief Justice he spent his vacations at Old Point Comfort in Virginia but he seems to have visited Richmond for the first time in the 1840s. In part, his lack of travel was due to lack of money. He found it very difficult to live on a salary of five thousand dollars a year and, despite his few prosperous years at the Baltimore bar, he had little besides his salary.

Nor did the society of the capital rub off any of his provincialism. A few years after he became Chief Justice some of the judges began to bring their wives to Washington with them and the old practice by which all the judges lived together during sessions of the Court was abandoned. Mrs. Taney usually stayed in Baltimore and her husband's constant ill health and natural tendency to solitude kept him from deriving much benefit from the society of Washington. He abhorred crowds of any kind to such an extent that the crowded condition of the railroad cars seems to have made the short journey from Baltimore to Washington an ordeal to him. After attending an evening party at President Tyler's he wrote his wife that he "was greatly oppressed, as I always am on such occasions, by the crowded state of the rooms." [30]

So far as he could he confined his social life to old friends. He had a great share of that localism which makes a man show a fondness for anybody from his own locality. When holding court on circuit in Baltimore he would always ask any juryman, even though he did not know him personally, who happened to be from Frederick, to call at his chambers. He took a particular delight in receiving visits from the children of his friends although he universally refused their requests for recommendations to political appointments. As old age narrowed his social circle even more it is not surprising that his most admiring friends remarked on the "great decisiveness" of "his opinions on all subjects, and on none more than on politics." [31] When this decisiveness was

_____
[30] TYLER, at 472-473.
[31] TYLER, at 119.

about to result in an explosion it was in his eyes that his intimates read the storm signals.

This provincialism, combined with the decisiveness of his political views, kept Taney from appreciating the nature of the struggle that was arising over slavery. Neither the free-soil sentiment of the North nor the plantation system of the deep South were familiar to him. To him the South was still typified by Frederick, or at most, Calvert County, Maryland while the North became assimilated in his mind to the tendency toward commercialism which he had fought in the Bank of the United States. This was his frame of mind when, near the close of the Pierce administration, an obscure case known as *Dred Scott* v. *Sandford* [32] appeared on the Court's docket.

In 1834 an army surgeon named Emerson was ordered to the army post at Rock Island, Illinois. He took his slave, Dred Scott, with him. Two years later Emerson was transferred to Fort Snelling in what is now Minnesota but was then known as Upper Louisiana and again the slave went along. After two years at Fort Snelling Dr. Emerson resigned from the army and settled in Missouri. Five or six years later legal proceedings were begun, in the slave's name, to establish that he was a free man; that he had become free under the Ordinance of 1787 when taken to Illinois and under the Missouri Compromise when taken to Minnesota. Once free, he claimed, he was free everywhere and for all time.

Dred Scott was not himself in any way a remarkable man and it is clear that he did not furnish any of the motive power to the proceedings. The question of who did actually furnish that motive power has always been a mystery. The charge was afterwards made by every Republican stump-speaker in the land that the case arose out of a plot by the slavery interests but in the beginning, at least, both sides seem to have been under the control of anti-slavery men.

---

[32] *Dred Scott* v. *Sandford*, 19 How. 393, 15 L. Ed. 691 (1857).

The only politically explosive element in the case, when it reached the Supreme Court, was the possibility that it might call for a decision on the validity of the Missouri Compromise. There were a number of obvious ways of disposing of the case without passing on that issue. It was doubtful whether Dred Scott had any status to bring the suit. It was doubtful whether the Court was not bound to follow the local law of Missouri and in an earlier case which Scott had brought in a state court he had been held to be a slave. Even if the Court was not bound to follow that adjudication it was doubtful whether it should not arrive at the same result by the same reasoning. That reasoning was that, irrespective of whether he was slave or free in Illinois or Minnesota, he resumed his original status upon his return to slave territory. The basis of this reasoning can be more clearly understood by considering the opposite type of status, that of nobility, as it has existed from time to time in various countries. The nobleman may travel into a country where that status is not recognized but it has always been agreed by everybody that upon his return to his native land he resumes his original rank.

In the earlier discussions among the judges the Missouri Compromise was scarcely mentioned. But there was no unanimity as to which of the other points properly governed the decision of the case. Finally Justice McLean let his colleagues know that whatever they decided he intended to write an opinion discussing the question of the validity of the Missouri Compromise. Dimly, through the veil of secrecy which has always surrounded the conference room of the Court, we can see Taney's wrath arise at this proposal. It was not difficult for him to find a motive for McLean's action. Both men had been appointed by Jackson but McLean, who had been Postmaster-General, had never sunk the politician in the judge. Ever since his appointment he had been fishing for a presidential nomination without being very particular as to the party from which he obtained the nomination, and Taney had no difficulty now in concluding that McLean's opinion was to be the opening gun in his campaign for nomination by the newly organized Republican Party. Mc-Lean's action gave Justice Wayne an unfortunate idea. If McLean was going to discuss the validity of the Missouri Compromise in his dissent why not base the decision of the majority squarely on the point of its invalidity? It would settle, forever, the vexed political question of slavery in the territories for it would be a holding that Congress had no power to forbid slavery in any of them.

Taney accepted the idea eagerly and in so doing he indicated how out of touch he was with public opinion. When we compare his action in this case with the care which Marshall always took to avoid arousing public resentment we get the full measure of the distance by which Taney fell short of his predecessor. Perhaps even Marshall could not have brought the Court unscathed through the slavery crisis but certainly he would have appreciated the explosive character of the *Dred Scott Case* and would have handled it with greater tact. Taney forgot that the power which the Court wielded rested on an almost purely moral basis and it was his forgetfulness here which was responsible for his impotence when he attempted to uphold the bill of rights during the storm of civil war.

He must take the full responsibility for the mistake. It is peculiarly the type of responsibility which belongs to the head of the Court. He could not, it is true, prevent his associates from delivering what opinions they pleased but the mischief would have been largely averted if the explosive question had been referred to only in dissenting opinions. It was Taney's own opinion which was the text on which stump-speakers descanted. Nor had the Court observed all the judicial proprieties. The case had attracted little notice at first but as months went by and still no decision was rendered the public gradually got an inkling of what was going on in the conference room. It does not appear that Taney himself revealed any confidential information but it is at least certain that one of the judges in the majority, very likely with Taney's acquiescence, kept President-elect Buchanan informed. The general respect with which the Court had been treated during the twenty years of Taney's Chief Justiceship had not been favorable to the growth of judicial propriety. The Republican press, from other sources, was as well informed as Buchanan and before the decision had been rendered the case had received ample publicity.

Buchanan's inaugural, which had been delivered a few days before the decision was rendered, had contained a veiled reference to the case which indicated that he knew what the decision was going to be. Out of this reference the Republican press and the Republican politicians soon concocted a story that the decision was a plot of the slave power, hatched between the President and the Chief Justice. In truth, the case was a godsend to the Republicans for they were badly in need of a more concrete issue than their general platform of opposition to the spread of slavery.

Taney's reaction to the onslaught against him—and the Republican attack on the decision largely took the form of a personal and very abusive attack on him—was one of outraged resentment. He gave no indication of any understanding of the reason for the onslaught. Age and the uniform respect with which he had now been treated for a good many years had not increased his ability to understand the viewpoint of his opponents. To him that opposition was merely another manifestation of that pecuniary tendency which dominated the life of the North and which now intended to attack the Jeffersonian ruralism of the South. He never directly admitted that his action in the *Dred Scott Case* had been a mistake but he was very careful not to allow his name to be dragged into the 1860 presidential campaign as favoring any candidate. The depth of his resentment against the attacks which had been made on him is only revealed by his declaration to an intimate friend that if Seward received the Republican nomination and was elected President he would refuse to administer the oath of office. That contingency did not happen but when the eighty-four year old Chief Justice swore in the gaunt frontiersman from Illinois both must have wondered whether another Chief Justice would ever administer the oath of office to another President.

It is difficult to determine Taney's attitude in regard to secession. Many of the Republicans believed that the only reason he did not join the Confederacy was that he was too old and feeble to travel to Richmond. Their belief would have been confirmed if they had known that he had told a young Marylander who joined the Confederate army that his action was like the action of those who had enlisted under Washington. Yet in 1859, two years after the *Dred Scott Case*, he had written the opinion of the Court in a decision [33] as nationalistic as any that Marshall ever rendered. It is probable that Taney felt that there was no problem for him to decide until his own state seceded yet he must have known that Maryland was kept in the Union only by military force. The view that his loyalty was stronger than that gains support from the action of his friend, Justice Wayne of Georgia, who remained on the Court despite the secession of his state. While Taney remained at his post he did not remain with any optimism and even as late as March, 1864, he wrote, "I have not only outlived the friends and companions of my early life, but I fear I have outlived the Government of which they were so justly proud. . . . The times are dark with evil omens, and seem to grow darker every day. . . ."[34]

He was careful to avoid any suspicion of sympathy with the Confederacy. The little money he had was invested in the stock of a Virginian bank and one of the first acts of that state had been to forbid the payment of dividends to the citizens of non-seceding states. The Virginian authorities offered to make an exception in his favor but he refused to

---

[33] *Ableman* v. *Booth*, 21 How. 506, 16 L. Ed. 169 (1859).
[34] Letter dated March 20, 1864 from Taney to S. T. Wallis. TYLER, at 459.

accept the money. When later his negro servant who, since the death of Mrs. Taney, had become indispensable to the Chief Justice, was drafted Taney refused to allow him to claim exemption on the ground of a bodily ailment and silently gave him the money with which to hire a substitute.

* * * * * *

It was in vain. Taney hovered around Washington like an unrespected ghost. His wife and his favorite daughter had died of yellow fever in 1855 and he no longer kept up a home of his own. During the sessions of the Court he would put up at one Washington boarding-house or another but Baltimore was his favorite city. While he spoke of Frederick City as his home he does not seem to have visited it after moving to Baltimore. When in the latter city he lived with his lawyer son-in-law, J. Mason Campbell. Taney's way of life was not due to the lack of a housekeeper for he was still supporting a spinster daughter and a daughter whose husband had deserted her. Campbell was never very prosperous and the families lived together to save expense. Taney had two other married daughters, one of whom was married to a purser in the navy who later joined the Confederate army and the other to a none too successful Baltimore merchant.

Taney's preternatural appearance had increased with age and he was well in his eighties when he swore in Lincoln. Taney had been a boy of twelve when Washington was inaugurated and his latest successor, Chief Justice Hughes, was a boy of two when he died. In this last period of his life Taney's physician described him as being "like a disembodied spirit; for . . . his mind did not, in any degree, participate in the infirmities of his body."[35] It increased the ecclesiastical aura which had always surrounded him but his moral authority as Chief Justice was gone. The Court itself was beginning to recover the prestige which it had lost in the *Dred Scott Case* but the recovery did not

---

[35] TYLER, at 457.

extend to Taney's personal prestige. Beginning with Swayne who was appointed in January of 1862 the Court was rapidly being filled with free-soilers for it is a curious thing that both Marshall's and Taney's courts died with them and that both Jackson and Lincoln had an opportunity to appoint a majority of the judges.

Taney viewed Lincoln with as grave distrust as Marshall had viewed Jackson but Taney had small hope of living until the election of a President with whom he would be more in sympathy. Taney stayed in office largely because he did not have any alternative. His salary was his only income and he needed the office in order to live.

Taney was horrified by the autocratic and dictatorial powers which the President was either assuming or was receiving by Act of Congress. The question of the constitutionality of most of the Civil War Acts was not to reach the Court until after Taney's death but in his capacity as a circuit judge he vigorously upheld the Bill of Rights. The first and most famous case in which he did so arose within a few weeks after Lincoln had taken office. In the effort to hold Maryland in the Union by main force a Baltimorean named Merryman was arrested by the military without process and imprisoned in Fort McHenry in that city. The next day Taney issued a writ of *habeas corpus* directed to the general in command. That functionary declined to admit the jurisdiction of the Court on the ground that he "was duly authorized by the President of the United States, in such cases, to suspend the writ of *habeas corpus* for the public safety."[36] There had not even been a proclamation of martial law and it is hard to find any legal excuse for the action which the general had taken undoubtedly with the backing of the President. The action of the executive did not meet with universal approval even among the most ardent Republicans but, as the Chief Justice had no physical power with which to enforce his opinion[37], Merryman re-

[36] Quoted in TYLER, at 421.
[37] *Ex parte Merryman,* Taney 246 (1861).

mained in jail. To many it seemed that Taney was to play the Boniface to Marshall's Innocent.

The Chief Justice had, in truth, outlived his time. Neither the North nor the South seemed to care much for that government of laws which he admired. If he sympathized with the South as the champion of Jeffersonian culture, he could not bear to think of the dissolution of the Union. The existence of civil war was something which had never been dreamed of in his philosophy. During his latter years he had become more and more out of touch with the currents of opinion. His mind had never been very flexible and old age had made it less receptive than ever to new ideas. From the period of his appointment until he rendered the Dred Scott decision he had been an eminently competent Chief Justice. His opinion in that case blasted his reputation in the greater part of the nation for the rest of his life and for many years after his death. There were few men in official Washington who regretted his death in the latter part of 1864. "The name of Taney," said Sumner when the death of the Chief Justice was announced, "is to be hooted down the page of history."[38]

It took many years to reverse that verdict but it has been reversed.

---

[38] WARREN, II at 393-394.